Fodor's InFocus

SINGAPORE

W9-AHY-286

Welcome to Singapore

Little did we realize that the emergence of a novel coronavirus in early 2020 would abruptly bring almost all travel to a halt. Although our Fodor's writers around the world have continued working to bring you the best of the destinations they cover, we still anticipate that more than the usual number of businesses will close permanently in the coming months, perhaps with little advance notice. We don't expect things to return to "normal" for some time. As you plan your upcoming travels to Singapore, please confirm that places are still open and let us know when we need to make updates by writing to us at this address: editors@fodors.com.

TOP REASONS TO GO

★ **Modern Marvels:** Sky-high pools, futuristic Supertrees, and an indoor waterfall await.

★ **Global Cuisine:** Singapore's local Peranakan, Chinese, Indian, and Malay food shines especially bright amid a global offering.

★ **Outdoor Adventures:** Take a city break at one of the many manicured gardens, nature reserves, and beaches.

★ **World-Class Shopping:** Splurge at the renowned megamalls and boutiques that line the famous Orchard Road.

Contents

MAPS

Chapter 1

EXPERIENCE SINGAPORE

15 ULTIMATE EXPERIENCES

Singapore offers terrific experiences that should be on every traveler's list. Here are Fodor's top picks for a memorable trip.

1 Futuristic Gardens

The extraordinary, 250-acre Gardens by the Bay has three waterfront gardens, air-conditioned conservatories, and a cluster of "Supertrees" linked by suspended walkways that soar up to 165 feet (Ch. 3).

2 Mosques and Murals

Kampong Glam, Singapore's Malay center, is home to the golden-domed Sultan Mosque, colorful murals, Malay eateries and hip cafes, and stores crammed with beautiful batik fabric (Ch. 5).

3 Action-Packed Beaches

Sentosa, a beachy paradise just off the coast of Singapore, has theme parks, resorts, and activities galore. Bungee jump or zip line on Siloso Beach or throw frisbees and order cocktails at Tanjong Beach Club (Ch. 9).

4 Singapore Sling

You can order a legendary Singapore Sling at just about any bar, but nothing beats sipping the coral-hued cocktail where it was first created—the Long Bar at Raffles Singapore (Ch. 3).

5 Chinatown

Red lanterns and ornate architecture mix with trendy restaurants, chic bars, and superlative hawker fare in this historic neighborhood (Ch. 4).

6 The World's Highest Infinity Pool

Marina Bay Sands' expansive swimming pool— the world's largest and highest at 650 feet above ground—offers a million-dollar view that blurs the line between sky and cityscape (Ch. 3).

7 A Stunning Waterfall...at the Airport

Changi International Airport isn't any ordinary airport. In its Jewel complex, the world's tallest indoor waterfall tumbles 130 feet from an oculus the size of a truck and is framed by a lush garden (Ch. 7).

8 Museum Hopping

Singapore's finest museums and monuments are housed in grand colonial buildings in the Civic District. The Asian Civilisations Museum and National Gallery Singapore are must-sees (Ch. 3).

9 Hawker Centers

No need to splurge for a taste of award-winning food. Hawker centers offer quick, delicious meals at low prices, making it easy to eat exceptionally well (Ch. 4).

10 The Singapore Botanic Gardens

This 184-acre oasis of calm, a UNESCO World Heritage Site, is threaded with landscaped gardens; swathes of rain forest; a tranquil lake; and a ravishing collection of orchids (Ch. 6).

11 Shopping on Orchard Road

Roam one of the world's most famous shopping streets, where glitzy megamalls are linked by underground tunnels so you don't have to duck traffic or brave the tropical swelter outside (Ch. 6).

12 Peranakan Culture

Named Singapore's first heritage town in 2011, Joo Chiat is the seat of Peranakan (local Malay) culture, dotted with well-preserved shophouses, time-honored businesses, and beloved eateries (Ch. 7).

13 Kopi Break in Tiong Bahru

Take a *kopi* (coffee) and cupcake break at Plain Vanilla or browse indie bookshop Books Actually in one of Singapore's oldest residential neighborhoods turned hipster haven (Ch. 4).

14 Bumboat Ride on Singapore River

Float by Merlion Park and the warehouses of Clarke Quay on the tranquil Singapore River, where hundreds of bumboats once transported goods daily (Ch. 3).

15 Little India's Markets and Temples

You could spend an entire day getting lost in Little India's warren of colorful streets and alleys, taking in temples, markets, and endless food stalls (Ch. 5).

WHAT'S WHERE

1 Civic District and Marina Bay. The colonial-era buildings and museums of the Civic District are a stark contrast to the futuristic skylines of Marina Bay across the water.

2 Chinatown and Tiong Bahru. Temples, parks, and street art meet food stalls and buzzing bars in Chinatown. Tiong Bahru is filled with cafes, boutiques, and murals.

3 Little India and Kampong Glam. Colorful temples dot the corners of Little India. Nearby in Kampong Glam you can stroll under the golden dome of Sultan Mosque.

4 Orchard Road. On Singapore's grand boulevard, shopping malls share space with the city's poshest hotels and restaurants. Just beyond, the Singapore Botanic Gardens provide a break from the city.

5 Eastern Singapore. In the East you'll find Changi, home to the world's best airport; Joo Chiat, a Peranakan enclave with colorful homes; and Geylang Serai, with a thriving market.

6 Western Singapore. The West is full of nature reserves like Bukit Timah, wildlife attractions like the Singapore Zoo; and posh neighborhoods like Dempsey Hill.

7 Sentosa and Pulau Ubin. Sentosa Island offers beach resorts and theme parks while Pulau Ubin is a slice of Singapore before modernization.

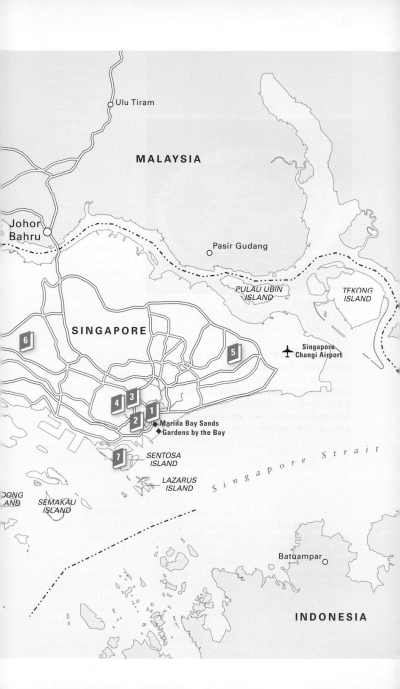

What to Eat and Drink in Singapore

CHILI CRAB

One of the country's signature dishes, chili crab is on the must-try list for seafood-loving visitors. It's typically made using mud crabs, which are cooked in a mildly spicy, tomato-based gravy. Try it at Long Beach Seafood.

HAINAN CHICKEN RICE

Although it originated in the Hainan Province of China, Hainanese chicken rice is considered one of Singapore's national dishes. A plump chicken is poached, and the stock is used, along with garlic and ginger, to cook the rice. Both are then served with a ginger-and-garlic dipping sauce. The most famous Hainan chicken rice stall is Tian Tian at the Maxwell Food Court.

SINGAPORE SLING

The signature pink drink, made with gin, brandy, pineapple juice, and grenadine, was created at the iconic Raffles Hotel back in 1915. You can still drink it in the hotel's legendary Long Bar while munching on peanuts and throwing their shells on the floor— the only place in Singapore you can legally litter.

LAKSA

Not to be confused with Malaysian assam laksa, Singaporean katong laksa is a bowl of rice noodles and seafood in a curry-like broth of coconut milk, dried shrimp, and spices. One popular place to try it is 328 Katong Laksa (who beat Gordon Ramsay in a cooking showdown).

BAK KUT TEH

This pork rib soup in herbal broth is commonly eaten for breakfast and makes for a great hangover cure (the name translates to "meat bone tea," but there is no tea in the broth).

DURIAN

It's an acquired taste, but fans of this fruit, which smells dreadful but tastes good once you get past it, know that Singapore is one of the best cities to get durian.

SOY SAUCE CHICKEN

The Hong Kong–style soy sauce chicken can primarily be found in Chinatown, but the dish recently gained popularity worldwide when Liao Fan's hawker stall was awarded a Michelin star for its version.

Bak Kut Teh

SALTED EGG FISH SKIN CHIPS

This recent food trend is currently Singapore's number-one snack—and it's addictive. Crispy fish skin is coated with salted egg yolk and spices for an umami bomb. Pick up a bag of Irvin's at Changi International Airport.

HOKKIEN MEE

This popular hawker dish consists of stir-fried egg and rice noodles with eggs, prawn, and pork.

KAYA TOAST

White bread toast with a creamy spread made of coconut milk, caramelized sugar, and eggs is served for breakfast with soft-boiled eggs and soy sauce.

ES POTONG

Singapore's take on the ice cream sandwich, *es potong*, or "cut ice," is ice cream cut into blocks and wrapped in white bread.

Best Hotel Pools in Singapore

MARINA BAY SANDS

There can be no list of Singapore's hotel pools that does not include the iconic infinity pool on the 57th floor—650 feet above the ground—of the Marina Bay Sands Hotel. The view is nothing short of spectacular (Ch. 3).

HOTEL JEN ORCHARDGATE-WAY

Although this infinity pool offers city views, it's surrounded by lush vegetation, making a dip here feel like a relaxing escape from the city life. Both this 19th-floor pool and the neighboring open-air rooftop bar are open until 11 pm, so come for sunset, and stay for the lights of Orchard Road. You can also get a massages in a poolside cabana or participate in a sunset yoga session on the deck (Ch. 6).

FAR EAST HOTELS OF SENTOSA

One amazing pool deck can be accessed from three Far East brand hotels: The Barracks Hotel Sentosa, Village Hotel Sentosa, and The Outpost Hotel Sentosa. Its highlight is a lazy river that flows through waterfalls (Ch. 9).

MANDARIN ORIENTAL

Lined with fountains and Italian mosaic glass, this luxurious 25-meter pool has an unobstructed view of downtown and Marina Bay Sands. Relax in one of the partially submerged chaise longues, or book a private cabana (Ch. 3).

CAPELLA SINGAPORE

For a tranquil escape—one that recalls the rice terraces of Bali—wade in this multi-tiered, Sentosa Island hotel pool set amid lush greenery and colonial build-ings next to Palawan Beach. The pool has ocean views and glimpses of the rain forest (Ch. 9).

PARKROYAL on Pickering

PARKROYAL ON PICKERING
This hotel's wellness floor features a spa, elevated garden, and this outdoor infinity pool, which offers city views. Greenery and partially enclosed cabanas shaped like birdcages give the pool a rather enchanted feel (Ch. 4).

FULLERTON BAY HOTEL
Built over the water, the luxurious hotel offers sweeping views of Marina Bay, including from its rooftop infinity pool and whirlpool tubs.

Framed by tropical plants, the pool sits next to the Lantern Rooftop Bar, so you can grab a cocktail between swims (Ch. 4).

ASCOTT RAFFLES PLACE
The "sexiness" factor of the 19th-floor infinity pool at this luxury, full-service apartment hotel has been amped up with the use of glass walls: from one end of the pool, you can glimpse the bay and high-rises of downtown; from the other, activities beyond the pool (Ch. 4).

SOFITEL SINGAPORE SENTOSA
Surrounded by colonial-style buildings and palm trees and adorned with aquamarine tiles, this Sentosa Island hotel pool is expansive enough for each guest to swim around with some privacy (Ch. 9).

W SINGAPORE SENTOSA COVE
In addition to a swim-up bar, this sleek hotel pool has complimentary private cabanas (first come, first served) with their own iPads. (Ch. 9).

Best Cocktail Bars in Singapore

NATIVE

This small Chinatown bar connects cocktails to the local heritage by foraging for local ingredients and using Asian spirits such as jackfruit rum or arrak from Sri Lanka in its unique concoctions (Ch. 4).

GIBSON BAR

Come to this cocktail and seafood bar with a casual vibe for the great oyster happy hour. The bar's namesake Gibson drink, created using house-made Ginjo sake vermouth, is a must-try. Seasonal offerings highlight Southeast Asian ingredients such as starfruit and pandan. (Ch. 4).

28 HONG KONG STREET

Hidden behind an unmarked door, 28 Hong Kong Street was named the best bar in Asia at the very first Asia's 50 Best Bars Awards. Years later, the speakeasy remains at the forefront of Singapore's craft-cocktail movement, offering creative libations and an energetic vibe (Ch. 3).

MANHATTAN BAR

Entering the Regent Hotel's bar is like stepping back into the golden age of New York City. The bar offers more than 150 whiskeys and crafts Negronis made with spirits that have been solera-aged in the hotel's own rickhouse (Ch. 6).

NUTMEG & CLOVE

To taste true local flavors, order from the Flavour and Memories menu, using herbs, fruits, spices, and other ingredients commonly found in Singapore. There is a variation of Singapore Sling, of course, but also a cocktail made with crab (Ch. 4).

Atlas

ATLAS
A grand art deco–style temple of cocktails inspired by the Jazz Age, Atlas Bar is a sight to behold. Located in the lobby of the Parkview Square building, between Bugis and Kampong Glam, it has a three-story tower filled with more than 1,000 bottles of gin (Ch. 5).

BITTERS & LOVE
Tell the bartenders at this 19th-century shophouse speakeasy your preferences and let them create a cocktail just for you. Prices are approachable, but if you're feeling more extravagant, request a bespoke cocktail made using rare spirits they've collected (Ch. 4).

JIGGER & PONY
This sultry bar and lounge specializes in traditional martinis and lesser-known Asian classics. The magazine-like menu offers lessons in cocktail history, and the renditions of the classics stand out (Ch. 4).

TIPPLING CLUB
Not only is Tippling Club an award-winning restaurant, but it also pushes the mixology boundaries. The chef and bartender collaborate closely to develop cocktails that are often inspired by culinary creations (Ch. 4).

OLD MAN
This outpost of Hong Kong's award-winning Hemingway-inspired bar has the same menu, but the bar is twice as big. Bartenders create drinks such as The Snows of Kilimanjaro, made with marshmallow gin and gruyere cheese, in a "mini-lab" (Ch. 4).

Outdoor Adventures in Singapore

MACRITCHIE NATURE TRAIL & RESERVOIR PARK

MacRitchie's highlight is its Treetop Walk, a suspension bridge that connects the park's two highest points and offers a bird's-eye view of the forest canopy (Ch. 8).

BUKIT TIMAH NATURE RESERVE

Some know Bukit Timah as an affluent residential district, but its name comes from an area hill, which, at just 537 feet, is the highest peak in Singapore. Declared an ASEAN Heritage Park in 2011, the hill's eponymous, 163-acre nature reserve contains one of Singapore's last remaining primary rain forests, so-called as they are untouched, original-condition forests. Hiking and cycling routes, including the city-state's first mountain-biking trail, lace the reserve, which also conducts a monthly nature walk (Ch. 8).

PALAWAN BEACH

One of Sentosa Island's best free beaches for families, Palawan has white sands and facilities that include lockers, free showers, nearby restaurants, and kid-friendly attractions like the aviary and the animal show at the Palawan Amphitheatre (Ch. 9).

CHESTNUT NATURE PARK

Singapore's largest nature park, at just over 200 acres, has two hiking trails: one on the north side that's just over 2 miles and a shorter route on the south-side that's 1.3 miles. There are also mountain biking trails (Ch. 8).

MARINA BAY WALK

You can take in several waterfront attractions along this easily accessible urban walk. Start at the Merlion statue in Merlion Park, and then stroll along the water to The Esplanade (Ch. 3).

Fort Siloso Skywalk

FORT SILOSO SKYWALK

This free skywalk on Sentosa Island was opened in 2015 as part of Singapore's Golden Jubilee celebration. The treetop trail is 11 stories high and 594 feet long, bringing explorers to historic Fort Siloso, a gun battery built in the late 1800s. The glass elevator up to the start of the skywalk runs from 9 am to 7 pm; in the off hours, you have to climb the stairs (Ch. 9).

SUNGEI BULOH WETLAND RESERVE

The island nation's first ASEAN Heritage Park encompasses 500 acres of wetlands, including a mangrove forest. It's a haven for bird-watchers year-round, but especially from September to March (Ch. 8).

EASTERN COASTAL PARK CONNECTOR NETWORK CYCLING TRAIL

This 26-mile cycling loop runs through diverse scenery that include beach parks, mangroves, and areas forested with heritage trees. One easy starting point is Sun Plaza Park, near the Tampines MRT station (Ch. 7).

MEGA ADVENTURE PARK

Thrill seekers love this park's attractions, which include the MegaZip, a 1,500-foot-long zip-line that starts off at 250 feet above the ground and traverses treetops before finishing just off Siloso Beach (Ch. 9).

Singapore's Most Luxurious Experiences

Many businesses in Singapore cater to the wealthiest of the wealthy, ready to pamper and impress with fine dining, high-end shopping, luxury hotels, and more. Despite the small size of the country, it's reportedly home to more than 30 billionaires and is ranked third in the world for GDP per capita. For those planning to enjoy Singapore like Crazy Rich Asians, here are the best luxurious experiences you can find.

MICHELIN-STARRED TASTING MENUS

Singapore might be famous for its cheap hawker fare (which, by the way, often attracts the wealthiest of food lovers), but the city is also home to a number of Michelin-starred fine-dining restaurants. The three-starred Odette has also recently been named the best restaurant in Asia. Waku Ghin's ten-course menu lines up the most coveted ingredients, from sea urchin to caviar to Ohmi wagyu. From the Nordic–Japanese restaurant Zen, named the most expensive restaurant in Singapore with its S$450 price tag, to edomae sushi at Shinji by Kanesaka, Singapore has something for every palate.

LUXURY SHOPPING MALLS

Singapore is one of Asia's top shopping destinations with no shortage of high-end luxury brands. ION Orchard, with more than 300 retail stores, is arguably the city's most famous mall, but luxury shoppers shouldn't miss The Shoppes at Marina Bay Sands, Paragon, and IMM. Capitol Piazza and Orchard Gateway are the places to check out local designers and brands. Shop right before your flight at the airport's Jewel Changi, which has 280 stores and restaurants.

BEST LUXURY SPAS

After a day of wandering around in Singapore's tropical weather, a refreshing spa treatment might be in order. ESPA has Singapore's first authentic Turkish hammam—in addition to onsen-style pools, a crystal steam room, and private beach villa suites—within its more than 107,000-square-foot space. For complete serenity, the ryokan-inspired Ikeda Spa Prestige offers an onsen bath and relaxation massages. Remede Spa at the St. Regis enhances the spa experience with eucalyptus-scented steam rooms and tea and treats after a treatment.

BEST LUXURY HOTELS

Plush beds, a majestic view, and unrivaled hospitality are all hallmarks of a luxury hotel. Stay at the posh Marina Bay Sands Hotel to gain access to its iconic infinity pool, open to hotel guests only. Some of the hotel's suites also come with a private gym and sauna. What could make a stay more luxurious than the 24-hour butler service at the St. Regis Singapore? Those interested in local culture can take advantage of the free heritage tour offered by Fullerton Bay Hotel, a five-star property built directly over the water with river views.

BEST GOLF CLUB

This small island nation surprisingly has the most golf courses per square mile in the world. Sentosa Golf Club is frequently named as Singapore's best, with two 18-hole courses that have both city and ocean views. Marina Bay Golf Course is Singapore's only public 18-hole golf course. Players can test their skills on the World Classic Course at Laguna National Golf and Country Club, known to be one of Asia's most challenging.

RENT A SUPERCAR

With the Formula 1 Grand Prix as one of the major annual events, Singapore certainly has proven interested in supercars. Visitors who want to experience driving around the island in a supercar need not bring their own, however: Ultimate Drive allows owners of luxury cars to rent their supercars to the public. For the ultimate driving experience,

book the Joyride with Ultimate Drive package, which lets you select a supercar ranging from a Ferrari or Lamborghini to a McLaren 12C to take for a lap around the official F1 circuit.

COCKTAILS WITH A VIEW

Sipping on a cocktail while enjoying the night lights is a fitting way to end any evening in the city. Thankfully, there are quite a few rooftop bars offering spectacular views of Singapore alongside great drinks. Situated on the 63rd floor of 1 Raffles Place, 1-Altitude is the highest rooftop bar in Singapore—not to mention the highest open-air bar in the world. Smoke & Mirrors, on the rooftop of the National Gallery of Singapore, offers panoramic views of the cityscape and creative craft cocktails. Beer lovers can also get their view at LeVel 33, a rooftop microbrewery. Of course, there's always Ce La Vi atop the iconic Marina Bay Sands.

Singapore Today

Singapore's reputation as "Asia light" is a well-earned one. Everyone speaks English, transportation is clean and efficient, and there's plenty to see and experience in its diminutive space. Whether it's your first trip or you're a well-seasoned traveler, here's what's to know about the island nation now.

POLITICS

The Republic of Singapore is a sovereign island city-state situated 137 kilometers (85 miles) north of the equator and founded in 1819 by Sir Stamford Raffles as a trading post of the British India Company. It came under direct British control in 1858 as a crown colony known as the Straits Settlements. Occupied by the Japanese during World War II, and again by Britain until it joined the short-lived federation of Malaya in 1963, Singapore became a fully sovereign state in 1965.

The President is head of state, voted for a renewable six-year term, while the Prime Minister is head of government appointed by the President to command the majority of Parliament. Lee Kuan Yew, the first Prime Minister of Singapore, governed for three decades from 1959 to 1990 and is recognized as the nation's founding father. He propelled the nation from third-world backwater to first-world country. Lee's rule was, however, criticized for exercising media control, limiting public protests, and bringing libel suits against political opponents. The nation's politics have been dominated by the People's Action Party (PAP) since Lee Kuan Yew came into power. As of 2016, the Worker's Party constitutes the main opposition in Parliament. Lee remained involved in politics until his death in 2015; now his son, Lee Hsien Loong, is PM.

CONSERVATIVE POLICIES

Singapore has a booming economy and one of Asia's most stable nations, but state control is also strong. The Ministry of Home Affairs Internal Security Department still enforces the Internal Security Act (ISA), a draconian law that permits indefinite detention without recourse. The press and the LGBTQ community also face challenges in Singapore, and no antidiscrimination laws exist to protect them. Same-sex relationships are not recognized under Singapore law.

DIVERSITY

Singapore is a remarkably peaceful multicultural society, where English acts as the common lingo. The city-state is composed by a majority of citizens of Chinese descent, followed by Malays and

Indians. A big number of working Western expatriates, and an even bigger number of foreign immigrant workers, add to the mix, contributing to the creation of a dynamic workforce and cohesive multicultural society.

THRIVING NIGHTLIFE

Singaporeans work hard and, maybe as a reflection of so many rules and fines, they also party very hard: clubs and discos stay open until the wee hours of the night, and in areas like Kampong Glam and the quays of the Singapore River, there's a bar on every corner.

CAFÉ CULTURE

Singapore's national obsession with *kopi* ("coffee" in Malay) means international cuppas are served everywhere, from the simple and ubiquitous hawker centers to all sorts of modern, stylish shops often housed in beautifully colored, century-old shophouses. Made with Robusta brew from nearby Indonesia, Singaporean coffee is usually long, frothy, and served with heavy doses of sugar or condensed milk.

FOOD AND SHOPPING

For foodies, Singapore offers the best of both worlds: both traditional, casual street food at hawker centers and upscale establishments, Michelin-starred restaurants, and world cuisines. And, Singapore has some of the best malls in the world—air-conditioned paradises filled with designer brands and the latest technological gadgets.

A JEWEL OF AN AIRPORT

Few countries in the world have an airport hub as good as Singapore's—or one as beautiful and visit-worthy. Opened in 2019, Jewel Changi is a rain forest–themed entertainment complex on the landside of Changi International Airport, whose main centerpiece, the Rain Vortex, is the world's highest indoor waterfall.

LOOKING AHEAD

Singapore's tourism is in constant flux, and moving well beyond the city center. A new integrated development will transform the Jurong Lake District by 2026, in line with the government's aim of spreading hotel offerings across non-central areas of the island. Many hotels have just opened in Singapore: think of Fraser Residence Orchard, with its sleek apartments set in the CBD, or the lavish Outpost Hotel and Village Hotel, two new offerings on Sentosa Island. Note that the coronavirus outbreak of 2020 caused many unexpected closures at the time of printing. If you're planning a visit, remember to call ahead to verify that the property is still in operation.

What to Read and Watch

CRAZY RICH ASIANS

Kevin Kwan's laugh-out-loud story of a Singaporean man bringing his American girlfriend home to meet his obscenely wealthy family and friends was a huge hit in theaters.

THE SINGAPORE GRIP

Centering on a British family who owns a trading company, J.G. Farrell's satirical book looks at Japan's entry into WWII and the occupation of Singapore.

FROM THIRD WORLD TO FIRST

How did tiny Singapore grow from a colonial trading post into one of the worlds richest countries? Singapore's first prime minister, Lee Kuan Yew, has the answer.

IN THE MOOD FOR LOVE

In Wong Kar-wai's award-winning film, two neighbors in Hong Kong fall in love; when one moves to Singapore, the other follows but is too late.

12 STOREYS

A look into the sometimes tumultuous lives of several people living in one apartment in Singapore; the film screened at Cannes in 1997.

15

An expansion of director Royston Tan's 2002 short film of the same name, 15 (2003) is about teenage gangsters in Singapore's suburbs.

CHICKEN RICE WAR (JIYUAN QIAOHE)

Can love bring two people divided by secret family recipes together? Meet the Chans and the Wongs, two generations of street hawkers, and learn about Singapore's daily life, and food, in this rom com from 2000.

LONG LONG TIME AGO

When Zhao Di, the unwanted and pregnant second wife of an older man, is forced to return to her own family to give birth to twins, life takes a sour turn. The 2016 film is beautiful, fun, and touching and captures Singapore's national development.

THE ART OF CHARLIE CHAN HOCK CHYE

Sonny Liew's *New York Times* bestselling graphic novel tells the story of a Singapore comic art genius. In truth, the fictional biography of Mr. Chan is a pungent metaphor of the autocratic development of Singapore's postwar politics.

GLASS CATHEDRAL

Winner of the 2014 Singapore Literature Prize Commendation Award, Andrew Koh's sensitive depiction of homosexuality in conservative Singapore is a landmark in local literature and part of a small wave of LGBT-themed fiction that appeared in Singapore during the early 1990s.

TRAVEL SMART

Updated by
Marco Ferrarese

★ **CAPITAL:**
Singapore

POPULATION:
5,821,788

LANGUAGE:
English, Malay,
Mandarin Chinese,
and Tamil

$ **CURRENCY:**
Singapore Dollars

AREA CODE:
65

⚠ **EMERGENCIES:**
Fire and Ambulance:
995; Police: 999

DRIVING:
On the Left

⚡ **ELECTRICITY:**
220/240V/50 cycles;
electrical plugs have
three flat prongs
forming a triangle

TIME:
12 hours ahead of
New York

**WEB
RESOURCES:**
www.visitsingapore.com
www.sethlui.com
www.changiairport.com

✈ **AIRPORT:**
SIN

MALAYSIA

SINGAPORE

Singapore Strait

INDONESIA

Know Before You Go

Is Singapore as strict as everyone says? Can you drink the water? Is it safe to travel alone? You may have a few questions before you head to this thriving city-state in Southeast Asia. Here, we give you a few tips and tricks to make your trip a whole lot smoother so you can focus on other things—like which walking shoes will best carry you across the city.

IT'S GENERALLY SAFE

Singapore is one of the safest, easiest, and most efficient cities to navigate, which is why it's often named one of the best cities for solo travelers. Petty crime is rare in Singapore and violent crime even more uncommon. The streets are well-lit, and the public transportation system is safe and efficient, even after hours. But even though Singapore is a very safe place to travel, use general caution.

YES, THE LAWS ARE STRICT

Singapore charges hefty fines for what may be trivial acts in other countries. It's not a myth that chewing gum is banned, and jaywalking, the act of crossing the road outside the white stripes, could result in a fine of S$50 the first time, and up to S$1,000 and a jail term of 3 months for repeat offenders. You can be fined up to S$1,000 for smoking in prohibited areas and S$1,000 for littering. Other criminal offenses include vandalism, not flushing the toilet, homosexual relations, and carrying or consuming drugs.

IT'S SUPER CLEAN AND GREEN

Lush greenery flourishes amid the urban sprawl, and the streets are so free of litter that you'd think thrice before dropping even the most miniscule of debris. And you won't have to—there's always a trash bin nearby whether you're indoors or out. The year-long tropical swelter is also real, which is where the verdant greenery comes in handy. When the unrelenting sun and humidity get to be too much, you'll be grateful for the benches beneath the tall, rainforest trees that line the streets.

DON'T BRING U.S. DOLLARS

Shops in Singapore only accept Singapore currency. If you prefer not to carry cash, credit cards are accepted everywhere except in places like hawker centers, wet markets, and neighborhood stores. Money changers are easy to find throughout the city. ATMs are widely available.

YOU'LL HEAR SINGLISH

Singapore's local patois is a mishmash of the island's four official languages—English, Mandarin, Malay, and Tamil—with regional dialects thrown in. Singlish is snappy, efficient, and casual, shortening words and sentences, and repeating things for emphasis ("ok ok" is a classic). Rather than say "yes, it can be done," Singaporeans will simply say "can." Rather than waste a full second on saying "excuse me," you might hear someone say, "scuse." And the most common word in the local parlance is "lah," which punctuates every sentence and can convey an exclamation, resignation, a question, or frustration. Singlish can be difficult to understand when spoken in its typical rapid-fire fashion. The good news is that Singaporeans are always happy to explain the nuances of Singlish to visitors—so use your questions as an ice breaker.

LOCALS CALL OTHERS "UNCLE" OR "AUNTY"

No, not everyone in Singapore is related—addressing someone (usually a stranger) who's older than you as "uncle" or "aunty" is a sign of respect. Most often, you'll hear Singaporeans addressing the likes of taxi drivers, hawkers, shopkeepers, and janitors in that manner. It's respectful to address your friends' parents and older relatives as "aunty" or "uncle" too.

YOU CAN DRINK THE WATER

Singapore's tap water is perfectly safe to drink (though some say poor tasting from chlorination), so fill your water bottles before heading out into the tropical heat.

DON'T HAGGLE

Prices in Singapore are almost always fixed, and bargaining is not part of the consumer culture in Singapore as it is in other Southeast Asian countries. If a product is marked with a price tag, it's not up for negotiation.

USE PUBLIC TRANSPORTATION

The Mass Rapid Transit (MRT) system is the quickest, easiest, and most comfortable way to get around Singapore. The under- and over-ground network stretches throughout the entire city, with many attractions within walking distance of MRT stations. Singapore's bus system also covers an extensive network of routes and is the most economical and scenic way to make your way across the city. Taxis and ride shares cover the rest.

FOLLOW LOCAL ETIQUETTE

There are a few cultural do's and don'ts. If you're invited for dinner by Chinese friends or acquaintances, leave some food on your plate to indicate that your host's generosity is so great, you can't eat another bite. There's no shame in asking for a knife and fork instead of chopsticks, which, by the way, should never be stuck straight up in your rice bowl, as this is considered bad luck (it recalls funerary offerings). Don't use your left hand for greeting, gesturing, giving something to, or eating with a Malay, Indonesian, or Indian person— it's the hand traditionally used for cleaning oneself with water after using the toilet. It's mandatory that you remove your shoes in places of worship.

Getting Here and Around

Sitting in the center of Southeast Asia, between Malaysia and the island of Sumatra in Indonesia, the small city-state of Singapore is one of the region's major transportation hubs. Most international air carriers fly direct to Singapore's modern Changi International Airport, connected to every point of interest in and around the city-state via an efficient and fairly inexpensive metro system. Taxis and buses are also plentiful and convenient, as are ride-hailing services like Uber.

✈ Air

Singapore is 14 hours and 30 minutes from San Francisco, 14 hours from Seattle and Vancouver, 20 hours from Chicago via Tokyo or Hong Kong, 18 hours from New York, and 8 hours from Sydney. The airport's four terminals are at Changi, in the southeast of the island, connected by a quick and free shuttle train. On popular tourist routes during peak holiday periods, flights to Singapore are often fully booked. Make sure you reserve well in advance of your travel date.

AIRPORT
International flights arrive and depart from Changi International Airport, which is on the island's eastern end and a 20-minute drive from downtown. It has four terminals, and all are connected by a free, two-minute ride on the Skytrain monorail.

Changi's facilities are second to none and contributed to making it the best airport in the world for seven years in a row. Each terminal is served by the Ambassador Transit Hotel, where you can shower or rent a room for six-hour periods. You take shorter naps at Terminal 2's Shower, Fitness and Lifestyle Centre. Terminal 2 also has a rooftop swimming pool and Jacuzzi, a movie theater, a supermarket, medical facilities, smoking rooms, and outdoor rest areas among other things. There are Free Internet Corners throughout the airport, as well as a children's playground, butterfly garden, and entertainment lounge. Just outside of the airport, the Jewel Changi Airport is Singapore's latest nature-themed entertainment and retail complex. Linked to three of the passenger terminals, it revolves around 130-foot-tall the Rain Vortex, the world's tallest indoor waterfall, surrounded by a stunning terraced forest setting. If you have at least 5.5 hours to kill between flights at Changi, register for one of three different 2.5-hour sightseeing tours of Singapore (Jewel, Heritage, or City Sights) at one of the clearly marked tour counters.

AIRPORT TRANSFERS
Buses 24, 27, 34, 36, 53, 110 and 858 stop at Terminal 1, 2 and 3 and, except for number 53 and 858, they all proceed to Terminal 4. Comfortable metro trains also run to the airport from 5:20 am to 11:50 pm. Catch the East West Line to Tanah Merah MRT Station, then transfer to the Changi International Airport MRT Station. Alternatively, use the Downtown Line to the Expo MRT Station, then transfer to Changi Airport MRT Station. From Monday to Friday, there is also a free, first come, first-served shuttle bus leaving from Terminal 3, as well as a bus to the Tanah Merah Ferry Terminal, the gateway to the nearby Indonesian islands of Batam and Bintan, which leaves frequently from Terminal 1 between 6:30 am and 7:30 pm. Taxis and app-based ride-hailing services are also available.

🚲 Bicycle

Singapore's low number of cars and well-organized streets make it an ideal place for bicycle riding even though, with the wealth of transport options covering the whole island, a bike is not really necessary to get around. Bike enthusiasts should consider instead taking a ferry to a former mining area on Pulau Ubin, now one of Singapore's most pristine natural spots, with few motorized vehicles and a limited number of roads. Cyclist can head out in the 111-acre Ketam Mountain Bike Park, an all-weather, man-made route endorsed by the International Mountain Bicycling Association.

🚢 Boat

There is frequent ferry service between Singapore and Indonesia's Pulau Batam and Pulau Bintan. Ferries are clean, fast, and air-conditioned, and they leave from the Tanah Merah Ferry terminal.

🚌 Bus

Big Bus Singapore Hop-on Hop-off Tour conducts 45-60 minutes long city tours in double-decker coaches from 9 am to 6 pm daily. Tickets start at S$43 per adult and can be booked online at ⊕ *www.duck-tours.com.sg*. Tickets are valid for 24, 48, or 72 hours across seven lines—four Hop On Hop Off lines and three feeder lines. The Yellow Line, or city route, connects Orchard Road past the Singapore Botanic

Getting Here and Around

Gardens and through the Civic District. The Red Line, or heritage route, crosses Chinatown, Little India, and Kampong Glam at a slower pace.

Air-conditioned private buses between Singapore and Malaysia are quite comfortable. The cheapest and best way to get to Singapore's nearest Malaysian city, Johor Bahru (aka JB), set right across the causeway, is to catch Singapore Bus Service (SBS) bus Number 170 to Larkin Terminal in JB. It's a two-hour ride that leaves from Queens Street bus station every 15 minutes and costs S$1.70 one-way. The bus will drop you at the Singapore checkpoint, but it will not wait, so bring all your belongings through immigration. Keep your bus ticket and hop on the next one that comes along.

🚗 Car

With the wealth of transportation options available in Singapore, you will not really need a car to get around. But if you are traveling with kids or a large group and plan on visiting the far reaches of the island, you may consider car rental. To be able to drive legally (for up to 12 months) in Singapore, you need either a valid driver's license in English or an International Driving Permit (IDP).

Check the AAA website for more information and getting an IDP ($20).

CAR RENTALS

All major and trusted car rental companies such as Avis, Budget, and Europcar have offices at Singapore's Changi International Airport and downtown. Prices start from S$50 per day for a regular five-seater, and about S$150 per day for vans. The longer the rental period, the cheaper the price. Be aware that not all rental companies allow drivers to take their cars into Malaysia.

DRIVING

Cars drive on the left, and there are strict speed limits of 50 kph (30 mph) in the city, 70 kph (roughly 44 mph) on rural roads, and 90 kph (about 55 mph) on highways. It is compulsory to wear seatbelts, and there's a strict limit of 80mg of blood alcohol content.

GASOLINE

Gasoline in Singapore is quite expensive at S$2.2 per liter and S$8.34 per gallon. This, coupled with the high costs of cars, is the main reason why very few Singaporeans can afford to have a vehicle.

PARKING

Parking in Singapore is not always easy and quickly gets expensive. On-street parking costs S$.60 per half hour outside the Central Business District (CBD) and S$1.20 per half hour within it. Having some time flexibility, however, helps with finding free parking even within the CBD: for example, popular Clarke Quay offers free parking from 12:30 to 1:30 pm on weekdays. Dempsey Hill has 24-hour free parking, and you can also park at the Gardens by the Bay without any charge from 12 to 2 pm on weekdays. Parking in the many multistory car parks around the city is even more expensive. Check a local-approved list of 20 free car parks at ⊕ *thesmartlocal.com/read/ free-carparks*

🚢 Cruise

Singapore has two separate cruise terminals. Star Cruises, Holland America, and some other lines operating smaller ships dock at the Singapore Cruise Centre, which is about a 10- to 15-minute taxi ride from downtown. The larger megaships operated by Celebrity, Cunard, Princess, and Royal Caribbean, use the newer Marina Bay Cruise Centre at the southernmost tip of the country.

🚡 Funicular/Streetcar

Singapore Cable Car is a gondola lift connecting Mount Faber on Singapore's mainland across the Keppel Harbour to the resort island of Sentosa. When opened back in 1974, it was the first aerial ropeway system in the world to span a harbor. A round-trip ticket costs S$35 for adults and S$25 for children, and it takes 15 minutes to ride across the 1,650-meter-long (5,400-foot-long) line.

Ⓜ Public Transport

Singapore's local buses are frequent, air-conditioned, clean and efficient. Together with an excellent subway system they cover routes across most of the island. The urban rail network in Singapore has 120 stations scattered over five metro lines and three light-rail lines. They referred to as the Mass Rapid Transit (MRT) and the Light Rail Transit (LRT) respectively and operate from 5:30 am to 1:00 am daily.

URBAN TRAIN LINES
The North South Line traverses the island connecting Jurong East to Marina Bay's South Pier, while the East West line cuts the island side to side from Pasir Ris to the Tuas Link, with an extension to Changi

Getting Here and Around

International Airport jutting out from the Tanah Merah station. The North East Line connects Harbour Front to Punggol Coast. The yellow Circle Line is very useful for visitors as it connects most of the central districts with the blue Downtown Line, with stops at important tourist attractions such as Little India, Chinatown, Bayfront, and Bugis. In addition, a system of three LRT loops extends from the MRT lines to service the areas of Bukit Panjang, Sengkang, and Punggol.

TICKETS

Trips on the MRT can be paid in cash or with foreign Mastercard and Visa bank cards, and their cost depends on the distance covered. A standard ticket contactless smart card for a single trip costs between S$2 and S$4 (inclusive of a S$1 refundable card deposit). If staying in Singapore for a few days, however, the Singapore Tourist Pass (STP) is a better deal. It's a special stored-value card allowing unlimited travel on both buses and urban trains at a cost of S$10 for one day, S$16 for two days, and S$20 for three days. The STP can be purchased at the Transit Link Ticket Offices at selected MRT stations, at the Concession Card Replacement Office at Somerset station, and at the Automated STP Kiosks at

Changi Airport MRT Station, which can be accessed from Terminal 2 and 3.

🚗 Ride-Sharing

Ride-hailing services are very popular and efficient in Singapore and are a safe and cheaper alternative to taxis. Since Grab (🌐 grab.com/sg) merged with Uber in March 2018, the city-state has welcomed a slew of new services to beat its monopoly. The most reliable are Gojek (🌐 gojek.com/sg), carpooling service RYDE (🌐 rydesharing.com) and TADA (🌐 tada.global), which emphasizes personalized rides and good customer service.

🚕 Taxi

Despite the numerous ride-hailing options available, taxis in Singapore are still plentiful. They are comfortable and handy if you need to go to places outside the bus or MRT radius, or if you are carrying heavy luggage after a long flight. You can easily engage a taxi by hailing one roadside or by lining up at the taxi stands found outside most shopping malls, MRT stations, hotels, and tourist attractions. Cabs in Singapore always use the meter, but there may be surcharges depending on the time of the day, or where and which company's taxi you board. The common taxi booking number 6-DIAL CAB ☎ 6342-5222 routes your call to the first available company.

🚆 Train

There is no longer a direct train from Singapore to anywhere other than Johor Bahru in Malaysia. The train ride is just 5 minutes long, which means that even after allowing for customs clearance and all, you can zip across the border in half an hour (citizens of the United States, the European Union, Australia, and New Zealand don't need a visa for stays of up to 90 days, but proof of onward travel may be required). From Singapore's Woodlands station there are 13 daily trains leaving roughly every hour and a half from 8:30 am to 11:45 pm.

JB Sentral station is the starting point of a single railway line that travels north through Greater Johor (Kluang, Segamat) and ends at Gemas interchange. This is where the train line splits into two: the main KTM railway line along Malaysia's western coast has Electric Train Service (ETS) trains going all the way to the Thai border at Padang Besar via Kuala Lumpur and Butterworth (for the island of Penang). The second line is fondly known as the Jungle Railway and runs across Malaysia's interior until the east coast city of Kota Bharu near Thailand's southeastern border. It's always best to reserve tickets online at ⊕ www.ktmb.com.my.

Essentials

🍴 Dining

Eating like a Singaporean can be a casual and cheap affair at one of the many open-air *kopitiams* (coffee shops) and food courts that serve great street food all over the island. Don't be put off by the less-than-stellar street-food environments, as dining in this manner is an authentic Singaporean experience, and you should try it at least once during your visit. First-timer visitors may prefer to dine at the hawker centers inside of shopping malls. Although such establishments cost a little more, they tend to be cleaner and fully air-conditioned. Beyond the food courts, Singapore's dining scene gets very sophisticated: from celebrated chef Violet Oon's National Kitchen to Janice Wong's acclaimed confection shops to the award-winning restaurant Iggy's, the city-state is a perfect place to experience some of the world's finest cuisine.

DISCOUNTS AND DEALS

Many upscale restaurants offer great lunch deals with special menus at cut-rate prices designed to give customers a true taste of the place. Singapore also has some interesting smartphone apps that can give you discounts on food and drinks. CHUG (⊕ *getchug.com*) offers an interesting S$19.90 deal to enjoy 30 drinks across 30 different outlets in 7 days, working out to only S$0.66 per drink. Chope (⊕ *www.chope. co/singapore-restaurants*) offers real-time reservation booking at a wide range of partner restaurants. Not only you will discover dining spots near you, but ChopeDeals has many buy one, get one free offers and 50-percent discounts at more than 700 different dining spots. Eatigo (⊕ *eatigo.com/sg/*) offers similar discounts.

PAYING

Most restaurants take credit cards, but some smaller places do not. It's worth asking. Waiters expect a 20-percent tip at high-end restaurants; some add an automatic gratuity for groups of six or more.

MEALS AND MEALTIMES

Many big-name restaurants shut down between lunch and dinner and close by 11 pm. Most restaurants are open seven days a week, but, for late-night dining, your best bets are food courts and kopitiams. Geylang Serai is a favorite late-night foodie hangout, as is Kampong Glam, where revelers head for quick, cheap bites after hitting the clubs.

SMOKING

Smoking is banned in all restaurants and bars, and like elsewhere in Singapore, it carries hefty fines of up to S$1,000.

What It Costs in Singapore Dollars			
$	$$	$$$	$$$$
AT DINNER			
under S$15	S$16-S$30	S$31–S$50	over S$50

⊕ Health

Each year, more than 200,000 people travel from neighboring countries to Singapore for top-notch medical care. First-rate doctors and well-equipped hospitals, all English-speaking, abound here.

FOOD AND DRINK

Tap water is safe to drink. Every eating establishment—from the most elegant hotel dining room to the smallest sidewalk stall—is regularly inspected by the strict health authorities. Look for "A" or "B" placards, meaning that these establishments have top-notch hygiene. If your stomach is delicate, watch out for the powerful local *chilli sambal* (chili paste), and be prepared for some minor upsets because your body may not be used to local herbs. MSG is still used in some food stalls or cheaper restaurants to enhance flavoring. It may be wise to pack a remedy for mild stomach upsets and also take a course of lactobacillus prior to your trip.

PESTS AND OTHER HAZARDS

With the relentless heat in Singapore it's important to be aware of dehydration and sunstroke. Pace yourself when planning outdoor activities, avoid long periods of time in direct sunlight, and drink at least 50 percent more water than you would at home. When swimming in the waters of Singapore's offshore islands, be aware not only of the water quality but also of the strong undercurrents. Although there's virtually no malaria risk in Singapore, there are occasional flare-ups of dengue fever, so protect yourself at all times from mosquitoes. Symptoms of dengue include a high fever, strong headache, joint and muscle pain, and sweating. Rashes on the chest and legs are clear signs. Singapore clinics are accustomed to treating these endemic diseases. If you plan to visit Bintan and Batam islands, Indonesia, you may consider taking precautions against malaria. Pack plenty of bug spray: note, however, that resorts on these islands will have netting, insect repellent, and mosquito coils.

Essentials

➕ Safety

Singapore has a very low crime rate; it's safe to walk around unaccompanied at night, and people often leave their bags unattended. Bear in mind, however, that low crime doesn't mean no crime. Use common sense.

Jaywalk at your own risk; besides the fact you may be fined by a passing policeman, Singapore drivers won't slow down or stop to let you cross.

✏️ Immunizations

Proof of vaccination against yellow fever is required if you're entering from an infected area (e.g., Africa or South America).

📶 Internet

Fast Internet broadband is the standard in Singapore. The three major Internet service providers—Singtel, StarHub, and M1—all offer good-value tourist SIM cards that are valid for stays of up to two weeks. Both Starhub and M1's tourist SIM cards cost $12, but Starhub offers more minutes of international calls and 1GB of roaming data. If you don't already own an EZ-link transport card and will need to take public transport when traveling to Singapore, it's best to get Singtel's **Hi!Tourist EZ-Link SIM Card,** which has a stored value of S$3 and can be used as an EZ-link card across the island's transport network.

Fast Internet, however, doesn't mean no censorship: website content is subject to regulation by the Media Development Authority (MDA), which blocks a number of websites containing "mass impact objectionable" material. The list of banned websites has not been revealed in public, but it includes pornography sites and Ashley Madison, an online dating service. A VPN is useful to protect your privacy but not really necessary for regular browsing while in Singapore.

🛏️ Lodging

Singapore has an incredible array of accommodation options to fit all price categories. From trusted luxury brands to vacation rentals to hostels, you will have plenty to choose from.

FACILITIES

You can assume that all rooms have private baths, phones, TVs, and air-conditioning, unless otherwise indicated. Breakfast is noted when it is included in the rate. Most hotels have pools, some of which are on the top floor or terrace.

APARTMENTS AND HOUSE RENTALS

It is possible to rent apartments or townhouses for longer stays in Singapore. Some popular vacation rental websites to check out are Airbnb, Property Guru, and Edge Prop.

PARKING

With the bounty of affordable transportation connecting the island, few hotels have proper parking facilities. It's not recommended to park or even drive in Singapore as costs get expensive quickly. If you need to rent a car, try to return it after a day trip to avoid the hassle and the costs of finding suitable overnight parking near your hotel.

PRICES

During peak tourist season, hotels are often fully booked, and rates soar. They climb even higher during holidays such as between Christmas and January, Chinese New Year (in January or February depending on the year), and Indian festivals such as Thaipusam and Deepavali.

RESERVATIONS

It pays to reserve a room before national holidays like Chinese New Year when demand for rooms increase.

What It Costs in Singapore Dollars

$	$$	$$$	$$$$
FOR TWO PEOPLE			
under S$100	S$101– S$250	S$251– S$400	over S$400

$ Money

The Singapore dollar (S$, known on the street as the "sing-dollar") is the city-state's official unit of currency, with an exchange rate of S$1 to USD0.77. Paper notes are denominated in S$2, S$5, S$10, and S$50 (less commonly seen are S$100, S$500, S$1,000, and S$10,000 bills). There 5-cent, 10-cent, 20-cent, 50-cent, and S$1 coins.

⊕ Passport

U.S. citizens need only a valid passport for stays of up to 90 days. Your passport must be valid for the next six months or more and in good condition. You also need a confirmed round-trip airline ticket or other proof of onward travel when entering the country.

Where Should I Stay?

	NEIGHBORHOOD VIBE	PROS	CONS
Orchard Road	Where all the shopping and high-life is. A true experience of Singapore's heart.	Safe area; close to both Marina Bay and the heritage districts.	Busy with cars and people; some areas are known for prostitution, but generally safe.
Marina Bay	Located in the center of the city, Marina Bay has glamorous high rises.	Super central; walking distance to the CBD and the Bay's main sights; good Metro access.	Expensive in general; can feel touristy.
Kampong Glam	Charming residential blocks of Chinese shophouses drawing artists and hipsters.	Great atmosphere; quiet yet vibrant; perfect MRT access.	Some streets are noisy at night; can become packed with tourists; not many high-end dining options around.
Chinatown	Iconic district strewn with temples, murals, and markets packed with both great finds and tourist tat.	Slightly removed from the busiest part of town, and yet super-central; large selection of hotels, shops, and restaurants.	Crowded in the daytime; can feel like a tourist trap.
Little India	A stunning mix of old lanes, temples, and simple eateries painted with stunning street art.	Safe area; historic charm on every street; cheap and delicious Indian food; wonderful photo opportunities.	Can get crowded; not many high-end dining options; backpacker-oriented area.
Dempsey Hill	Cosmopolitan, lively neighborhood on the western fringes of the city.	Plenty of modern hotels; good selection of bars and restaurants.	Few budget hotel options; not so well connected by MRT; highbrow vibe may not be for everyone.
Sentosa	The island center of family entertainment, sun, and sea.	A one-stop-shop for theme parks, kid-friendly attractions, and family-oriented accommodations.	On the expensive side; very touristy; as far from Singapore's old heritage feel as it gets.
Clarke Quay (Singapore River)	Super-central and flashy neighborhood on the Singapore River.	Safe; easy walk to the MRT and the Bay; more restaurants than you can try.	Can be noisy at night; at times it feels like an entertainment den for expatriates.

💼 Shopping

Singapore is a real shopping paradise. Start on Orchard Road and its many shopping malls filled with high-end boutiques and designer ware. Marina Bay has more malls that close late (11 pm during the week and 11:30 pm on Fridays and Saturdays). Besides its many bars, popular Clarke Quay on the Singapore River also packs many signature boutiques worth a browse. In Holland Village, you'll find made-in-Asia trinkets, carpets, antiques and vintage furnishings. VIVOCity, on the western side of the Harbour Front, is the city's biggest mall, with every major international outlet.

Even Singapore's artsy districts have great shopping: Haji Lane in Kampong Glam is lined with cute vintage stores, and its Arab quarter offers an interesting mix of clothes, vintage cameras, and accessories. Little India is perfect for silks, jewelery, and Indian sarees. You'll get more bargains in Chinatown, the perfect place to buy spices, souvenirs, and low-cost clothing. Continue to Bugis Street Market, between Little India and north Marina Bay, where you'll find 800-odd stalls loaded with the cheapest bargains, from clothes to electronics, house wares, and footwear.

💲 Taxes

Everyone leaving Singapore by air pays a hefty departure tax, known as a Passenger Service Charge, of S$32.90. Add to that an Aviation Levy of S$6.10, plus a new Airport Development Levy of S$10.80, for a grand total of S$49.80. The fee will be further increased by $2.50 annually until April 1, 2024 to fund developments for the airport's expected and hyper-technological Terminal 5. Transiting passengers only pay S$9 tax. In the rare case it's not already included with the price of your ticket, tax is payable at the airport. To save time and avoid standing in line, buy a tax voucher at your hotel or any airline office. Passengers who are in Singapore for less than 24 hours may leave the airport without paying this tax.

VALUE-ADDED TAX

There's a 7% sales tax, called the Goods and Services Tax (GST), the equivalent of a value-added tax. You can get the tax refunded at Global Refund Singapore counters in the airport as you leave the country for purchases of at least S$100 made at a store or retail chain displaying the Tax Free Shopping sticker (you can pool together a maximum of three same-day individual receipts to reach the minimum S$100).

Essentials

💲 Tipping

Tipping isn't common in Singapore; however, if you feel that the service was exceptional you can leave a small tip. High-end hotels and restaurants automatically levy a 10% service charge. Taxi drivers don't receive tips from Singaporeans.

🏳️ U.S. Embassy/Consulate

The Embassy of the United States in Singapore at 27 Napier Road offers consular services in the embassy building.

🛂 Visa

U.S. passport holders (regular, official, and diplomatic) do not require a visa to enter Singapore for business or pleasure and can remain in the country for up to 90 days. The same rule applies to citizens of the United Kingdom, Australia, Canada, and the European Union.

📅 When to Go

High Season: It's hot and humid all year, but peak travel season is between December and June. Mid-December through Chinese New Year (falling in January or February depending on the lunar calendar) is when flights and hotels are often booked up, so it pays to book and plan in advance.

Low Season: Singapore is always humid, but rainy season is between November and January. Showers can last for hours or be heavy and finish within minutes, but full-out storms are rare. January is also the coolest month, but by only a few degrees.

Value Season: Summer is no hotter than the rest of the year and, although schools are on vacation, you won't find attractions to be very crowded. Because many office workers go on vacation themselves, hotel prices can be more reasonable during the summer months.

Contacts

📍 Visitor Information

TOURISM BOARD Visit Singapore. ⊕ *www.visitsingapore. com.*

VISITOR CENTERS Orchardgateway Visitor Centre. ✉ *216 Orchard Rd., Orchard* Ⓜ *Somerset.* **Chinatown Visitor Centre.** ✉ *2 Banda St., Chinatown* Ⓜ *Chinatown.* **Kampong Glam Visitor Centre.** ✉ *55 Bussorah St., Kampong Glam* Ⓜ *Bugis.*

🏳️ Embassy

U.S. Embassy. ✉ *27 Napier Rd.* ☎ *6476-9100* ⊕ *sg.usembassy. gov.*

🆚 Visa

Ministry of Foreign Affairs. ☎ *6379-8000* ⊕ *www.mfa. gov.sg.*

Immigration and Checkpoints Authority. ✉ *10 Kallang Rd.* ⊕ *www.ica.gov.sg.*

🛏️ Lodging

Airbnb. ⊕ *www.airbnb.com/s/ Singapore.*

Property Guru ☎ *6238-5971* ⊕ *www.propertyguru.com.sg.*

✈️ Air Travel

Changi International Airport. ✉ *Airport Blvd.* ☎ *6595-6868* ⊕ *www.changiairport.com.* **AirAsia.** ☎ *80/4666-2222* ⊕ *www.airasia.com.* **Scoot.** ☎ *3138-4047* ⊕ *flyscoot.com.* **Singapore Airlines.** ☎ *3027-7900* ⊕ *www.singaporeair.com.*

🚕 Taxi Travel

Gojek. ☎ *3135-3135* ⊕ *www. gojek.com/sg.*

RYDE. ⊕ *www.rydesharing. com.*

TADA. ⊕ *tada.global.*

🚆 Train Travel

Singapore MRT. ⊕ *mrt.sg.*

Singapore Land Transport Authority. ☎ *800/2255-582* ⊕ *www.lta. gov.sg.*

➕ Health

Alexandra Hospital. ✉ *378 Alexandra Rd.* ☎ *6472-2000* ⊕ *www.ah.com.sg.* **Mount Elizabeth Hospital.** ✉ *3 Mount Elizabeth, Orchard* ☎ *6737-2666* ⊕ *www.mountelizabeth.com. sg.* **Singapore General Hospital.** ✉ *Outram Rd.* ☎ *6222-3322* ⊕ *www.sgh.com.sg* Ⓜ *Outram Park.*

Great Itineraries

THE BEST OF SINGAPORE: CITY, ARTS, AND NATURE IN 7 DAYS

Singapore is compact and very well-connected by public transport, and you can definitely visit its main sights in just a couple of days. A week, however, is the perfect amount of time to experience the best of Singapore's nature, modernity, and rich heritage, as well as to sample its food at casual and trendy restaurants—with a few nights out hitting the best bars and live music joints.

DAY 1: BAYFRONT EXPLORATION

If you are flying in, visit **the Jewel** at Changi International Airport before catching an MRT or taxi to your hotel. You should start your Singapore exploration by the bay, visiting the iconic **Merlion Park**, the city-state's landmark. But first, grab breakfast at **Lau Pa Sat**, a popular food court in the Central Business District (CBD)—arrive before noon to avoid the crowds, or return in the evening for barbecue fish and casual outdoor dining. Then head to Marina Bay's **Gardens By the Bay**. You'll need about three hours to walk around these 250 acres of reclaimed land and three waterfront gardens. Explore the **Cloud Forest**, the **Flower Dome**, and the futuristic electric trees of the **Supertree Grove**. In the evening,

the nearby **Marina Bay Sands Skypark**, perched 55-stories above ground like a surfboard on top of three hotel towers, is a perfect spot to catch a sunset over the bay.

Logistics: Wear comfortable shoes as you'll have to walk a lot. MRT: Raffles Place.

DAY 2: DOWNTOWN EXPLORATION

Start your day in the Civic District with a walking tour of the beautiful heritage buildings around the **Padang**, the immaculate lawn that marks the center of old Singapore. Before lunch, move to nearby **Chinatown**, where you can walk along historic streets to understand more about the lifestyles of Singapore's early immigrants. In addition to shopping for souvenirs, be sure to visit some of Singapore's most important temples, like **Thian Hock Keng**, a Hokkien shrine dedicated to Sea Goddess Mazu, and the Hindu **Sri Mariamman**. You can have lunch at **Chinatown Food Street**, or keep that for dinner and hop to nearby **Tiong Bahru**, an old neighborhood transformed into hipster heaven, with plenty of cool cafes, indie boutiques, and iconic wall murals.

After lunch, head back to the Bugis and **Kampong Glam** area, a former red-light district turned artsy neighborhood, for more shopping and cafe hopping. For a stark change of atmosphere, visit the **National Museum of Singapore**, the oldest in town, and the **Malay Heritage Centre**. From here, skirt the golden-domed **Sultan Mosque** totake in the heritage charm and abundant shops of hip **Haji Lane**.

Reserve your second evening for more window shopping at **Orchard Road**, Singapore's glitziest thoroughfare, stopping for a casual-chic dinner in one of **Emerald Hill's** al fresco restaurants, or catch a live band or poetry slam at the **Aliwal Arts Center** in Kampong Glam, where artsy types fill attractive local bars.

DAY 3: INTO THE WILD

Singapore Zoo, in Western Singapore, is one of the best in the world, and you should dedicate a solid day to see it. Start with the zoo's four- to six-hour custom tour in the morning, and see how you feel by noon. You can take the afternoon off at your hotel, or take a break at a cafe downtown, but you shouldn't miss a chance to experience the zoo's **Night Safari**, dining in a tepee tent before you start your night walk.

Logistics: Get an early start, or you won't see many active animals in the hottest hours of the day. MRT: Ang Mo Kio.

DAY 4: LITTLE INDIA AND THE GARDENS

After a break with nature, continue your exploration of Singapore's heart with breakfast in **Little India**. Browse the hawker stalls of **Tekka Market**, or try a *dosa* (crispy pancake) at the 70-year-old **Komala Villas** before you start traipsing down streets lined with shops and temples. Peek at the elaborate pantheon of Gods etched on the *gopurams* (entrance towers) of the **Sri Veeramakaliamman** and **Sri Srinivasa Perumal** Hindu shrines. Continue your heritage hunt at the **Indian Heritage Centre**.

If you still have time before lunch, stroll through **Little India Arcade** to enjoy the 1920s architecture and the stacks of Indian textiles and flower garlands on offer. Have lunch at **Banana Leaf Apolo**, and then sweat off the calories by walking down glitzy **Orchard Road**. Stop as much as you need, but try to reach **Singapore Botanic Gardens**, a UNESCO World Heritage Site, by 3:30 pm. Check out the rain forest, the Ethnobotany, and the Orchid Gardens, with more than a thousand rare species on display.

Logistics: MRT: Little India, Orchard Road.

Great Itineraries

DAY 5: EXPLORE PULAU UBIN

Tucked in the northeastern corner of Singapore right across from Malaysia, **Pulau Ubin** is an island stuck back in time. Shaped like a boomerang, this 2,500-acre land mass is home to Singapore's last village as well as the Chek Jawa Wetlands, one of the city-state's richest ecosystems. Pulau Ubin is great for cyclists, with a highlight being the 10-km (6.2-mile) **Ketam Mountain Bike Park** trail skirting around the Ketam Quarry. Otherwise, try to time your visit with one of the 2.5-km (1.5-mile) guided walking tours that showcase Pulau Ubin's kampung heritage and cultural, economic, and natural history.

Logistics: Board a bumboat at Changi Point Ferry Terminal and you'll reach Pulau Ubin's shores in about 15 minutes.

DAY 6: THEME PARK FUN AT SENTOSA

Singapore's entertainment island may not be everyone's cup of tea, but it's so packed with attractions that it's a must visit. The **Universal Studios** here should top your list, with its 28 rides, as well as shows and attractions, across seven zones, including Ancient Egypt and Madagascar. If you still have time, check out the 1,000 species on display at **S.E.A.**

Aquarium, or visit the **Butterfly Park and Insect Kingdom**. And if you are not exhausted, consider catching Universal Studios' nightly fireworks show at around 9 pm or 9:30 pm.

Logistics: Sentosa can be reached on foot or by car, bus, monorail, and cable car. For those heading to Sentosa by train, take the MRT to Harbourfront Station, which is found on the North East Line.

DAY 7: SHOPPING AND DINING

Reserve your final day for last-minute shopping and relaxation. Start at **Orchard ION** for luxury branded items, and swing by **Lucky Plaza** for perfumes at bargain prices. In hip Bugis, **Bugis Junction** and **Bugis Plus** are two shopping arcades combined under one roof. You could also head farther west to **VivoCity** and experience the largest shopping mall in Singapore. For electronics, try **Sim Lim Square** in Rochor, the city-state's IT hub, but skip the pushy sellers on Level 1 and 2. Make time for a relaxing evening at **Dempsey Hill**, filled with upscale stores and award-winning restaurants. Get one last nightcap in nearby **Holland Village**, where al fresco eateries, unusual craft ateliers, dessert bars, and old-fashioned cafes will make you feel sad to leave Singapore.

On the Calendar

January

Singapore Art Week. A nine-day annual celebration of the visual arts, from screenings to talks and exhibits, that spruce up museums, art galleries and precincts, and plain odd spaces island-wide.

February

Chinese New Year. The Lunar New Year is celebrated with particular fervor in Singapore, home to a majority Chinese population. It can take place in January or February depending on the year's calendar.

Thaipusam. Celebrated on the full moon day of the Indian month of Thai, between the end of January and February in honor of Lord Murugan, the destroyer of evil, this religious festival attracts thousands of Hindu devotees who fulfill their vows (*kavadi*, ranging from pots of milk hauled over the head to skewers pierced through their cheeks and tongues) with a 4- km walk from the Sri Srinivasa Perumal Temple to the Sri Thendayuthapani Temple.

March

Singapore Festival of Fun. Three festivals in one enliven Clarke Quay's scene for ten days of comedy, street performances, and more.

April

Sing Jazz. Three nights of international jazz and blues descend on the glittering Marina Bay Sands.

May

Singapore International Festival of Arts. Going strong for more than 40 years, this illustrious event has long been a jewel in Singapore's cultural calendar, presenting theatrical performances, music, and conferences by global luminaries and groundbreaking local artists alike.

Sundown Marathon Taking place between May and June every year, this is Asia's biggest night run. ⊕ *www.sundownmarathon.com/sg/.*

On the Calendar

June

Ultra Singapore. This outdoor electronic music festival at Marina Bay debuted in 2015 in Singapore as part of Ultra Music Festival's worldwide expansion, part of a dance empire spread across twenty countries.

July

Singapore Food Festival. Singapore food is celebrated in all its forms, including in workshops, chef collaborations, and food-themed tours of the tastiest neighborhoods in town.

August

Baybeats. Baybeats is an annual 3-day alternative music festival organized by Esplanade. It showcases various Singaporean bands, who share an outdoor stage with Southeast Asian and international artists. The festival happens at Esplanade-Theatres on the Bay and is 100% free ⊕ *http://www.sifa.sg.*

Singapore Night Festival. A line-up of arts, heritage, and cultural experiences transforms the Bras Basah and Bugis districts into an ethereal wonderland. ⊕ *www.nightfestival.sg.*

September

Hungry Ghost Festival. Just as Americans have Halloween, the Chinese have the Hungry Ghost Festival ("Zhong Yuan Jie"). According to local folklore, this is the time when the souls of the dead come back to earth and roam the streets looking for entertainment. Locals celebrate in the streets, knowing well that ignoring the ghosts can lead to mischief.

Singapore Grand Prix. Cars run a 3.14-mile F1 route at night during this event, which sees racers zipping around Marina Bay. ⊕ *www.singaporegp.sg.*

November

Deepavali. During the Indian festival of lights, Singapore's Little India fills with a thousand lamps and colors.

Singapore Writers Festival. One of Southeast Asia's most celebrated literary events returns every year to bring together an international array of writers and readers.

December

Marina Bay Countdown. End the year in a smorgasbord of fireworks and light shows at Singapore's enticing show by the bay.

Chapter 3

CIVIC DISTRICT AND MARINA BAY

Updated by
Audrey Phoon

⦿ Sights　　🍴 Restaurants　　🛏 Hotels　　🛍 Shopping　　🍸 Nightlife

★★★★★　　★★★★★　　★★★★★　　★★★★☆　　★★★★☆

NEIGHBORHOOD SNAPSHOT

TOP EXPERIENCES

■ **Gardens by the Bay:** This man-made nature park (and architectural marvel) houses hundreds of thousands of plants in fantastical structures.

■ **Singapore by boat:** Take a bumboat ride down the Singapore River and admire the colorful heritage shophouses.

■ **Sundown at Marina Bay Sands:** The hotel's stunning 150-meter infinity pool is the world's largest elevated outdoor body of water.

■ **World-Class museums:** The National Gallery, Peranakan Museum, and Asian Civilisations Museum are top-notch.

■ **Fort Canning Park:** This beautiful, historic park has nine gardens inspired by Singapore's heritage.

GETTING HERE

The Civic District is easily reachable via the Bras Basah MRT station on the Circle Line (yellow) and the City Hall MRT station on the North South Line (red). The Marina Bay area is accessible via the Bayfront MRT station on the Downtown and Circle lines or on a pleasant waterside walk from Raffles Place MRT station on the North South and East West (green) lines. The districts are compact and walkable.

PLANNING YOUR TIME

Allow at least one full day for exploring. Restaurants get busy during weekdays with the after-office crowd, so check out hawker stalls ahead of lunchtime. On weekends, the area is much quieter, though not as many restaurants and shops are open.

QUICK BITES

■ **Gather.** Located in a quiet corner of Raffles Hotel is a stylish French cafe-boutique known for speciality coffee and handmade crepes. ⊠ *328 North Bridge Rd., Civic District* ⊕ *www.gathershop. co* Ⓜ *City Hall*

■ **Yet Con Restaurant.** Take a trip to Singapore in the '40s at this charmingly old-school Hainanese cafeteria; the speciality is chicken rice. ⊠ *25 Purvis St., City Hall* Ⓜ *Bugis, Bras Basah, and Esplanade*

■ **Makansutra Gluttons Bay.** This centrally located, open-air food court is a great option for those tight on time but determined to sample as many of Singapore's local dishes as possible. ⊠ *#01–15 Esplanade, 8 Raffles Ave., City Hall* ⊕ *www. makansutra. com* Ⓜ *City Hall, Esplanade, and Promenade*

Many of Singapore's top attractions are a short walk within or from this central part of the city. Singapore's earliest example of urban planning is the Civic District, which runs alongside the Singapore River between the City Hall and Dhoby Ghaut MRT stations. The birthplace of the country's modern historical, architectural, and cultural heritage, it's dotted with imposing reminders of British rule.

Many of these colonial markers been conserved and converted into government offices and museums (this is also the museum district), the stateliest of which is the National Gallery Singapore. It occupies two national monuments, the former Supreme Court building and City Hall. Other majestic landmarks include the storied Raffles Hotel—which completed an extensive renovation in 2019 and has accommodated many notable guests, from Charlie Chaplin to Elizabeth Taylor to Michael Jackson—and the Fullerton Hotel, which was once Singapore's first general post office.

Set along the mouth of the Singapore River are Clarke Quay, Boat Quay, and Robertson Quay. Clarke Quay stands upstream from Boat Quay, which was a trading center during the colonial era. Its once-abandoned warehouses and shophouses have now become part of a brightly colored maze of restaurants, bars, and clubs. Farther upstream is the more laid-back Robertson Quay, a residential area popular among expats for its numerous, upscale, food-and-beverage options. Mohamed Sultan Road, to the north, is a quieter stretch of shophouses containing restaurants and offices.

Across from the Civic District and the Marina Bay waters, the futuristic buildings of the Marina Bay area sprout from 890 acres of reclaimed land. This is where some of Singapore's most famous skyline landmarks are located, from the iconic Marina Bay Sands and gleaming Marina Bay Financial Centre to Gardens By The Bay, a waterfront garden complex known for its larger-than-life Supertrees.

Civic District

Bras Basah Road and the surrounding streets were marked out by Sir Stamford Raffles as the European portion of the city in the 1800s. They're now home to many of the city's most important museums and national monuments. Although it's small, the area is highly concentrated, so allow a couple of days to explore thoroughly, especially if you love art and architecture.

◉ Sights

Armenian Church

RELIGIOUS SITE | Also known as the Church of St. Gregory the Illuminator, this is one of Singapore's most elegant buildings. Built in 1835, this is the republic's oldest surviving church. The Armenians were but one of many minority groups that came to Singapore in search of better lives. A dozen wealthy Armenian families (and several non-Christian merchants) donated the funds for renowned colonial architect George Coleman to design this church. The main internal circular structure is imposed on a square plan with four projecting porticoes. In the churchyard is the weathered tombstone of Agnes Joaquim, who bred the orchid hybrid that has become Singapore's national flower. The pink-and-white orchid, with a deeper purplish pink center, was discovered in her garden in 1893 and still carries her name: Vanda Miss Joaquim. ✉ *60 Hill St., Civic District* ☎ *6334–0141* ⊕ *www.armeniansinasia.org* 🎫 *Free* Ⓜ *City Hall.*

★ The Arts House

ARTS VENUE | George Coleman designed the Parliament House in 1827 as a mansion for wealthy merchant John Maxwell. Maxwell never occupied it, and instead leased it to the government, which eventually bought it in 1841 for S$15,600. It is considered Singapore's oldest government building, housing the Supreme Court until 1939 followed by the Legislative Assembly in 1953 and then the Parliament in 1965. The building now contains The Arts House, a multidisciplinary venue offering film retrospectives, photo exhibitions, musicals, plays, and talks by experts. Note the bronze elephant statue on a plinth in front of the building; it was a gift from King Chulalongkorn of Siam during his state visit in 1871. ✉ *1 Old Parliament Ln., Civic District* ☎ *6332–6900* ⊕ *www.theartshouse.sg* 🎫 *Free* Ⓜ *City Hall.*

Did You Know?

Fort Canning Park, once known as Forbidden Hill, is home to ancient artifacts, gardens, and a striking underground staircase.

Civic District and Singapore River

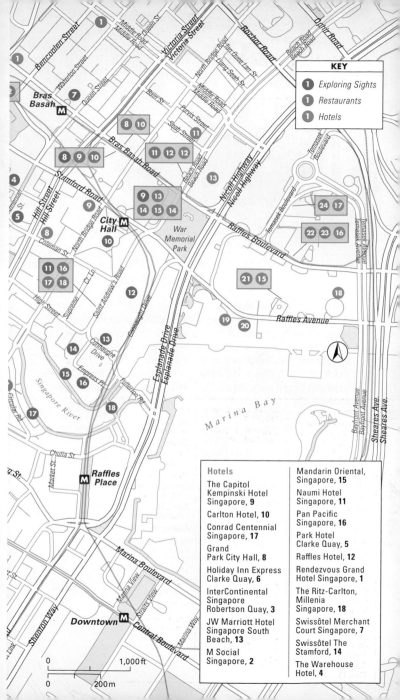

KEY

- ① Exploring Sights
- ① Restaurants
- ① Hotels

Hotels

The Capitol
Kempinski Hotel
Singapore, **9**

Carlton Hotel, **10**

Conrad Centennial
Singapore, **17**

Grand
Park City Hall, **8**

Holiday Inn Express
Clarke Quay, **6**

InterContinental
Singapore
Robertson Quay, **3**

JW Marriott Hotel
Singapore South
Beach, **13**

M Social
Singapore, **2**

Mandarin Oriental,
Singapore, **15**

Naumi Hotel
Singapore, **11**

Pan Pacific
Singapore, **16**

Park Hotel
Clarke Quay, **5**

Raffles Hotel, **12**

Rendezvous Grand
Hotel Singapore, **1**

The Ritz-Carlton,
Millenia
Singapore, **18**

Swissôtel Merchant
Court Singapore, **7**

Swissôtel The
Stamford, **14**

The Warehouse
Hotel, **4**

The Asian Civilisations Museum's fascinating galleries are dedicated to Asian heritage.

★ Asian Civilisations Museum

MUSEUM | FAMILY | Constructed in the 1860s as a courthouse, the huge, white, Neoclassical Empress Place building has housed nearly every government body, including the Registry of Births and Deaths and the Immigration Department. It's now home to the Asian Civilisations Museum, the nation's first to look comprehensively at the east, south, southeast, and west Asian regions, each of which has its own timeline and permanent displays. Spread over three levels, the 11 galleries have state-of-the-art interactive features, and there's also an educational center for kids. ⊠ *1 Empress Place, Civic District* ☎ *6332–7798* ⊕ *www.acm. org.sg* 🖅 *S$20* Ⓜ *Raffles Place.*

Cavenagh Bridge

BRIDGE/TUNNEL | This gracious steel bridge, the oldest surviving bridge across the Singapore River, is named after Major General Orfeur Cavenagh, governor of the Straits Settlements from 1859 to 1867. Built in 1868 with girders imported from Glasgow, Scotland, it was the main route across the river until 1909. It's now a pedestrian bridge with a spectacular view of the Fullerton Hotel. On the riverbank, the whimsical sculptures of boys in half-dive over the water by local sculptor Chong Fah Cheong make for great pictures. ⊠ *Connaught Dr., Civic District* ⊕ *www.cavenagh-bridge. com* Ⓜ *City Hall.*

Chijmes

PLAZA | The oldest building in this walled complex is the Coleman-designed Caldwell House, a private mansion built in 1840. In 1852, this, together with other buildings, became the Convent of the Holy Infant Jesus, where nuns housed and schooled abandoned children. A church was added between 1901 and 1903. After World War II, both the convent and the church fell into disrepair. The buildings received a S$100 million renovation in 1996 and were reopened as a shopping and entertainment complex that's a good spot to catch live sport screenings or have a romantic dinner. The lovingly restored church is also rented out for private functions, and the grounds are used for the occasional arts market. The name Chijmes (pronounced "chimes") is an acronym of the convent's name. ⊠ *30 Victoria St., Civic District* ☎ *6337–7810* ⊕ *www.chijmes.com.sg* Ⓜ *Bras Basah.*

Fort Canning Park

NATIONAL/STATE PARK | **FAMILY** | Offering a green sanctuary from the bustling city below, Fort Canning is where modern Singapore's founder, Sir Stamford Raffles, built his first bungalow and experimented with a botanical garden. Massive fig trees, luxuriant ferns, and abundant birdlife—including piping black-naped orioles and chattering collared kingfishers—flourish here. The hill's trails are well marked by signs, or you can explore the area with the help of augmented reality via the free BalikSG app offered by the National Heritage Board. In addition to the lush greenery, there are ancient artifacts for history buffs and occasional theater productions and music festivals for arts lovers. ⊠ *River Valley Rd., Civic District* ☎ *1800/471–7300* ⊕ *www.nparks.gov.sg* Ⓜ *Fort Canning.*

★ National Gallery Singapore

MUSEUM | **FAMILY** | A restoration and integration of Singapore's former City Hall and Supreme Court, this Southeast Asian visual arts museum is a work of art in itself. Immerse yourself in its extensive collection of modern art from the region—the world's largest public display—before grabbing a bite at one of the many globally acclaimed restaurants on site. ⊠ *1 St Andrew's Rd., Civic District* ☎ *65/6271–7000,* ⊕ *www.nationalgallery.sg* 🎫 *S$20* Ⓜ *City Hall.*

National Museum of Singapore

MUSEUM | **FAMILY** | Known as the Raffles Museum when it opened in 1887, this building with a silver dome has 20 dioramas depicting the republic's past. It's also home to the Revere Bell, donated to the original St. Andrew's Church in 1834 by the daughter of American patriot Paul Revere; the 380-piece Haw Par Jade Collection, one of the largest of its kind; the exquisite

Farquhar Collection of regional flora and fauna paintings execut-
ed in the 19th century; occult paraphernalia from Chinese secret
societies; and lots of historical documents. ✉ *93 Stamford Rd.,
Civic District* ☎ *6332–3659* ⊕ *www.nationalmuseum.sg* ⊙ *S$15*
Ⓜ *Bencoolen, Bras Basah, Dhoby Ghaut.*

Padang

SPORTS VENUE | Used primarily as a playing field, the Padang (Malay
for "field" or "plain") is behind the Singapore Cricket Club and
has traditionally been a social and political hub. Once called the
Esplanade, it was half its current size until an 1890s land reclamation expanded it. During World War II, the Japanese gathered
2,000 British civilians here before marching them off to Changi
Prison and, in many cases, to their deaths. Today, it serves as a
sports facility for cricket, hockey, and rugby teams, hosting such
international events as the SCC 7s, Asia's oldest international
rugby tournament.

Beyond the Padang's northeastern edge, across Stamford Road
and the Stamford Canal, are the four 220-foot (67-meter) tapering
white columns of the **Civilian War Memorial,** known locally as the
Four Chopsticks. The monument honors the thousands of civilians
from Singapore's four main ethnic groups (Chinese, Malay, Indian,
and "others," including Eurasians and Europeans) who lost their
lives during the Japanese occupation or were dispatched to build
the Burma–Siam Railway. ✉ *3 St. Andrew's Rd., Civic District*
⊕ *www.scc.org.sg/padang-field* Ⓜ *City Hall.*

★ Peranakan Museum

MUSEUM | Formerly the Tao Nan School, built in 1910, this grand
colonial building now houses the first museum in Southeast
Asia devoted to the story of the Peranakans, the descendants of
17th-century Chinese and Indian immigrants who married local
Malays. Its 10 galleries display artwork, jewelry, furniture, and
clothing from members of the community. The museum was
closed for major redevelopment in 2019 and is slated to reopen
mid 2021, but the Peranakan Gallery at Changi International
Airport Terminal 4 features a rotation of its exhibits, and pop-up
displays will also be held at public libraries throughout the closure
period. ✉ *39 Armenian St., Civic District* ☎ *6332–3015* ⊕ *www.
peranakanmuseum.sg* 🎫 *S$6* Ⓜ *Bras Basah.*

Raffles City

STORE/MALL | Designed by the famed Chinese-American architect
I. M. Pei, the towering Raffles City complex contains an office
tower; a variety of retail stores, including Robinsons Department
Store; and two hotels, the Swissôtel The Stamford and the Fair-
mont Singapore. There's a stunning view of downtown and the

harbor from the Swissôtel's 70th-floor restaurants, contemporary grill Skai and mod British fine diner Jaan by Kirk Westaway. ✉ *252 North Bridge Rd., Civic District* ☎ *6338–7766* ⊕ *www.rafflescity. com.sg* Ⓜ *City Hall.*

St. Andrew's Cathedral

RELIGIOUS SITE | The first church at this site was constructed in 1834 but demolished in 1852 following two lightning strikes. Some suggested that before another place of worship was built, the spirits should be appeased with the blood from 30 heads. This suggestion was ignored. Indian convicts were brought in to construct this cathedral in the English Gothic style. The structure, completed in 1861, has bells cast by the firm that made Big Ben's, and it resembles Netley Abbey, in Hampshire, England. The British overlords were so impressed by the cathedral that the Indian convict who supplied the working drawings was granted his freedom. The church was expanded in 1952 and again in 1983. Its lofty interior is white and simple, with stained-glass windows coloring the sunlight as it enters. On the walls are marble-and-brass memorial plaques, including one commemorating the British who died in a 1915 mutiny of native light infantry and another in memory of 41 Australian army nurses killed in the Japanese invasion. Services are held every Sunday. A showcase of historical artifacts and a history video are in the south transept. Guided tours are available. ✉ *11 St. Andrew's Rd., Civic District* ☎ *6337–6104* ⊕ *www.cathedral.org.sg* ⚟ *Free* Ⓜ *City Hall.*

Singapore Art Museum

MUSEUM | **FAMILY** | This art museum opened in 1996 in what was once a Catholic boys' school. It draws from some 10,000 works in the national collection to present exhibitions on contemporary Southeast Asian art. The permanent collection is rotated regularly, displaying such important pieces as the evocative *Pinkswing Park* installation by Agus Suwage and Davy Linggar, the 6-meter-long (20-foot-long) photorealist work *Fall Leaves After Leaves Fall* by Nona Garcia, or the monumental *Status* by Jane Lee. A museum extension, SAM at 8Q, displays a selection of multidisciplinary and interactive works. ✉ *71 Bras Basah Rd., Civic District* ☎ *65/6332–3222* ⊕ *www.singaporeartmuseum.sg* ⚟ *S$6, free on Friday after 6pm* Ⓜ *Bras Basah.*

Statue of Sir Thomas Stamford Raffles

PUBLIC ART | Raffles' likeness keeps permanent watch over the spot where he first landed in Singapore on the morning of January 29, 1819. The location has changed a lot since then: previously, this river was the artery feeding Singapore's commercial life, packed with barges and lighters that ferried goods from cargo ship to dock. There were no cranes—the unloading was done by teams of laborers who tottered back and forth between lighters and riverside godowns (warehouses). ⊠ *North Boat Quay, Civic District* Ⓜ *Raffles Place.*

🍴 Restaurants

★ Artichoke

$$ | **MIDDLE EASTERN** | This restaurant helmed by local celebrity chef Bjorn Shen serves up playful (and unabashedly inauthentic) Middle Eastern–inspired dishes like the cheekily titled Lambgasm, a 5.2-pound hunk of slow-roasted lamb; hummus with Iraqi spiced mushrooms; and raw tuna kebabs. The tranquil, tucked-away location in a cluster of historical buildings known as Sculpture Square only adds to the fun vibe. **Known for:** funky food with Middle Eastern flair; excellent playlist; chill vibes. ⑤ *Average main: S$25* ⊠ *Sculpture Square, 161 Middle Rd., Civic District* ☎ *6336–6949* ⊕ *www.bjornshen.com/artichoke* ⊘ *Closed Mon.*

Art Restaurant

$$$$ | **ITALIAN** | Locally sourced ingredients, including produce from head chef and restaurateur Beppe de Vito's family farm, take center stage at this ritzy Italian fine-dining restaurant. With artfully prepared dishes made with exotic ingredients like fennel pollen, ancient wheat from Puglia, and water from the Dolomites, your meal will be one to remember. **Known for:** refined Italian cooking; interesting ingredients and flavor pairings; tasting menu. ⑤ *Average main: S$78* ⊠ *National Gallery Singapore, 1 St Andrew's Rd., #05–03, Civic District* ☎ *6866–1977* ⊕ *www.artrestaurant.sg* Ⓜ *City Hall.*

BBR by Alain Ducasse

$$$ | **MEDITERRANEAN** | Take your taste buds on a journey across Portugal, Spain, Italy, and France at globally acclaimed chef Alain Ducasse's shared-plate and grill restaurant and bar. The lively eatery, complete with an open kitchen retrofitted with a wood-fired rotisserie and pizza oven, serves up bold food, including a flavorful shrimp and shellfish stew and a surprising dark and milk chocolate pizza. **Known for:** celebrity chef; creative Mediterranean food; energetic vibe. ⑤ *Average main: S$50* ⊠ *Raffles Singapore, 1 Beach Rd., Civic District* ☎ *6337–1886* ⊕ *www.bbr-byalainducasse.com. sg* ⊘ *Closed Tues.-Wed.* Ⓜ *City Hall.*

Flutes at the Fort

$$$ | **MODERN EUROPEAN** | Frangipani perfumes the air as you ascend the steps to this former colonial house among the well-manicured gardens of Fort Canning. The menu, which changes with the season, includes homemade breads and a hearty selection of international dishes, such as seared scallops, pan-fried foie gras, rack of lamb, and lobster. **Known for:** romantic setting; business lunch; wedding venue. ⑤ *Average main: S$50* ⊠ *National Museum of Singapore, 93 Stamford Rd., #01–02, Civic District* ☏ *6338–8770* ⊕ *www.flutes.com.sg* ⊙ *No dinner Sun.* Ⓜ *City Hall.*

Golden Peony

$$ | **CANTONESE** | Join the power-lunchers at this swanky, Michelin-starred hotel dining room for what has been described as "maverick Hong Kong cuisine." Alongside an impressive selection of conventional dim sum delicacies you'll also find more adventurous Cantonese dishes, like crispy prawns with walnuts or golden crispy chicken stuffed with glutinous rice. Both prix-fixe and à la carte menus are available for lunch and dinner. **Known for:** business lunches; Chinese fine dining; classic cooking with a contemporary twist. ⑤ *Average main: S$25* ⊠ *Conrad Centennial Singapore, 2 Temasek Blvd., Civic District* ☏ *6432–7482* ⊕ *conrad-hotels3.hilton.com* ⊙ *No dinner Mon.-Tues.* Ⓜ *City Hall.*

Hai Tien Lo

$$$ | **CHINESE** | You'll enjoy sweeping views of Singapore from most tables at this contemporary Cantonese restaurant high up in the Pan Pacific hotel. Dim lighting, carved wooden screens, and waitresses in cheongsams (Chinese-style dresses with Mandarin collars and side slits) all contribute to the restaurant's distinct sense of place. **Known for:** dim sum; great views; business lunches. ⑤ *Average main: S$34* ⊠ *Level 3, Pan Pacific Singapore, 7 Raffles Blvd., Marina Square* ☏ *6826–8240* ⊕ *www.panpacific. com/en* Ⓜ *City Hall.*

Keyaki Japanese Restaurant

$$$ | **JAPANESE** | This upscale, rooftop, Marina Square restaurant is within a tranquil garden replete with a koi pond, stone lanterns, bamboo, and a pavilion. Keyaki's attentive staff is dressed in kimonos and *happi* coats, and the menu includes what is perhaps Singapore's best teppanyaki , a mix of meat and vegetables stir-fried right at your table, as well as delicious sushi and sashimi and good-value bento lunches. **Known for:** urban oasis; set lunches; traditional Japanese fare. ⑤ *Average main: S$22* ⊠ *Level 4, Pan Pacific Singapore, 7 Raffles Blvd., Marina Square* ☏ *6826–8240* ⊕ *www.panpacific.com* Ⓜ *Promenade.*

★ Labyrinth

$$$$ | **ASIAN FUSION** | The inventive dishes at this one-Michelin-star restaurant reinvent Singaporean classics with local produce. Within its five-course lunch (S$78) and nine-course dinner (S$188) menus, chicken rice is packaged into dainty dumplings, chilli crab is transformed into ice cream, and kaya toast is elevated with caviar—but the flavors stay distinctively Singaporean. **Known for:** modern Singaporean cuisine; inventive flavor pairings; chilli crab ice cream. ⑤ *Average main: S$80* ⊠ *Esplanade Mall, 8 Raffles Ave., #02–23, Civic District* ☎ *6223–4098* ⊕ *labyrinth.com.sg* ⊙ *Closed Mon. No lunch weekends* Ⓜ *Esplanade.*

La Dame De Pic

$$$$ | FRENCH FUSION | French, Michelin-starred chef Anne-Sophie Pic's first foray into Asia is a sensory delight with its soft, pastel space and delicate French creations imbued with Asian flavors. The food includes the restaurant's iconic *berlingots* (pyramid-shaped pasta parcels) filled with a French cheese fondue and complemented by red Kampot peppers native to Cambodia. **Known for:** picture-perfect furnishings; French-Asian creations; first Anne-Sophie Pic restaurant in Asia. ⑤ *Average main: S$218* ⊠ *Raffles Singapore, 1 Beach Rd., Grand Lobby, Civic District* ☎ *6337–1886* ⊕ *www.ladamedepic.com.sg* ⊙ *Closed Sun.-Mon.* Ⓜ *City Hall.*

Lei Garden Restaurant

$$$ | CANTONESE | FAMILY | Located within the Civic District's historic Chijmes building, Lei Garden is known for having one of the best dim sum spreads in Singapore (prixe-fixe and à la carte menus are also available). It's packed with lunching office workers on weekdays and with families on weekends, but the jostle is worth it to savor such standout dishes as Peking duck, grilled rib-eye beef, and scallops with bean curd in black bean sauce. **Known for:** dim sum; big-group dining; sophisticated setting. ⑤ *Average main: S$50* ⊠ *Chijmes, 30 Victoria St., #01–24, Civic District* ☎ *6339–3822* ⊕ *www.leigarden.hk* Ⓜ *City Hall.*

Makansutra Gluttons Bay

$ | ASIAN | Located just off the boardwalk by the Esplanade–Theatres on the Bay, this outdoor, hawker-style cluster of food stands offers a delicious variety of local specialties. Here you'll find chili crab, grilled prawns, chicken rice, fried carrot cake, meat satay, and much more served into the wee hours of the morning. **Known for:** authentic hawker fare; wide variety of food in one spot; local vibes. ⑤ *Average main: S$14* ⊠ *#01–15, 8 Raffles Ave., Civic District* ☎ *6438–4038* ⊕ *www.makansutra.com* ▭ *No credit cards* ⊙ *No lunch* Ⓜ *City Hall.*

Morton's The Steakhouse

$$$$ | AMERICAN | This outpost of Morton's U.S. steakhouses is an adopted favorite among Singaporean carnivores. Morton's characteristic dark-wood paneling, linen napkins and tablecloths, and subdued lighting are all here, as are the juicy cuts of filet mignon, porterhouse steak, and USDA prime-aged beef. **Known for:** huge, pricey portions; free happy hour filet mignon sandwiches; power lunches and dinners in the private boardrooms. $ *Average main: S$90* ⊠ *Level 4, Mandarin Oriental, Singapore, 5 Raffles Ave., Marina Square* ☎ *6339–3740* ⊕ *www.mortons.com/singapore* ☾ *No lunch* Ⓜ *City Hall.*

★ National Kitchen by Violet Oon

$$ | ASIAN FUSION | Get a taste of Singapore's culinary heritage at this luxurious, colonial-style dining destination helmed by veteran local chef Violet Oon. It's known for serving elevated local and Peranakan classics like fish head curry and *mee siam* (thin rice vermicelli noodles), as well as modern reinventions like pasta tossed with spicy *buah keluak* (a bitter and earthy nut labelled the "truffle of the east") sauce. **Known for:** refined Singaporean fare for lunch, dinner, and high tea; lovely ambience; local approval. $ *Average main: S$30* ⊠ *National Gallery Singapore, 1 St. Andrew's Rd., #02–01, Civic District* ☎ *9834–9935* ⊕ *violetoon.com* Ⓜ *City Hall.*

★ New Ubin CHIJMES

$$ | ASIAN FUSION | With creations like Heart Attack Fried Rice (rice stir-fried in beef drippings and served with U.S. Angus beef cubes on the side) and foie-gras satay, this Michelin Bib Gourmand listee specializing in creative Singaporean food is decidedly not for those on a diet. **Known for:** local foodie favorite; innovative use of flavors; Heart Attack Fried Rice. $ *Average main: S$20* ⊠ *CHIJMES, 30 Victoria St., #02–01B/01C, Civic District* ☎ *9740–6870* ⊕ *newubin-seafood.com* Ⓜ *City Hall, Bras Basah, Esplanade.*

Odette

$$$$ | EUROPEAN | Any self-proclaimed gourmand needs to add this three-Michelin-star recipient and "Asia's Best Restaurant" title-holder to their culinary bucket list. The dishes in its four- to six-course lunches (S$188 and S$248) and eight-course dinners (S$358) vary seasonally but boast the same respect for great artisanal produce, brought to life by French culinary arts and a touch of Japanese flair. **Known for:** mod-French fine dining; numerous accolades; cozy and minimalist space. $ *Average main: S$358* ⊠ *National Gallery Singapore, 1 St Andrew's Rd., #01–04, Civic District* ☎ *6385–0498* ⊕ *www.odetterestaurant.com* ☾ *Closed Sun. No lunch Mon.* Ⓜ *City Hall.*

Shahi Maharani

$$ | INDIAN | Teak tables, gold-plated chairs, Indian artifacts, and live Nepalese music combine for a regal experience at this lavish North Indian restaurant, where each dish is categorized as mild, spicy, or very spicy (though the chef can turn the heat up or down based on your preference). You can't go wrong with any of the biryani (rice casserole) or tandoori meals, and the well-chosen wine list, which includes labels from many of the world's top wine-producing regions, runs surprisingly deep. **Known for:** North Indian fine dining; value-for-money lunch buffet; refined biryani dishes. ⑤ *Average main: S$30 ⊠ Raffles City, 252 North Bridge Rd., #03–21B, Civic District* ☎ *6235–8840* ⊕ *www.shahimaharani. com* Ⓜ *City Hall.*

Shinji by Kanesaka

$$$$ | SUSHI | For some of the best sushi outside of Japan, make your way to this spartan Edo-style restaurant by Michelin-starred chef Shinji Kanesaka, where you'll be served sublime nigiri sushi across a counter carved from a single, 220-year-old, Japanese cypress tree. Here, simplicity takes precedence so that the cultural and culinary traditions can shine. **Known for:** true-to-tradition sushi; elegant Japanese setting; acclaimed chef. ⑤ *Average main: S$250 ⊠ Carlton Hotel Singapore, 76 Bras Basah Rd., L1, Civic District* ☎ *6338–6131* ⊕ *www.shinjibykanesaka.com/raffles-place* ⊘ *Closed Sun.* Ⓜ *City Hall.*

SKAI

$$$$ | MODERN EUROPEAN | This contemporary restaurant on the 70th floor of the Swissôtel The Stamford hotel doesn't just serve up beautifully plated sharing dishes, it also doles out fabulous views of Singapore (and, on a clear day, Malaysia and Indonesia). The staff's quiet, attentive service contributes to the elegance, as does the warm, modern decor. **Known for:** panoramic views; Instagrammable interiors; refined sharing plates. ⑤ *Average main: S$60 ⊠ Swissôtel The Stamford, 2 Stamford Rd., Level 70, Civic District* ☎ *6837–3322* ⊕ *www.swissotel.com* Ⓜ *City Hall.*

Szechuan Court & Kitchen

$$$ | CHINESE | FAMILY | The extensive menu at this contemporary Szechuan and Cantonese restaurant includes dishes designed to be *xian* (salty), *tian* (sweet), *suan* (sour), *la* (hot), *xin* (pungent), and *ku* (bitter). Specialties include thinly sliced beef rolls with garlic sauce, spare ribs in honey sauce, and spicy rice noodles with diced chicken; dim sum and six- to eight-course prix-fixe menus are also available. **Known for:** dim sum; refined Szechuan and Cantonese cooking; hairy crabs (when in season). ⑤ *Average main: S$40 ⊠ Fairmont Singapore, 80 Bras Basah Rd., Level 3, Civic District* ☎ ⊕ *www.fairmont.com* Ⓜ *City Hall.*

🛏 Hotels

★ The Capitol Kempinski Hotel Singapore

$$$ | **HOTEL** | No two rooms are the same at this luxury hotel set in the neoclassical, 1930 Capitol Building and the Venetian Renaissance–style, 1904 Stamford House, where it took Pritzker Prize–winning architect Richard Meier years to renovate in a way that seamlessly marries European elegance with local heritage. **Pros:** steps from City Hall MRT station and Raffles City shopping mall; walking distance to top sights; beautifully restored heritage site. **Cons:** lowest-tier room option feels small and closed-in; small pool; poorer-than-average breakfast selection. ⑤ *Rooms from: S$340* ✉ *15 Stamford Rd., Civic District* ☎ *6368–8888* ⊕ *www.kempinski. com* ⬎ *157 rooms* ⑩ *No meals* Ⓜ *City Hall.*

Carlton Hotel

$$$ | **HOTEL** | Raffles City, Chijmes, the arts and cultural district, the convention and business areas, and major public transportation are all near this understated, contemporary hotel, where the marble lobby is dotted with modern artwork, and the lounges are perfect spots for sipping afternoon tea. **Pros:** center of town; spacious rooms; poolside drinks. **Cons:** some wings have rooms that are better than others; not a showstopper like some other hotels in the area. ⑤ *Rooms from: S$260* ✉ *76 Bras Basah Rd., Civic District* ☎ *6338–8333* ⊕ *www.carlton.com.sg* ⬎ *940 rooms* ⑩ *No meals* Ⓜ *Bras Basah.*

Conrad Centennial Singapore

$$$ | **HOTEL** | Spaces throughout this swank business hotel—situated near Suntec City, three national museums, and the CBD—are brightened by original Asian-influenced artwork, and guest rooms have pillow menus, Conrad teddy bears, bath salts, and other little extras. **Pros:** 24-hour restaurant; convenience; great service. **Cons:** swimming pool is showing its age; limited spa treatments; rooms can be noisy. ⑤ *Rooms from: S$400* ✉ *2 Temasek Blvd., Civic District* ☎ *6334–8888* ⊕ *conradhotels3.hilton.com* ⬎ *512 rooms* ⑩ *Free Breakfast* Ⓜ *City Hall.*

Grand Park City Hall

$$ | **HOTEL** | **FAMILY** | Revamped in 2019, this stylish heritage hotel in the heart of the Civic District now offers tech conveniences like app-controlled check in, lights, and temperature as well as inclusive features like grab bars and wheelchair accessibility. **Pros:** walking distance to many historic landmarks; thoughtfully designed family suites; reasonable pricing for the location. **Cons:** some rooms are small; check-in app requires pre-registration; limited dining options on site. ⑤ *Rooms from: S$200* ✉ *10 Coleman*

The Singapore Sling

Like the legendary shooting of Singapore's last wild tiger under the billiard table at Raffles Hotel (that's for another time), the Singapore Sling is part of Singaporean folklore. The consensus is that Ngiam Tong Boon, a Raffles Hotel bartender, created the pink-colored drink with ladies in mind. That's where the agreement ends: some claim the first Sling was concocted in 1915, others contend that it was given life in 1913, and the hotel insists that it was created prior to 1910. Many purists insist that the original recipe was lost in the 1930s. They contend that the drink, in its current incarnation, is based on the memories of retired bartenders. The hotel's museum shop has what it claims is the safe where Mr. Ngiam locked away his recipe books, and the original Sling recipe. Leave the debate to the die-hards. Order a tall glass at the peanut shell–covered Long Bar at Raffles Hotel or make your own version with these ingredients:

1½ ounces gin

½ ounce Cherry Herring brandy

¼ ounce Cointreau

¼ ounce Benedictine

4 ounces pineapple juice

½ ounce lime juice

⅓ ounce grenadine

a dash of bitters

Shake the mix with ice, pour it into a chilled glass, and garnish the drink with cherries or pineapple. Sip with care: the juices often mask the gin, brandy, Cointreau, and Benedictine.

St., Civic District ☏ *6336-3456* ⊕ *www.parkhotelgroup.com/en/cityhall* ⇱ *343 rooms* ⏐ *No meals* Ⓜ *City Hall.*

JW Marriott Hotel Singapore South Beach

$$$ | HOTEL | Sophistication meets eccentricity at this towering, artsy JW Marriott outpost with contemporary rooms designed by Philippe Starck and five eclectic bars—from a jazz joint to a Champagne bar with mermaids. **Pros:** sky gardens, a spa, and two infinity pools; plenty of dining in the hotel and connected buildings; underground passage links hotel to subway stations. **Cons:** poor views from low-level rooms; some rooms are small; not many attractions in the immediate vicinity. ⑤ *Rooms from: S$360* ✉ *30 Beach Rd., Civic District* ☏ *6818–1888* ⊕ *www.marriott.com* ⇱ *634 rooms* ⏐ *No meals* Ⓜ *City Hall.*

★ Mandarin Oriental, Singapore

$$$$ | HOTEL | FAMILY | Subdued, modern elegance and personal attention are the hallmarks of this luxurious hotel, where guest rooms feature soft peach and green color schemes, handwoven carpets, paintings of old Singapore, and Italian-marble-tile bathrooms. **Pros:** great views; excellent service; connected to the Marina Square mall and train stations. **Cons:** all of this attention comes with a big price tag; rooms are starting to show their age; lobby can get busy. $ *Rooms from: S$600* ⊠ *5 Raffles Ave., Civic District* ☎ *6338–0066* ⊕ *www.mandarinoriental.com* ⇨ *527 rooms* ❍ *No meals* Ⓜ *City Hall.*

★ Naumi Hotel Singapore

$$$ | **HOTEL** | In an effort to pay tribute to the Peranakan-style townhouses used to form this hotel, its designers left details like the original timber flooring and French-style windows intact. **Pros:** free snacks and minibar; Nespresso machines; rooftop infinity pool. **Cons:** TV reception could be better; noise from traffic; rooms could do with a refresh. $ *Rooms from: S$300* ⊠ *41 Seah St., Civic District* ☎ *6403–6000* ⊕ *www.naumihotels.com/singapore* ⇨ *79 rooms* ❍ *No meals.*

Pan Pacific Singapore

$$$ | **HOTEL** | **FAMILY** | The vast, 35-story atrium of this luxury hotel is filled with greenery and has an exterior elevator with impressive city views. **Pros:** central location; award-winning spa; great views. **Cons:** not overly baby-friendly; bathroom taps aren't in a user-friendly position; turndown service is by request only. $ *Rooms from: S$380* ⊠ *7 Raffles Blvd., Civic District* ☎ *6336–8111* ⊕ *www.panpacific.com* ⇨ *821 rooms* ❍ *No meals* Ⓜ *City Hall.*

★ Raffles Hotel

$$$$ | **HOTEL** | An extensive 2019 makeover added elegant new suites, restaurants, and bars to this 1887 Grande Dame, which was once the home of a British sea captain and is still Singapore's history-steeped showpiece—not only has its guest list included the likes of Rudyard Kipling, Somerset Maugham, Elizabeth Taylor, and Michael Jackson, but its chic plantation-themed Long Bar is the original purveyor of the Singapore Sling cocktail and the only place where you can litter legally (help yourself to peanuts from the gunny sack, then throw their shells onto the floor). **Pros:** a Singapore landmark; legendary service; Long Bar, the original purveyor of the Singapore Sling cocktail. **Cons:** very expensive; lots of curious non-guests milling around; still somewhat old-fashioned after the renovation. $ *Rooms from: S$950* ⊠ *1 Beach Rd., Civic District* ☎ *6337–1886* ⊕ *www.raffles.com/singapore* ⇨ *115 suites* ❍ *No meals* Ⓜ *City Hall.*

Rendezvous Grand Hotel Singapore

$$$ | HOTEL | With its mix of colonial and modern architecture, this hotel retains its '30s charm; the rooms are styled with warm, bright colors, and the retro bathroom tiles reflect shades of days gone by. **Pros:** Balinese-inspired swimming pool; Straits Café restaurant on site; central location. **Cons:** rooms could use updating; busy road; limited dining options within the hotel. $ *Rooms from: S$270* ⊠ *9 Bras Basah Rd., Civic District* ☎ *6336–0220* ⊕ *www. rendezvoushotels.com.sg/en* ⊐ *298 rooms* ◯| *No meals* Ⓜ *Dhoby Ghaut.*

★ The Ritz-Carlton, Millenia Singapore

$$$ | HOTEL | One of the most dramatic of the luxury hotels in Marina Bay has 32 floors of unobstructed harbor and city views; sculptures by Frank Stella; prints by David Hockney and Henry Moore; and large rooms with sofas as well as bathrooms where tubs have pillows and large octagonal windows. **Pros:** top floors have great views; top-notch service; central. **Cons:** some corner rooms overlook the highway; all this luxury is costly; doesn't participate in Marriott's Bonvoy loyalty rewards program. $ *Rooms from: S$400* ⊠ *7 Raffles Ave., Marina Square* ☎ *6337–8888* ⊕ *www. ritzcarlton.com* ⊐ *608 rooms* ◯| *No meals* Ⓜ *City Hall.*

Swissôtel The Stamford

$$$ | HOTEL | Catering to business executives, this 70-story hotel, among the tallest in the world, is connected to the busy Raffles City office and retail tower, with dozens of restaurants, more than 100 shops, and convention facilities. **Pros:** all rooms have balconies; central location; five-star business hotel. **Cons:** busy lobby; might be too crowded for some people; getting public transport can be challenging, especially during peak hours. $ *Rooms from: S$372* ⊠ *2 Stamford Rd., Civic District* ☎ *6338–8585* ⊕ *www. swissotel.com/hotels/singapore-stamford/* ⊐ *1,261 rooms* ◯| *No meals* Ⓜ *City Hall.*

ⓨ Nightlife

Bar Rouge

DANCE CLUBS | Experience a wild night out in Singapore at this posh club perched on the 71st floor of Swissôtel the Stamford. Popular regional guest DJs often take the decks. ⊠ *Swissôtel the Stamford, 2 Stamford Rd., #71–01, Civic District* ☎ *9177–7307* ⊕ *barrougeclubs.com/sg* Ⓜ *City Hall.*

Long Bar

BARS/PUBS | The home of the Singapore Sling cocktail reopened in 2019 after a major makeover and now sports stylized, earthy decor inspired by the Malayan plantations of the 1920s. But some things haven't changed: you can still knock back the original-recipe Singapore Sling and chuck peanut shells on the floor, technically the only place you're allowed to litter legally in Singapore. As you might expect of a bar inside Singapore's best-known and most historic hotel, it's touristy and pricey. ⊠ *Raffles Arcade, 328 North Bridge Rd., Civic District* ☎ ⊕ *www.rafflessingapore.com/dining/long-bar* Ⓜ *City Hall.*

Loof

BARS/PUBS | At what's billed as Singapore's first standalone rooftop bar, local flavors come through in both the appetizers by celebrated local chef Bjorn Shen and Southeast Asian–inspired cocktails. Resident DJs often take the deck, and themed party nights are frequent. ⊠ *Odeon Towers, 331 North Bridge Rd., #03–07, Civic District* ☎ *6337–9416* ⊕ *www.loof.com.sg* ☞ *Closed Sun.*

★ Smoke and Mirrors

BARS/PUBS | Cocktail aficionados need to make a pit stop at this rooftop bar, where mixologists favor adventurous ingredients such as gentian root and "pencil aroma" and create experimental concoctions such as a whisky sour with Asian flavors like black sesame and rice. Bonus: There are unblocked views of the Marina Bay skyline. ⊠ *National Gallery Singapore, 1 St Andrew's Rd., #06–01, Civic District* ☎ *9380–6313* ⊕ *www.smokeandmirrors. com.sg* ☞ *Closed Sun.-Tues.* Ⓜ *City Hall.*

🎭 Performing Arts

Drama Centre

THEATER | The Drama Centre on the third floor of the National Library is a key platform for many of Singapore's theater companies and often hosts performances from overseas companies as well. There are two performance spaces here, the 615-seat Drama Centre Theatre and the 120-seat Black Box. ⊠ *National Library Building, 100 Victoria St., #03–01, Civic District* ☎ *6837–8400* ⊕ *www.dramacentre.com* Ⓜ *City Hall.*

The Esplanade–Theatres on the Bay

ARTS CENTERS | FAMILY | The Esplanade hosts many of Singapore's top ticketed performances, but it also offers free concerts, shows, and talks every week. Most take place at the Esplanade Concourse or the Outdoor Theater in the evenings when the weather is cooler—all you have to do is drop by and take a seat. There's a performance schedule on the Esplanade website, but it's much more fun to visit and be surprised by what's on, which could be anything from a classical guitar performance from Latin America to a Chinese puppet show. ✉ *1 Esplanade Dr., Civic District* ☎ *6828–8377* ⊕ *www.esplanade.com* Ⓜ *Esplanade.*

Singapore Film Society

FILM | The respected Singapore Film Society, founded in 1958, holds regular screenings of art-house and foreign films. You have to be a member to participate, but membership starts at a reasonable S$18 per month, barely the price of two movie tickets. Everything in Singapore goes through the censors, but they usually let Film Society films go uncut as a gesture to the nation's small but serious film-buff community. (Generally, sexual themes, especially homosexuality, and certain political topics are the first to be cut.) ✉ *Suntec City Mall , 3 Temasek Blvd., #03-373, Civic District* ☎ *90–170–160* ⊕ *www.singaporefilmsociety.com* Ⓜ *Suntec City.*

Singapore Symphony Orchestra

CONCERTS | The nearly 100 members of the Singapore Symphony Orchestra, Singapore's flagship orchestra, regularly deliver a mix of Western classical music and new Asian compositions. Performances are usually held at the Esplanade Concert Hall. ✉ *Victoria Concert Hall, 11 Empress Place, #01–02, Civic District* ☎ *6602–4200* ⊕ *www.sso.org.sg* Ⓜ *City Hall.*

The Substation

ARTS CENTERS | This independent establishment, which has its own theater, art gallery, and dance studio, aims to nurture the city's up-and-coming artists with spaces in which to learn and exhibit. It also schedules events that include short film festivals, experimental theater, and poetry readings. ✉ *45 Armenian St., Civic District* ☎ *6337–7535* ⊕ *www.substation.org* Ⓜ *City Hall.*

🛍 Shopping

The Camera Workshop

CAMERAS/ELECTRONICS | This shop in Peninsula Shopping Centre carries not just the latest cameras and accessories from Nikon, Canon, Pentax, and Mamiya, but also analogue models and serious shutterbug equipment like dry cabinets. You can even get camera issues diagnosed by the staff, have your cam cleaned, or sell a pre-loved gadget. ✉ *Peninsula Shopping Centre, 3 Coleman St., #01–06, Civic District* ☎ *6336–1956* ⊕ *www.thecameraworkshop.sg* Ⓜ *City Hall.*

Capitol Piazza

CLOTHING | Within its four sleek floors, this swanky mall that's part of the historic Capitol Singapore complex houses many cult labels from around the globe, including the flagship stores for local designers like SABRINA GOH and Max Tan. There are also three art galleries for you to visit amid all your shopping. ✉ *13 Stamford Rd., Civic District* ☎ *6499–5168* ⊕ *capitolsingapore. com* Ⓜ *City Hall.*

The Cathay

SHOPPING CENTERS/MALLS | This complex, inside what was Singapore's first skyscraper when it was built in 1939, has eight floors of quirky stores and entertainment outlets, including an eight-screen cineplex and the funky Brunswick Pool & Billiards. Check out Leftfoot (#01–19/20) for an excellent selection of hard-to-find sneakers and VOL.TA Marque (#02–09) for sharp men's fashion. The complex is across the street from the Dhoby Ghaut MRT station; look for the building's original art deco facade. ✉ *2 Handy Rd., Civic District* ☎ *6732–7332* ⊕ *www.thecathay.com.sg* Ⓜ *Dhoby Ghaut.*

★ Funan

SHOPPING CENTERS/MALLS | Following a renovation that was completed in 2019, this electronics and tech-lifestyle center now has funky retail, dining, and entertainment offerings like a food court where you can pay with cryptocurrency, an urban farm, a theater, a rock-climbing wall, and more. ✉ *107 North Bridge Rd., Civic District* ☎ *6970–1665* ⊕ *www.capitaland.com/sg/malls/funan/en* Ⓜ *City Hall.*

Marina Square

SHOPPING CENTERS/MALLS | **FAMILY** | Home to more than 250 shops and restaurants, Marina Square was once the largest shopping mall in Singapore, an honor that now belongs to VivoCity. Banks, convenience stores, a movie theater, a bowling alley, a large food court, coffee shops, and spas and salons are all here. Some nearby hotels and attractions, including Esplanade–Theatres on the Bay, Pan Pacific Singapore, and Suntec City, can be accessed directly from here via underground walkways. ✉ *6 Raffles Blvd., Civic District* ☎ *6339–8787* ⊕ *www.marinasquare.com.sg* Ⓜ *City Hall.*

Millenia Walk

SHOPPING CENTERS/MALLS | Near Suntec City in Millenia Singapore, this upscale complex has a mix of audiovisual stores—including the sprawling flagship store of electronics retailer Harvey Norman—designer house-ware boutiques, quirky retail outlets, and a clutch of Japanese restaurants and contemporary cafes. ✉ *9 Raffles Blvd., Civic District* ☎ *6883–1122* ⊕ *www.milleniawalk.com* Ⓜ *Promenade.*

Raffles City

SHOPPING CENTERS/MALLS | Get everything you need at this mega mall, which has more than 200 tenants within its walls, including Robinsons Department Store and Ode to Art, a contemporary art gallery. Both traveling to and spending time in the mall is a breeze—it is easily accessed from the City Hall and Esplanade train stations. It also offers services like the loan of portable chargers and umbrellas. ✉ *252 North Bridge Rd., Civic District* ☎ *6318–0238* ⊕ *www.capitaland.com/sg/malls/rafflescity* Ⓜ *Esplanade.*

Suntec City Mall

SHOPPING CENTERS/MALLS | This sprawling complex has more than 600 stores, including local designer boutiques and the funky Pasarbella food court featuring stalls by some of Singapore's most creative culinary entrepreneurs. In the middle is the photo-worthy Fountain of Wealth, which was listed in the 1998 Guinness Book of Records as the world's largest fountain. There are nightly laser shows, and walking around the fountain supposedly brings good luck. ✉ *3 Temasek Blvd., Civic District* ☎ *6825–2669* ⊕ *www. sunteccity.com.sg* Ⓜ *Suntec City.*

🏃 Activities

Jane's Tours

WALKING TOURS | The buildings in the Civic District, Singapore's earliest example of urban planning, are clustered in the downtown area, so they're easy to cover on foot. You can do the walk yourself using Google Maps (just search for "Singapore Civic District DIY Walk Itinerary"), or go with a tour agency like Jane's Tours, a small-group operator offering out-of-the-ordinary and bespoke tours that focus on culture and history. Either way, sunscreen, comfortable shoes, and a bottle of water are essential take-alongs. ✉ *Civic District* ⊕ *janestours.sg* Ⓜ *City Hall, Bras Basah, Esplanade, Promenade.*

Singapore River

Just below the Civic District is a group of quays running along the Singapore River. Once the center of commercial Singapore, this area hummed with energy from bumboats that transported goods to and from its warehouses along the water. Now, Clarke Quay and Boat Quay are best visited at night, when herds of partygoers descend on the area. The more laid-back Robertson Quay neighborhood is good for weekend brunch or a riverside run. A river cruise on a bumboat is a good way to get another perspective on this busy area. Use the Clarke Quay MRT station stop on the North East Line (purple) to get here.

👁 Sights

Boat Quay

HISTORIC SITE | Local entrepreneurs have created a mélange of eateries and bars to satisfy diverse tastes at this dining and drinking stretch along the Singapore River, the country's trading hub from colonial times to the 1970s. Between 7 pm and midnight, the area swells with an after-work crowd enjoying drinks along the water. At the end of Boat Quay and named after Lord Elgin, a British governor-general of India, **Elgin Bridge** links the colonial quarter to Chinatown. The original rickety wooden structure was replaced in 1863 with an iron bridge imported from Calcutta. The current concrete bridge was installed in 1926. ✉ *Boat Quay, Clarke Quay* Ⓜ *Raffles Place.*

★ Clarke Quay

PEDESTRIAN MALL | Stretching along the riverfront, Clarke Quay is canopied by space-age umbrellas and filled with a smorgasbord of entertainment venues, restaurants, bars, and clubs. Come nightfall, the pedestrian-only streets are packed with a mix of visitors and locals hitting up the latest eateries and bars. With its bright lights and festive nightlife, the river along the quay is a world away from the sleepy waterway it was when Raffles first arrived. Get a view from the river by boarding one of the many bumboats that offer daily 30-minute cruises. Thrill seekers will love the **G-MAX Reverse Bungy**, a ride at the river's edge, open from 2 pm until late into the night. Zouk, the city's most-celebrated nightclub, draws partygoers from Wednesday to Saturday with its roster of top global DJs. ✉ *3 River Valley Rd., Clarke Quay* ☎ *6337–3292* ⊕ *www.capitaland.com* Ⓜ *Clarke Quay.*

Sri Thendayuthapani Temple

RELIGIOUS SITE | Also known as Chettiars' Temple, this southern Indian temple, a national monument that's home to numerous shrines, is a replacement for the original, which was built in the 19th century. The 75-foot-high gopuram, with its many colorful sculptures of godly manifestations, is astounding. The chandelier-lighted interior is lavishly decorated; 48 painted-glass panels are inset in the ceiling and angled to reflect the sunrise and sunset. The temple is the main gathering point for devotees during the Tamil festival Thaipusam and a sight to watch, as attendees pierce their bodies with metal spikes and hooks and walk over burning coals as part of the festival's pilgrimage.

✉ *15 Tank Rd., Clarke Quay* ☎ *6221–4853* ⊕ *www.sttemple.com* ⬛ *Free* Ⓜ *Clarke Quay.*

🍴 Restaurants

Braci

$$$$ | **MODERN ITALIAN** | When you have a meal at this cozy, 20-seat, open-kitchen restaurant with a rooftop bar, it feels like you're dining at a friend's—a friend with one-Michelin-star culinary chops. Here, the flame-kissed grilled mains are the draw, but you should also leave room for popular starters like the foie-gras semifreddo and the house-made charcoal-baked bread. **Known for:** riverside views; homey but refined food; amazing bread. Ⓢ *Average main: S$60* ✉ *52 Boat Quay, Level 5/6, Clarke Quay* ☎ *6866–1933* ⊕ *www.braci.sg* ⊗ *Closed Sun. No lunch Sat.-Mon.* Ⓜ *Clarke Quay.*

Brewerkz

$$ | **AMERICAN** | **FAMILY** | This buzzy, breezy microbrewery, sprawling along a prime stretch of real estate on the Singapore River, across from Clarke Quay, serves Western-friendly favorites like burgers and pizzas, buffalo wings, beer-battered fish-and-chips, and chargrilled steaks, along with lighter fare like grilled fish and soups. The portions are hearty—perfect for soaking up pours of Brewerkz's award-winning craft beers. **Known for:** locally brewed beers; hearty portions; casual business lunches. Ⓢ *Average main: S$30* ✉ *#01–07 Riverside Point, 30 Merchant Rd., Clarke Quay* ☎ *6438–7438* ⊕ *www.brewerkz.com* Ⓜ *Clarke Quay.*

★ Hai Di Lao at Clarke Quay

$$$ | **CHINESE** | Robust soup bases, gourmet ingredients, and hand-pulled noodles aside, what makes this hotpot joint in a heritage warehouse one of the most popular in Singapore is its next-level service. Free manicures, a children's playroom, and complimentary drinks and snacks are offered even as you wait for your table—a nice touch, albeit a move to placate customers stuck in the notoriously long lines. **Known for:** satisfying hotpot; above-and-beyond service; freebies like takeaway popcorn and crackers. Ⓢ *Average main: S$35* ✉ *Clarke Quay, 3D River Valley Rd., #02–04, Clarke Quay* ☎ *6337–8626* ⊕ *www.haidilao.com/sg* Ⓜ *Clarke Quay.*

Jumbo Seafood, Riverside Point

$$$ | **CHINESE** | **FAMILY** | As the crowds that permanently pack it show, Jumbo Seafood is the place to get your hands dirty while savoring award-winning chilli and black-pepper crab, freshly snapped up from on-site seafood tanks. This riverside branch offers views of Clarke Quay and the Singapore River; other less atmospheric locations include Ion Orchard and Jewel Changi International Airport. **Known for:** chilli crab; live seafood; big-group gatherings. $ *Average main: S$50* ✉ *Riverside Point, 30 Merchant Rd., #01–01/02, Clarke Quay* ☎ *6532–3435* ⊕ *www.jumboseafood. com.sg* Ⓜ *Clarke Quay.*

Rendezvous Restaurant Hock Lock Kee

$$ | **INDONESIAN** | **FAMILY** | Long-standing Rendezvous is known for its luxe, pricey rendition of *nasi padang* (Indonesian-style cooked dishes with rice), including *beef rendang* (beef curry), *sayur lodeh* (vegetable in spicy coconut milk), *sambal sotong* (chili squid), and *sambal brinjal* (spicy eggplant). Servings are small and meant to be shared like tapas; meat and seafood dishes are charged by the piece. **Known for:** spicy Indonesian-style dishes; smorgasbord of items; retro setting. $ *Average main: S$18* ✉ *The Central, 6 Eu Tong Sen St., #02–72 to 75/77/92, Clarke Quay* ☎ *6339–7508* ⊕ *www.rendezvous-hlk.com.sg* Ⓜ *Clarke Quay.*

🛏 Hotels

Holiday Inn Express Clarke Quay

$$ | **HOTEL** | One of the more sophisticated Holiday Inn Express options around (the building was initially constructed for a four-star hotel until the Holiday Inn chain took over), this comfortable lodging provides lush amenities like a pillow menu, free breakfast, and a rooftop pool with views of Robertson Quay. **Pros:** rooftop pool; central; guide dogs allowed. **Cons:** lack of storage space in rooms; no laundry service; common areas can get crowded. $ *Rooms from: S$170* ✉ *2 Magazine Rd., Clarke Quay* ☎ *6589–8000* ⊕ *www. hiexpress.com* 🛏 *442 rooms* ⦿⃝ *Free Breakfast* Ⓜ *Clarke Quay.*

InterContinental Singapore Robertson Quay

$$ | **HOTEL** | This stylishly masculine hotel has ultra modern rooms that are smaller than at most InterContinental hotels but have well-utilized spaces and floor-to-ceiling windows with views of the Robertson Quay area. **Pros:** plenty of dining options nearby; DIY cocktail kit in room; right next to the Singapore River. **Cons:** location isn't the most accessible; rooms are on the small side; design is not the most suitable for families. $ *Rooms from: S$220* ✉ *1 Nanson Rd., Clarke Quay* ☎ *6826–5000* ⊕ *robertsonquay.inter-continental.com* 🛏 *225 rooms* Ⓜ *Clarke Quay.*

M Social Singapore

$$ | **HOTEL** | It's clear this mod boutique hotel designed by Philippe Starck is for the digital nomad generation: each loft-style room includes a snug workspace on the mezzanine, and the common spaces feature interactive elements like iPads on the walls and a

robot to cook your breakfast eggs for you. **Pros:** free shuttle buses; homey design; features for solo travelers, like single rooms and single-portion bottled wines. **Cons:** rooms are small; not family-friendly; 15-min walk to the nearest train station. Ⓢ *Rooms from: S$220* ✉ *90 Robertson Quay, Robertson Quay* ☎ *6206–1888* ⊕ *www.millenniumhotels.com* ➘ *293 rooms* ⦿ *No meals* Ⓜ *Clarke Quay.*

Park Hotel Clarke Quay

$$ | HOTEL | Find respite in the city's party central—Clarke Quay—at this quaint enclave with restful rooms in neutral tones and a relaxing, award-winning pool. **Pros:** walking distance to Clarke Quay; close to MRT stations; complimentary shuttle bus to Orchard and Marina Bay areas. **Cons:** rooms are on the small side; thin walls; some upkeep needed. Ⓢ *Rooms from: S$199* ✉ *1 Unity St., Clarke Quay* ☎ *6593–8888* ⊕ *www.parkhotelgroup.com/en/clarkequay* ➘ *336 rooms* Ⓜ *Clarke Quay, Fort Canning.*

Swissôtel Merchant Court Singapore

$$ | HOTEL | At this business hotel, standard rooms, albeit small, are comfortable; larger executive rooms have a few more amenities, and the Premier Rooms have balconies. **Pros:** next to the Singapore River and Clarke Quay; balcony rooms available; free portable Wi-Fi device for guests. **Cons:** inconsistent water temps in the shower; some rooms don't have views; expensive laundry service. Ⓢ *Rooms from: S$200* ✉ *20 Merchant Rd., Clarke Quay* ☎ *6337–2288* ⊕ *www.swissotel.com* ➘ *476 rooms* ⦿ *No meals* Ⓜ *City Hall.*

★ The Warehouse Hotel

$$$ | HOTEL | Occupying a restored godown (or warehouse), this progressive, distinctively designed boutique hotel by the river partners with local makers and creators to showcase environmentally sound Singapore amenities such as eco-certified bath products from Ashley & Co. and eco-friendly water, bottled in-house, by Nordaq Fresh. **Pros:** eco-friendly environment; hip local flavor; riverside location. **Cons:** some rooms are windowless; a distance from the nearest train station; no on-site gym (although there's a gym partnership with a nearby establishment). Ⓢ *Rooms from: S$260* ✉ *320 Havelock Rd., Robertson Quay* ☎ *6828–0000* ⊕ *www.thewarehousehotel.com* ➘ *37 rooms* ⦿ *No meals* Ⓜ *Fort Canning.*

Nightlife

★ Crazy Elephant

MUSIC CLUBS | Dedicated to the blues, with occasional forays into R&B and rock, this popular, laid-back bar in a heritage shophouse by the river hosts jam sessions that draw gifted musicians. ⊠ *3E River Valley Rd., #01–03/04, Clarke Quay* ☎ *6337–7859* ⊕ *www. crazyelephant.sg* Ⓜ *Clarke Quay.*

Harry's

BARS/PUBS | At this long-standing bar by the water you can watch rugby, Australian football, and soccer matches. English-style lunches (fish-and-chips, bangers and mash, bread pudding with rum sauce) are served upstairs on weekdays; bar food and tapas are dished daily until 11:30 pm. Expats and business executives make up most of the crowd, which spills out onto the sidewalk on the weekend. The bar has cloned itself at over 20 other locations, including those at the Esplanade theater complex, Dempsey Hill, and Changi International Airport. ⊠ *28 Boat Quay, Clarke Quay* ☎ *6538–3029* ⊕ *www.harrys.com.sg* Ⓜ *Raffles Place.*

★ Headquarters by The Council

DANCE CLUBS | The music takes center stage at this underground club, where you can dress down and party alongside a like-minded community to sub-genres like acid house, techno, and disco. There's no cover charge on Wednesday and Thursday. ⊠ *66 Boat Quay, Level 2, Clarke Quay* ⊕ *thecouncil.sg* Ⓜ *Clarke Quay.*

Molly Malone's Irish Pub & Brasserie

BARS/PUBS | Stacked sandwiches and fish-and-chips join the beers and cocktails at this friendly bar, where the TVs screen soccer and rugby matches throughout the week and where there's live music on Wednesday, Thursday, and Friday nights. On the second floor, heartier dishes such as British sausage platters are served. ⊠ *56 Circular Rd., Clarke Quay* ☎ *6536–2029* ⊕ *www.molly-malone. com* Ⓜ *Clarke Quay.*

★ 28 Hong Kong Street

BARS/PUBS | Don't be fooled by the fact that the name of this bar is its address—it can still be easy to miss. Opened in 2011, 28 Hong Kong Street was one of the early pioneers of Singapore's speakeasy cocktail scene. Inside the cozy space, you'll find American-style craft cocktails. Order the Five Foot Assassin or the Stone Fence for a feel of what this bar is all about. ⊠ *28 Hong Kong St., Clarke Quay* ⊕ *www.28hks.com* Ⓜ *Clarke Quay.*

★ Zouk

DANCE CLUBS | The long-running Zouk always manages to reinvent itself. The huge dance club, carved out of renovated riverside warehouses, is four venues in one: Zouk, the main dance room that specializes in all genres of electronic music; the more sophisticated and intimate Capital; and Phuture for hip hop lovers; and Red Tail Bar for cocktails and sharing bites. Visiting international DJs take the decks weekly, and the club consistently gets rave reviews overseas. ✉ *The Cannery, 3C River Valley Rd., Clarke Quay* ☎ *6738–2988* ⊕ *www.zoukclub.com.sg* Ⓜ *Clarke Quay.*

🎭 Performing Arts

Singapore Repertory Theatre

THEATER | The popular Singapore Repertory Theatre stages plays and musicals. Its subsidiary, the Little Company, produces children's plays. ✉ *KC Arts Centre, 20 Merbau Rd., Robertson Quay* ☎ *6221–5585* ⊕ *www.srt.com.sg.*

Singapore Tyler Print Institute

ARTS CENTERS | At this American-inspired venture dedicated to print- and paper-making and paper-based artwork, there's a free admission gallery for exhibits, which change frequently. ✉ *41 Robertson Quay, Robertson Quay* ☎ *6336–3663* ⊕ *www.stpi.com.sg.*

TheatreWorks

THEATER | Under director Ong Keng Sen, this internationally known theater company has staged daring cross-cultural productions, such as Asian versions of *King Lear* and *Desdemona* (derived from *Othello*), and has traveled to Denmark to workshop *Hamlet*. Workshops, readings and comedy nights, are held regularly on its premises. ✉ *Mohamed Sultan Rd., 72-13, Robertson Quay* ☎ *6737–7213* ⊕ *www.theatreworks.org.sg* Ⓜ *Fort Canning.*

🛍 Shopping

Laurent Bernard Chocolatier

FOOD/CANDY | The chocolate desserts at this specialist cafe are delightful, but it's the handcrafted souvenirs available seasonally that are truly memorable. Think giant chocolate Easter bunnies and tiny chocolate chickens containing painted chocolate eggs—the perfect edible gifts for foodie friends. ✉ *The Pier at Robertson Quay, 80 Mohamed Sultan Rd., #01–11, Robertson Quay* ☎ *6235–9007* ⊕ *www.laurentbernard.com.sg* Ⓜ *Fort Canning.*

The Flower Dome at Gardens by the Bay is the largest glass greenhouse in the world.

The Patissier

FOOD/CANDY | This homegrown takeaway patisserie melds intricate French baking techniques with innovative flavor combinations to create unique treats. It's famous for its passion-fruit meringue—meringue sponge cake filled with passion-fruit mousse and fruit—but other easier-to-transport goodies like cookies and tarts are also available. ✉ *4 Mohamed Sultan Rd., Clarke Quay* ☎ *6737–3369* ⊕ *www.thepatissier.com* Ⓜ *Fort Canning.*

🏃 Activities

★ Singapore River Cruise

BOAT TOURS | **FAMILY** | Early in Singapore's history, bumboats were were used to transport goods up and down the Singapore River, from the businesses in Boat Quay to warehouses in Clarke Quay. These days, there's no better way to see the river and modern Singapore than from one of these retrofitted barges. You can choose to take a bumboat "taxi" service from jetties that line a route running from the Esplanade to Robertson Quay (this allows you to board and get off at different points) or a 40-minute fixed-route cruise that will take you through Boat Quay, Clarke Quay, and Marina Bay. Both options can be booked through operator Singapore River Cruise at kiosks along the river. ✉ *Clarke Quay* ☎ *6336–6111* ⊕ *rivercruise.com.sg* Ⓜ *Raffles Place, Bayfront, Clarke Quay.*

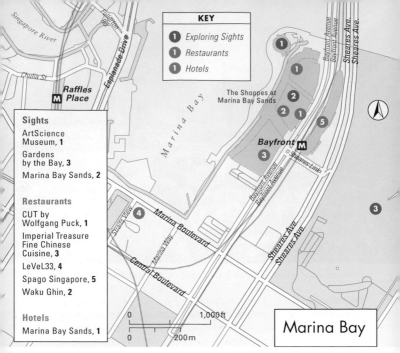

Marina Bay

Across the water from the Civic District is Marina Bay, an extension of the business district that was created through land reclamation in the 1970s. It's now one of the most architecturally significant parts of town, with Marina Bay Sands hotel-casino and the futuristic Gardens by the Bay.

⊙ Sights

ArtScience Museum

MUSEUM | FAMILY | Part of **Marina Bay Sands**, this Moshe Safdie–designed structure is often compared to an open hand or a lotus flower. Inside, the exhibitions combine—you guessed it—art and science. Since its opening in 2011, major international exhibitions have been set up within the 21 gallery spaces, totaling 50,000 square feet. ⊠ *Marina Bay Sands, 6 Bayfront Ave, CBD* ☎ *6688–8868* ⊕ *www.marinabaysands.com/singapore-museum* ⊠ *From S$19 for a single exhibition* Ⓜ *Bayfront.*

★ Gardens by the Bay

GARDEN | **FAMILY** | The government-funded, large-scale gar
next to Marina Bay Sands opened with much well-deserv
in 2012. Highlights include a futuristic grove of "Supertree
giant vertical gardens—and two armadillo-shaped conservatories.
The Flower Dome is home to plants from the Mediterranean and
subtropical regions, while the Cloud Forest is veiled in mist and
houses the world's largest indoor waterfall. The OCBC Skyway is a
420-foot (128-meter) walkway that connects several of the Supertrees and offers a great view from above. While fees apply for
both the Skyway and conservatories, visitors can wander around
the Gardens until 2 am free of charge. ⊠ *18 Marina Gardens Dr.,
Marina Square* ☎ *6420–6848* ⊕ *www.gardensbythebay.com.sg*
Ⓜ *Bayfront.*

★ Marina Bay Sands

BUILDING | One of the most iconic structures on the Singapore
skyline, Marina Bay Sands includes the biggest hotel in Singapore;
The Shoppes at Marina Bay Sands, a glitzy mall filled with top fashion
brands and its own casino; celebrity-chef restaurants; and the cav-
ernous Marquee nightclub. There's also the SkyPark, an observation
deck that's 660 feet (200 meters) high and home to the hotel's
much-Instagrammed, 150 meter-long infinity pool—the world's
largest outdoor elevated body of water. ⊠ *1 Bayfront Ave., Marina
Square* ☎ *6688–8868* ⊕ *www.marinabaysands.com* Ⓜ *Bayfront.*

🍴 Restaurants

CUT by Wolfgang Puck

$$$$ | **STEAKHOUSE** | Dine with Adele, Denzel Washington, and Katy
Perry—or their portraits by award-winning photographer Martin
Schoeller, at least—at this storied steakhouse by Wolfgang Puck.
The Austrian-American celebrity chef's first foray into Asia offers
up an amazing selection of USDA Prime, Australian Angus, American, and Japanese wagyu cuts and an impressive list of artisanal
cocktails with not-suitable-for-work names, including Bound &
Gagged (vodka, elderflower liquer, yuzu, and shiso) and The Full
Frontal (gin, pineapple, and orgeat). **Known for:** perhaps the best
steak in Singapore; celebrity status; sharp service. Ⓢ *Average
main: S$90* ⊠ *The Shoppes at Marina Bay Sands, 2 Bayfront Ave.,
#B1–71, Marina Square* ☎ *6688–8517* ⊕ *wolfgangpuck.com/din-
ing/cut-singapore* ◷ *No lunch* Ⓜ *Bayfront.*

Imperial Treasure Fine Chinese Cuisine

$$$$ | **CANTONESE** | Ogle the hopefuls in the Marina Bay Sands casi-
no while enjoying a meal at this Cantonese fine-dining restaurant
overlooking the slot machines and gaming tables. Choose from

set menus featuring simple yet refined seafood-forward dishes or such à la carte signature options as Australian lobster baked in superior broth or braised bird's nest with crab meat and roe. **Known for:** delicious fine Cantonese food; fresh seafood; big-group gatherings. $ *Average main: S$88* ⊠ *The Shoppes at Marina Bay Sands, 2 Bayfront Ave., #02–04, Marina Square* ☎ *6688–7788* ⊕ *www.imperialtreasure.com* Ⓜ *Bayfront.*

LeVeL33

$$$ | INTERNATIONAL | At what's billed as "the world's highest urban craft brewery," the pricey platters of meat and seafood served in the slick indoor dining area are beside the point. Instead, get here no later than 6 pm on a clear day, hunker down in one of the too-few outdoor deck tables, and bask in the stunning panoramas over the marina, with the spaceship-like pool deck of the Marina Bay Sands hotel to your right and the impressive CBD skyscrapers to your left. **Known for:** panoramic views; craft beers; sharing plates. $ *Average main: S$36* ⊠ *Marina Bay Financial Centre Tower 1, 8 Marina Blvd., #33–01, Marina Square* ☎ *6834–3133* ⊕ *www.level33.com.sg* Ⓜ *Bayfront.*

★ Spago Singapore

$$$$ | MODERN AMERICAN | The second Singaporean venture by Wolfgang Puck serves up Californian food with an Asian twist, including a locally-inspired "kaya toast" with foie gras. Perched on the 57th floor of Sands SkyPark in the Marina Bay Sands, the restaurant offers unparalleled views of the hotel's famed infinity pool and the city skyline from its alfresco bar and lounge and its indoor dining room. **Known for:** sky-high views; celebrity chef; casual chic ambience. $ *Average main: S$80* ⊠ *Sands SkyPark, 10 Bayfront Ave., Level 57, Marina Square* ☎ *6688–9955* ⊕ *wolfgangpuck.com/dining/spago-singapore* Ⓜ *Bayfront.*

Waku Ghin

$$$$ | MODERN AUSTRALIAN | Celebrated chef Tetsuya Wakuda expertly melds Australian, Japanese, and classic French cuisine to craft the innovative menus at this two-Michelin-starred spot. The dinner experience begins with a 10-course degustation meal in one of the three private cocoon rooms, which is followed by dessert in the drawing room with a view of Marina Bay and then a Japanese-style cocktail or sake at The Bar at Waku Ghin. **Known for:** memorable experience; fusion that isn't confusion; intimate, personal service. $ *Average main: S$450* ⊠ *The Shoppes at Marina Bay Sands, 2 Bayfront Ave., #02–01, Marina Square* ☎ *6688–8507* ⊕ *tetsuyas.com/singapore/waku-ghin-about-us* ⊘ *No lunch Sat.-Thurs.* Ⓜ *Bayfront.*

Hotels

Marina Bay Sands

$$$$ | **HOTEL** | It's all about the view at this world-famous hotel, with its three towers offering plenty of vantage points from which to enjoy Singapore's cityscape. **Pros:** iconic rooftop infinity pool; lots of excellent restaurants; award-winning Banyan Tree Spa. **Cons:** very expensive; large crowds milling about; service can feel impersonal. Ⓢ *Rooms from: S$530* ✉ *10 Bayfront Ave., Marina Square* ☎ *6688–8868* ⊕ *www.marinabaysands.com* ⇆ *2,561 rooms* ❗️◯❗️ *No meals* Ⓜ *Bayfront.*

Nightlife

Cé La Vi Singapore

TAPAS BARS | At this stunning restaurant-bar 57 stories above ground, you can take in Singapore's late-night vistas while vibing to resident and celeb DJs. Start with a mod-Asian dinner at Cé La Vi Restaurant, before enjoying a tipple at the Skybar and then hitting the dance floor at the Club Lounge. ✉ *Marina Bay Sands SkyPark, 1 Bayfront Ave., Level 57, Marina Square* ☎ *6508–2188* ⊕ *www.celavi.com* Ⓜ *Bayfront.*

★ Marquee Singapore

DANCE CLUBS | For a night you will (or likely, won't) remember, party at this glittering club kid hotspot with Vegas vibes. Also Singapore's largest nightclub, it goes big with eight private dance pods suspended 20 meters in the air as well as a massive ferris wheel you can board for a spin. ✉ *The Shoppes at Marina Bay Sands, 2 Bayfront Ave., #B1-67, Marina Square* ☎ *6688-8660* ⊕ *marqueesingapore.com* Ⓜ *Bayfront.*

🎟 Performing Arts

Sands Theatre

THEATER | When big performances like The Lion King and The Phantom of the Opera come to Singapore, this glitzy 2,155-seat theater is where they often drop. The best seats in the three-level space are the Orchestra seats; skip the Dress Circle ones on the upper deck if you want a full view of the stage. ✉ *The Shoppes at Marina Bay Sands, 4 Bayfront Ave., B1, Marina Square* ☎ *6688-8826* ⊕ *www.marinabaysands.com/entertainment/shows* Ⓜ *Bayfront.*

🛍 Shopping

The Shoppes at Marina Bay Sands

CLOTHING | You can while away a whole day at this mega mall that has over 170 stores and restaurants. Look out for the contemporary cuts of local fashion label In Good Company (#B1–65) and the unique handiwork of custom sneaker design artist SBTG at Limited Edt Chamber (#B2–112). While you're at it, make time for the mall's casino, theater, and boat rides along its indoor river. ⊠ *2 Bayfront Ave., Marina Square* 🕾 *6688–8868* ⊕ *www.marinabay-sands.com/shopping* Ⓜ *Bayfront.*

🏃 Activities

Banyan Tree Spa

SPA—SIGHT | There's a more relaxing way to take in the views than from the perpetually packed Marina Bay Sands rooftop: from a spa bed. The award-winning Banyan Tree Spa sits just two stories below the hotel's famous infinity pool, so you can enjoy the same stunning views through floor-to-ceiling windows as your knots get kneaded. There are more than 30 treatments available, from facials, massages, and body scrubs to hand, foot, and hair treatments. Post session, further unwind in the tea lounge, or visit the in-house boutique to stock up on products so you can re-create the experience at home. ⊠ *Marina Bay Sands Tower 1, 10 Bayfront Ave., Level 55, Singapore* 🕾 *6688–8825* ⊕ *www.banyantreespa. com* Ⓜ *Bayfront.*

Marina Bay Golf Course

GOLF | Singapore's only public 18-hole green is an award-winning links-style course—and it's one of the best in Asia. Course A has an outer and inner loop of two nines and Course B (a new configuration) has holes crossing over to the inner loop after hole 5. It's also one of the few golf courses in Singapore to have night golfing. ⊠ *80 Rhu Cross, Marina Square* 🕾 *6345–7788* ⊕ *www. mbgc.com.sg* 🏌 *18 holes, 7100 yd, par 72* Ⓜ *Bayfront.*

Ultimate Drive

AUTO RACING | Feel like one of the racers in the Formula 1 Grand Prix (one of Singapore's most anticipated annual events) by renting a super car from a local owner. If you book the Joyride with Ultimate Drive package, you'll get to choose from a number of supercars from Ferraris and Lamborghinis to McLaren 12C and take it for a lap around the official F1 circuit. ⊠ *#01–14 Hotel Tower 3 , 1 Bayfront Ave., Marina Square* 🕾 *6688–7997* ⊕ *www.ultimat-edrive.com* ☞ *From $400 per half hour* Ⓜ *Bayfront.*

CHINATOWN AND TIONG BAHRU

Updated by
Olivia Lee

👁 Sights ⭐ Restaurants 🛏 Hotels 🛍 Shopping 🍸 Nightlife
★★★★☆   ★★★★★   ★★★★☆   ★★★★☆   ★★★★☆

NEIGHBORHOOD SNAPSHOT

TOP EXPERIENCES

- **Brunch like a local:** Sip coffee and eat French toast along with trendy locals in Tiong Bahru's hip café hotspots.

- **Bargain hunt:** Browse Chinatown's colorful market stalls in search of silk fabrics, trinkets, and charms.

- **Fashion a bar crawl:** Tiong Bahru has trendy craft beer bars that you can hop between, and Chinatown has some of the city's top cocktail bars.

- **Snack along Chinatown Food Street:** Eat your way along Chinatown's open-air food street where vendors serve everything from crispy duck to dim sum.

- **Hunt for murals:** Both Tiong Bahru and Chinatown are known for their vibrant street murals.

GETTING HERE

The Chinatown MRT stop is on the North East Line (purple), though you can also reach area sights from the Outram Park MRT and Tanjong Pagar MRT stations on the East West Line (green). For Tiong Bahru, take the East West Line (green) to the Tiong Bahru MRT station, which is within walking distance of the sights. Several buses (including the 5, 16, and 33) also traverse the neighborhood. Bus stops and taxi stands line Eu Tong Sen Street and New Bridge Road.

PLANNING YOUR TIME

Chinatown is particularly pretty at night, when the neon lights flick on, but it's also a good place for shopping at the market stalls by day. Tiong Bahru has an excellent brunch and bar scene, which makes it popular on weekends.

QUICK BITES

- **Creamier Handcrafted Ice Cream and Coffee.** This hip store serves some of the best ice cream in Singapore—a fact the locals will testify to, given it's crowded from noon until night each day. ⊠ #01–18 Yong Siak St., Blk 78, 163078 ⊕ creamier.com.sg Ⓜ Tiong Bahru

- **Foong Kee Coffee Shop.** This shop looks so local it's almost intimidating, but don't be deterred: the staff is always friendly, and the Chinese delicacies are always delicious. ⊠ 6 Keong Saik Rd., 089114 Ⓜ Outram Park

- **Nanyang Old Coffee.** This traditional coffee shop, open since the 1940s, is a great place to sip a cup of *kopi*: black coffee with sugar and condensed milk. ⊠ 268 South Bridge Rd., 058817 ⊕ nanyang-goldcoffee.com Ⓜ Chinatown

Chinatown and Tiong Bahru lie only two miles apart but offer wildly different Singaporean experiences. The former is a place for sizzling street food and bargain shopping, where you can explore the twisting streets packed with vibrant market stalls. The latter is chic and elegant, a place to brunch by day and sip craft beer by night. And adjacent to Chinatown is a neighborhood with a completely different vibe: the Central Business District (CBD), where locals shuffle to work in shiny high rises.

Chinatowns are typically found in cities where the Chinese are a minority. In Singapore, though, where ethnic Chinese substantially outnumber all other groups, a Chinatown may seem out of place. This Chinatown was formed back in colonial times, when Sir Stamford Raffles was attempting to organize immigrants by their race. The Chinese received the largest portion of land, south-west of the Singapore River. Over the years, the neighborhood has had its ups and downs, but recently it's gotten a lot more touristy. Smith, Temple, and Pagoda streets are filled with shops selling souvenir Buddhas and tea sets, "I Love SG" key chains, and T-shirts poking fun at Singapore's love for strict fines. It's a fun place to explore at night, with traditional lanterns lighting the streets and the smell of deep-fried food filling the air.

Tiong Bahru, by contrast, feels far more trendy and upscale. The neighborhood was built in the 1930s as Singapore's first public housing estate. The low-rise art deco buildings initially housed res-idents from overcrowded parts of Chinatown, but they were grad-ually taken over by the city's trendsetters, turning the area into one of the most sought-after residential addresses in Singapore. And as the number of young and wealthy people in the area grew, so too did the number of funky coffee shops, craft breweries, and bookstores. Today, it's one of Singapore's coolest neighborhoods, where indie boutiques and vegetarian cafés are the norm. Still, beneath the hipster veneer, there's a huge amount of history to uncover, including the fact that Tiong Bahru used to be home to the largest Chinese burial site in the country.

Chinatown

Chinatown is a dynamic and colorful part of the city, where you feel Singapore's heritage along every street. There are plenty of individual sights to explore, but the greatest experience is taking in the neighborhood as a whole. Red lanterns, masterful street art, and ornate architecture lie around each corner, and chaotic market stalls and street vendors offer up all kinds of goods.

Sights

Al-Abrar Mosque
RELIGIOUS SITE | Standing on a busy corner of Chinatown, this ornate mosque was once just a thatched hut, built in 1827 as one of Singapore's first mosques for Indian Muslims. Also known as Kuchu Palli (Tamil for "mosque hut"), the existing structure dates from 1850. Though much of the mosque's original ornamentation has been replaced, its original timber panels and fanlight windows have remained. You can visit during the week except on a Friday lunchtime, when devotees flock in for the midday prayers. ⊠ *192 Telok Ayer St., Chinatown* ☎ *6220–6306* ⊕ *www.muis.gov.sg* ⊙ *Closed Fri. pm and Sun.* Ⓜ *Tanjong Pagar.*

Baba House
SPECIAL-INTEREST | Take the hour-long heritage tour (S$10) to explore the ancestral home of a Chinese Peranakan family who lived in this three-story townhouse in 1895. The building and furnishings are stunning, with gold-gilded beds, mother-of-pearl inlay chairs, and striking works of calligraphy art. Heritage tours take place Tuesday to Friday at 10 am. You can also opt for a self-guided tour. ⊠ *157 Neil Rd., Chinatown* ☎ *6227–5731* ⊕ *babahouse.nus. edu.sg* Ⓜ *Outram Park.*

Blair Road
NEIGHBORHOOD | The heritage houses that line Blair Road are a site to be seen with their beautiful Peranakan floor tiles, mint green facades, and French-style shutters. They were built in the 1900s in response to the increasing demand from well-to-do Chinese merchants who wanted new homes for their families. Nowadays, they look too pretty to live in, but some people are lucky enough to call them home—which means you can't go inside and should

be conscientious with your photography. Still, just strolling the street outside is enough to give you a taste of what it might be like to live here. ⊠ *Blair Rd., Chinatown* Ⓜ *Outram Park.*

Chinatown Complex
MARKET | Typically, this market is swamped. On the first floor, hawker stalls sell local eats that are great for a quick, cheap meal, but it's the basement floor that fascinates. Here, you'll find a wet market—so called because water is continually sloshed over the floors to clean them—where meat, fowl, and fish are bought and sold. There's also an open-air produce market where you can find bargain local fruit—including the infamous durian—for an after-lunch snack. ⊠ *335 Smith St., Chinatown* Ⓜ *Chinatown.*

Chinatown Heritage Centre
MUSEUM | These three painstakingly restored shophouses show-case Chinatown's rich heritage, serving as a repository for the area's memories, sights, and sounds. The shophouse at No. 48 is the center's highlight, with replicas of an early settler's living quarters and tailor shop. There are also a number of exhibition galleries devoted to the trials and tribulations of Chinese immigrants and Chinatown's evolution, as told through the stories of past and current residents. ⊠ *48 Pagoda St., Chinatown* ☎ *6224–3928* ⊕ *www.chinatownheritagecentre.sg* ☎ *S$18* Ⓜ *Chinatown.*

Jamae Mosque
RELIGIOUS SITE | Popularly called Masjid Chulia, this simple, almost austere mosque was built in 1826 by Chulia Muslims from India's Coromandel Coast, on its southeast shore. So long as it's not prayer time and the doors are open, you're welcome to step inside for a look. Note that you must be dressed conservatively and take your shoes off before entering. ⊠ *218 South Bridge Rd., Chinatown* ☎ *6221–4165* ⊕ *www.masjidjamaechulia.sg* Ⓜ *Chinatown.*

Speakers' Corner
PLAZA | Also known as Hong Lim Park, this spot was declared a "free speech zone" by the government in 2001. It looks like nothing more than a small patch of grass, but from 7 am to 7 pm on some days, you may be able to catch carefully crafted words and speeches from people with an opinion to share. Those who wish to speak need to register with the police at the park station or online. This was intended as a place for people to express their opinions freely, but it hasn't been very successful: you can't address religious or racial issues, and having to register means that your presence has been noted. ⊠ *Hong Lim Park, bounded by North Canal Rd., South Bridge Rd., Upper Pickering St., and New Bridge Rd., Chinatown* Ⓜ *Clarke Quay.*

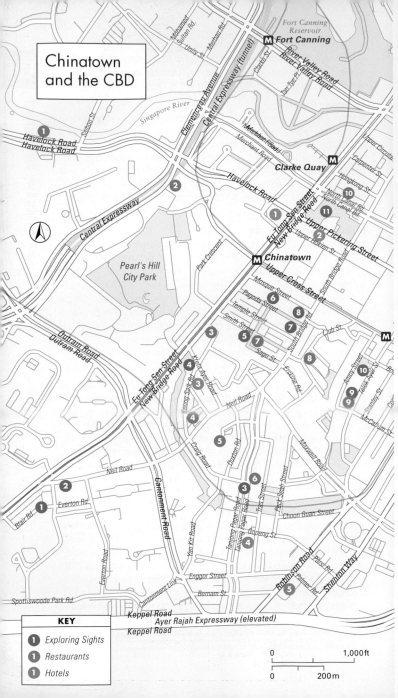

Chinatown and the CBD

KEY

- ① *Exploring Sights*
- ① *Restaurants*
- ① *Hotels*

0 ————— 1,000ft

0 ————— 200m

Sights

Al-Abrar Mosque, **9**

Baba House, **2**

Blair Road, **1**

Chinatown Complex, **5**

Chinatown Heritage Centre, **6**

Collyer Quay, **14**

Jamae Mosque, **8**

Lau Pa Sat, **13**

Merlion Park, **15**

Speakers' Corner, **11**

Sri Layan Sithi Vinayagar Temple, **4**

Sri Mariamman Temple, **7**

Tanjong Pagar Road, **3**

Thian Hock Keng Temple, **10**

Wak Hai Cheng Bio Temple, **12**

Restaurants

The Black Swan, **11**

Blue Ginger, **6**

Chinatown Food Street, **7**

Imperial Herbal Restaurant, **1**

L'Angelus, **8**

Lime House, **4**

Lucha Loco, **5**

My Awesome Café, **9**

Red Star Restaurant, **2**

Saint Pierre, **13**

Settler's Café, **10**

Shoukouwa, **14**

Tiong Shian Porridge, **3**

Zafferano Italian Restaurant and Lounge, **12**

Hotels

Amara Singapore Hotel, **4**

The Fullerton Bay Hotel, **6**

The Fullerton Hotel, **7**

Furama City Centre, **1**

Hotel 1929, **3**

M Hotel Singapore, **5**

PARKROYAL on Pickering, **2**

Keong Saik Road buzzes at night with Singapore's top restaurants and bars.

★ Sri Mariamman Temple

RELIGIOUS SITE | Singapore's oldest Hindu temple has a pagoda-like entrance topped by one of the most ornate *gopurams* (pyramidal gateway towers) you're likely to ever see outside of South India. Hundreds of brightly colored statues of deities and mythical animals line the tiers of this towering porch; glazed concrete cows sit, seemingly in great contentment, atop the surrounding walls. The story of this temple begins with Naraina Pillay, Singapore's first recorded Indian immigrant, who arrived on the same ship as Raffles in 1819 and started work as a clerk. Soon he'd set up his own construction business, often using convicts sent to Singapore from India, and quickly made a fortune. He obtained this site for the temple, so that devotees could pray on the way to and from work at the harbor. The first temple, built in 1827 of wood and *attap* (wattle and daub), was replaced in 1843 by the current brick structure. The gopuram was added in 1936. Inside are some spectacular paintings that have been restored by Tamil craftsmen brought over from South India. This is where Hindu weddings, as well as the firewalking festival *Thimithi*, take place. ⊠ *244 South Bridge Rd., Chinatown* ☎ *6223–4064* ⊕ *www.smt.org.sg* Ⓜ *Chinatown.*

Sri Layan Sithi Vinayagar Temple

RELIGIOUS SITE | This small but incredibly ornate temple is covered with tiny pale blue and baby pink statues in typical Hindu style. It was first built in 1925 in honor of Lord Vinayagar—also known as Lord Ganesha, the most widely worshipped Hindu god. He has three deity statues dedicated to him in the main sanctum, one of

which was brought from India. It's worth visiting just to adm
from the outside as you breathe in the heavy scents of incens
but you can go inside as long as there isn't a worship session
taking place. ⊠ *73 Keong Saik Rd., Chinatown* ⊕ *www.sttemple.*
com Ⓜ *Outram Park*.

Tanjong Pagar Road
NEIGHBORHOOD | You'll struggle not to pull out your camera as you
walk along this road. The 220 shophouses that line the street
have been restored to an idealized version of their 19th-century
appearance—a collection of brightly-colored facades standing in
symmetrical unity. The buildings contain tea houses, calligraphers,
mahjong tile makers, shops, bars, and restaurants, and although
there is no one house that is especially worth visiting, the road
itself makes for a pleasant stroll as you admire the striking architecture. ⊠ *Chinatown* Ⓜ *Tanjong Pagar*.

★ Thian Hock Keng Temple
RELIGIOUS SITE | This structure—the Temple of Heavenly Happi-
ness—was completed in 1842 to replace a simple shrine built 20
years earlier. It's one of Singapore's oldest and largest Chinese
temples, built on the spot where, prior to land reclamation,
immigrants stepped ashore after a hazardous journey across the
China Sea. In gratitude for their safe passage, the Hokkien people
dedicated the temple to Ma Chu P'oh, the goddess of the sea.
It's richly decorated with gilded carvings, sculptures, tile roofs
topped with dragons, and fine carved-stone pillars. On either side
of the entrance are two stone lions. The one on the left is female
and holds a cup symbolizing fertility; the other, a male, holds a
ball, a symbol of wealth. If the temple is open, note that as you
enter, you must step over a high threshold board. This serves a
dual function. First, it forces devotees to look downward, as they
should when entering the temple. Second, it keeps out wandering
ghosts—ghosts tend to shuffle their feet, so if they try to enter,
the threshold board will trip them.

Inside, a statue of a maternal Ma Chu P'oh surrounded by masses
of burning incense and candles dominates the room. On either
side of her are the deities of health (on your left) and wealth. The
two tall figures you'll notice are her sentinels: one can see for
1,000 miles; the other can hear for 1,000 miles. The gluey black
substance on their lips—placed there by devotees in days past—is
opium, meant to heighten their senses. Although the main temple
is Taoist, the temple at the back is Buddhist and dedicated to Kuan
Yin, the goddess of mercy. Her many arms represent how she
reaches out to all those who suffer on earth.

Singapore's Hawker Centers

👁

Singapore's hawker centers are a way of life. These vibrant food markets, dotted across the island in large numbers, play an integral role in the country's heritage and identity. They act as a kind of community dining center, full of stalls selling everything from Chinese and Malay to Indian and Thai, where people from all walks of life can gather to eat, drink, and bond over the cheap, local food.

The hawker centers started out in the 1800s as street food stalls and grew rapidly until the colonial British government attempted to stop them in the early 1900s. But as the population expanded, so did the centers. The government eventually issued licenses, and in the 1970s, moved them to new centers in residential areas—ones that still exist today.

These days, a trip to Singapore wouldn't be complete without eating at a hawker center: Chinatown has **Maxwell Food Centre**, **Amoy Street Food Centre**, and **Chinatown Complex Food Centre** and Tiong Bahru has **Tiong Bahru Food Centre**, though you can find centers in just about every central neighborhood.

There are no real rules to observe: simply turn up, eat, and enjoy. Many like to find a seat first, a practice called "choping" in Singlish, in which you leave a personal item (like a packet of tissues) on a table while you line up for their meal. Usually you wait while the food is cooked, then pay when you collect it a few minutes later. When you're done, leave the tray on the table. No napkins are provided, but there are sinks for washing your hands.

🌿 This is a good place to learn your fortune. Choose a number out of the box, then pick up two small stenciled pieces of wood at the back of the altar and let them fall to the ground. If they land showing opposite faces, then the number you have picked is valid. If they land same-side up, try again. From a valid number, the person in the nearby booth will tell you your fate, and whether you like the outcome or not, you pay for the information. Leave the grounds by the alley that runs alongside the main temple. The two statues to the left are the gambling brothers. They will help you choose a lucky number for your next betting session; if you win, you must return and place lighted cigarettes in their hands. ✉ *158 Telok Ayer St., Chinatown* ☎ *6423–4616* ⊕ *www.thianhockkeng. com.sg* Ⓜ *Tanjong Pagar.*

🍴 Restaurants

★ Blue Ginger

$$ | **ASIAN FUSION** | Come to this beautifully restored shophouse for such well-prepared Malaysian/Chinese fare as *udang goreng tauyu lada* (sautéed prawns with pepper in sweet soy sauce), *ayam panggang Blue Ginger* (grilled boneless chicken grilled in spiced coconut milk), and *ngo heong* (rolls of ground pork and prawns seasoned with five spices). The specialty dessert, a sweet mixture of red beans, pandan (screw-pine)-flavored jelly, and coconut milk, is finished with puréed durian, perhaps the most polarizing fruit on the planet: you'll either love it or hate it, but you should try it at least once. **Known for:** historical setting; authentic Southeast Asian fare; specialty dessert made with durian. ⑤ *Average main: S$25* ✉ *97 Tanjong Pagar Rd., Tanjong Pagar* ☎ *6222–3928* ⊕ *www. theblueginger.com* Ⓜ *Tanjong Pagar.*

★ Chinatown Food Street

$ | **CHINESE** | A stretch of Smith Street that is closed to traffic, this outdoor eating area packed with stalls is the only place you'll find real "street food" in Singapore. Though it isn't totally open-air (there is a high-ceiling glass canopy in case of rain), it makes a welcome change from the often hot and sweaty hawker centers. **Known for:** street food in a novel setting; open rain or shine; cold beer and chicken satay. ⑤ *Average main: S$5* ✉ *41 Smith St., Chinatown* ⊕ *chinatownfoodstreet.sg* Ⓜ *Chinatown.*

Imperial Herbal Restaurant

$$$ | **CHINESE** | Located roughly between Tiong Bahru and Chinatown, Imperial Herbal is not your average Chinese restaurant: the enormous menu is packed with everything from braised crocodile tail and quick-fried eel to stewed deer tendon and braised goose. If, however, such unusual dishes aren't to your liking, you can order classics like glazed spare ribs or juicy pork dumplings. **Known for:** large and varied menu; picturesque wooden carvings; a focus on Chinese herbal recipes. ⑤ *Average main: S$31* ✉ *Riverview Hotel, 382 Havelock Ave., Chinatown* ☎ *6337–0491* ⊕ *www. imperialherbal.com* Ⓜ *Chinatown.*

L'Angelus

$$$ | **FRENCH** | Potted plants line the entrance of this chic, Parisian-style restaurant, and, in its casual dining area, French film posters cover the walls from floor to ceiling. Daily specials are scrawled on chalkboards, but the set menu includes meat, seafood, and such French specialties as baked foie gras and crème brûlée, and there's an exhaustive selection of French wines, as well as a large range of whiskies, vodkas, gins, liqueurs, rums, and Armagnacs. **Known for:** poster-covered walls; perfectly cooked steaks; French wine. $ *Average main: S$50* ⊠ *85 Club St., Chinatown* ☎ *6225–6897* ⊕ *www.langelus.sg* ☾ *Closed Sun. No lunch Sat.* Ⓜ *Chinatown.*

Lime House

$$ | JAMAICAN | Spend time "liming"—the Caribbean slang for "hanging with friends"—at this vibrant eatery inside a four-story heritage shophouse decorated with leafy plants, natural woods, and colorful prints. Wash down such classic Caribbean dishes as jerk chicken and curry goat with a rum cocktail from the restaurant's tiki-style bar, Bago. **Known for:** Caribbean classics; tiki bar; light and airy atmosphere. $ *Average main: S$30* ⊠ *2 Jiak Chuan Rd., Chinatown* ☎ *6222–3130* ⊕ *limehouse.asia* ☾ *Closed Sun. and Mon. No lunch* Ⓜ *Outram.*

★ Lucha Loco

$ | MEXICAN | This lively restaurant is a real treat in a country where good Mexican cuisine can be hard to come by. While the inside is lovely, it's the large, leafy garden adorned with wall posters and bunting that provides the perfect setting for tucking into great food and even greater tequila. **Known for:** garden seating; street food menu of tacos and quesadillas; great happy hour; weekdays until 7 pm. $ *Average main: S$12* ⊠ *15 Duxton Hill, Chinatown* ☎ *6226–3938* ⊕ *www.super-loco.com* ☾ *Closed Sun.* Ⓜ *Outram.*

My Awesome Café

$$ | CONTEMPORARY | Inside a historic shophouse tucked away on a quiet street, this café-by-day, bar-by-night has all the makings of a hipster hangout. Seated at a table with legs made out of old piping—amid fairy lights and exposed brickwork—you can order fresh salads, sandwiches, or platters, as well as excellent coffees and even better wine. **Known for:** hearty sandwiches by day; great wine by night; lively evening atmosphere. $ *Average main: S$15* ⊠ *202 Telok Ayer St., Chinatown* ☎ *6222–2007* ⊕ *www.myawesomecafe.com* Ⓜ *Tanjong Pagar.*

★ Red Star Restaurant

$ | CANTONESE | Shuffling waiters push dim sum trolleys from table to table at this wonderfully outdated Cantonese restaurant. Although the old-school decor (red carpets, cream table cloths, strip lights) makes it feel like a giant community center, the crispy spring rolls, siew mai dumplings, fried wantons, and egg tarts are classic and delicious. **Known for:** suckling pig; roast duck; delicious dumplings (served at lunchtime only). $ *Average main: S$10* ⊠ *#07–23 Block 54, Chin Swee Rd., Chinatown* ☎ *6532–5266* ⊕ *redstarrestaurant.com.sg* Ⓜ *Chinatown.*

★ Settler's Café

$$ | **AMERICAN** | Of all Singapore's popular themed cafés, Settler's Café is considered the first board game café in the country. There are more than 600 games on offer, which you can enjoy as part of a package that includes food and drink alongside a few hours of game play. **Known for:** games like Pictionary; dinner and wine packages; fun for friends. ⑤ *Average main: S$25* ✉ *39 North Canal Rd., Clarke Quay* ☎ *6535–0435* ⊕ *www.settlers.sg* ☉ *Closed Mon.* Ⓜ *Clarke Quay.*

Tiong Shian Porridge

$ | **CHINESE** | This humble store on the edge of Chinatown, with its metal chairs and bright strip lights, doesn't look very inviting—until you see the hoards of people waiting to get inside. *Congee*, or savory porridge, is a popular local dish, and nowhere does it better than Tiong Shian, where thick, hot white rice is served with everything from meatballs to frogs legs. Service is brisk and comfort is minimal but you can be guaranteed a good meal. **Known for:** cheap prices; delicious congee; quick service. ⑤ *Average main: S$4* ✉ *265 New Bridge Rd., Chinatown* ☎ *6222–3911* Ⓜ *Outram Park or Chinatown.*

🛏 Hotels

Staying in Chinatown means you're always at the heart of the action: just seconds away from great food, quirky bars, and huge markets made for shopping. With the convenient location, however, comes noise from the people who throng the streets. Still, the neighborhood's good selection of hotels makes it an ideal place to stay if you're okay with the hustle and bustle.

Amara Singapore Hotel

$$ | **HOTEL** | This 18-story hotel—part of a vibrant entertainment and shopping complex in the business district's south end and convenient to the MRT station, the commercial and port facilities, and Chinatown's shops and restaurants—is soothing, thanks to a minimalist lobby, a Balinese-style pool, and guest rooms decorated in earth tones and timber. **Pros:** central location; business center; spacious bedrooms. **Cons:** breakfast is crowded; rooms are a little tired looking; internet could be faster. ⑤ *Rooms from: S$200* ✉ *165 Tanjong Pagar Rd., Chinatown* ☎ *6879–2555* ⊕ *singapore. amarahotels.com* ⬳ *380 rooms* ⑩ *No meals* Ⓜ *Tanjong Pagar.*

Furama City Centre

$$ | **HOTEL** | This modern curvilinear building stands out amid the surrounding shophouses on the edge of Chinatown. **Pros:** great views from high floors; easy access to Chinatown; 24-hour

`ons:` amenities are outdated; some rooms have `windows`; check-in and check-out can take a `ns from: S$200` ⊠ *60 Eu Tong Sen St., Chinatown* `3` ⊕ *www.furama.com/citycentre* ☞ *445 rooms* ❑| *No inatown.*

Hote.

$$ | HOTEL | Comprising five converted shophouses that were built in 1929, this hotel successfully blends old-style architecture with a modern interior. **Pros:** in the heart of Chinatown; hip and stylish decor; great if you stay in a suite. **Cons:** small rooms; basic breakfast; glass door on bathrooms. Ⓢ *Rooms from: S$150* ⊠ *50 Keong Saik St., Chinatown* ☎ *6347–1929* ⊕ *www.hotel1929.com* ☞ *34 rooms* ❑| *Free Breakfast* Ⓜ *Outram Park.*

★ PARKROYAL on Pickering

$$$ | HOTEL | The stunning architecture at this hotel integrates environmental principles both inside and out, including lush sky gardens almost 1,000 feet above street level, floor-to-ceiling glass windows throughout to decrease the need for artificial lighting, use of recycled stone and glass in guest room baths, and rainwater used to water greenery in the lobby. **Pros:** great spa facilities; eco-conscious initiatives; city views from infinity pool. **Cons:** limited in-house restaurants; rooms could be considered small for price; outdoor walkways not so great in the rain. Ⓢ *Rooms from: S$310* ⊠ *3 Upper Pickering St., Chinatown* ☎ *6809–8888* ⊕ *www. panpacific.com* ☞ *367 rooms* ❑| *No meals* Ⓜ *Chinatown.*

☯ Nightlife

Chinatown is one of the best places to spend an evening in Singapore. Not only is it draped in lanterns and neon lights that transform the neighborhood into a kaleidoscope after dark, but it's also packed with top-notch bars that'll keep you entertained all night.

Bitters and Love

BARS/PUBS | A 19th-century shophouse in Chinatown is the perfect location for this speakeasy-like cocktail bar, where you'll have a one-of-a-kind experience. Tell the bartenders what you like, and they'll create a cocktail especially for you. There are also signature cocktails and bar bites available. Be sure to call for reservations in advance. ⊠ *118 Telok Ayer St., Chinatown* ☎ *6438–1836 Reservations* ⊕ *www.bittersandlove.com* ☞ *Closed Sun.–Mon.* Ⓜ *Telok Ayer.*

Chinese Theatre Circle

THEMED ENTERTAINMENT | The Chinese Circle Theatre (CTC) is a nonprofit organization that's been cultivating an appreciation of Cantonese opera since 1981. Check out one of their dinner performances every Friday and Saturday night from 7 to 9 pm and gain some insight into this particular art form (translations are provided). For S$40, you can dine on a set Chinese dinner with special-brewed tea while you watch, or for S$25 you can simply sit back and enjoy the show. The Theatre Circle is set up along a stretch of Smith Street that transforms into a pedestrian zone nightly and brings to mind the hustle and bustle of the street hawkers from the 1970s. ⊠ *5 Smith St., Chinatown* ☎ *6323–4862* ⊕ *www.ctcopera.com.sg* Ⓜ *Chinatown.*

Employees Only

BARS/PUBS | Conceived in downtown New York City back in 2004, Employees Only has become one of the most iconic cocktail bars in Singapore since it opened here in 2016. Describing itself as a "neo-speakeasy restaurant and bar," this slice of the Big Apple has been ranked among Asia's 50 best bars in the annual "Best Bars" awards every year since its inception. Enjoy small plates like bone marrow poppers and spicy smothered shrimp as you drink the innovative NYC cocktails. ⊠ *112 Amoy St., Chinatown* ☎ *6221–7357* ⊕ *employeesonlysg.com* Ⓜ *Chinatown.*

★ Gibson Bar

BARS/PUBS | This casual cocktail and seafood bar comes from the team behind Jigger & Pony (another Chinatown hot spot), so you already know it's good. Their seasonal cocktail menu does a good job of highlighting Southeast Asian ingredients such as starfruit. Try the happy hour oysters along with their namesake cocktail, the Gibson, which incorporates a homemade Ginjo sake vermouth. ⊠ *20 Bukit Pasoh Rd., Level 2, Chinatown* ☎ *9114–8385* ⊕ *www.gibsonbar.sg* Ⓜ *Outram.*

★ Jigger and Pony

BARS/PUBS | Yet another of the city's establishments to make the list of the "World's 50 Best Bars," Jigger & Pony serves up exceptional classic cocktails such as negronis, martinis, and Old Fashioneds, as well as signature cocktails with a local twist (think gin fizz with orange flower bubbles or whiskey sour with a touch of yuzu marmalade). Located in the Amara hotel, the dimly lit space is cozy and inviting. ⊠ *Amara Singapore Hotel, 165 Tanjong Pagar Rd., Chinatown* ☎ *9621–1074* ⊕ *www.jiggerandpony.com* Ⓜ *Tanjong Pagar.*

★ Native

BARS/PUBS | At this top-ranked bar, the goal is to connect with Singapore through local flavors. Many of the cocktails are made using ingredients foraged from nearby areas and local alcohol like jackfruit rum. ⊠ *52A Amoy St., Chinatown* ⊕ *tribenative.com* Ⓜ *Chinatown.*

Nutmeg and Clove

BARS/PUBS | This avant-garde cocktail bar recalls the days when rickshaws rolled through the streets of Chinatown. Drawing inspiration from illustrations in the books of William Farquhar, the first British Resident and Commandant of colonial Singapore, this bar uses herbs, fruits, spices, and flora in concoctions that reflect Singapore's history in every sip. ⊠ *10A Ann Siang Hill, Chinatown* ☎ *9389–9301* ⊕ *nutmegandclove.com.sg* ☞ *Closed Sun.* Ⓜ *Chinatown.*

Olde Cuban

BARS/PUBS | In this plush bar, you can sink into leather sofas with a glass of aged whiskey in one hand and a rare cigar in the other. The Olde Cuban is home to a collection of more than 100 whiskies and over 200 types of cigars, with an old-fashioned aesthetic straight out of a scene from *Mad Men*. ⊠ *#02–01, 2 Trengganu St., Chinatown* ☎ *6222–2207* ⊕ *www.oldecuban.com* Ⓜ *Chinatown.*

★ The Old Man Singapore

BARS/PUBS | Opened in 2019, this Hemingway-inspired bar is an outpost of Hong Kong's Old Man bar, which was deemed "Best Bar in Asia" by the World's 50 Best Bars. The cocktails live up to the hype, and there's even a small "laboratory" where bartenders create drinks such as The Snows of Kilimanjaro made with marshmallow gin, citrus, lacto-fermented raspberries, and gruyere cheese. ⊠ *55 Keong Saik Rd., Chinatown* ☎ *6909–5505* ⊕ *theoldmanhk.com* Ⓜ *Outram.*

★ Operation Dagger

BARS/PUBS | This basement drinking den, dreamed up by an Aussie bartender, combines modern cocktails with a medieval, apothecary-style design. The drinks are original and inventive, from a honeycomb and liquid nitrogen concoction to a "not a Margarita" drink made from agave, pea husks, and salt. If you don't know what to pick, they also serve an omakase menu made of three or five "courses" of cocktails the mixologist whisks up based on your preferences. ⊠ *#B1–01, No. 7 Ann Sian Hill, Chinatown* ☎ *6438–4057* ⊕ *operationdagger.com* Ⓜ *Chinatown.*

★ Potato Head

BARS/PUBS | Hailing from the sandy shores of Bali, this bar with a cult following brings a beach-chic aesthetic to the art deco heritage building it occupies. Although it has an Asian burger restaurant and quirky speakeasy-style bar, head for the rooftop bar—a place of fairy lights, bright murals, lush greenery, lovely night views over the city, and tropical cocktails that will have you believing you're really in Bali. ✉ *36 Keong Saik Rd., Chinatown* ☎ *6327–1939* ⊕ *potatohead.co/singapore* Ⓜ *Outram Park.*

★ Screening Room

BARS/PUBS | This five-floor film, food, and bar complex is part of a cluster of trendy shophouse bars and restaurants. A lounge area takes up the basement and first floor, but the biggest draw is on the third floor, where there's a small, funky theater with its own bar. Classic films from around the world are shown, and menus are created to match the theme. (The film schedule is online, and reservations can be made via email or phone.) The rooftop bar attracts a cool after-work crowd. ✉ *12 Ann Siang Rd., Chinatown* ☎ *6532–3357* ⊕ *www.screeningroom.com.sg* Ⓜ *Chinatown.*

★ Smith Street Taps

BARS/PUBS | Occupying two hawker stalls on Level 2 of the Chinatown Complex Food Centre, this tiny bar is the definition of "hidden gem." It would be easy to mistake it as just one of the hundreds of food vendors that occupy the center if it weren't for the number of people drinking its excellent craft drafts at the tables that surround it. One stall is dedicated to international brews, the other to local ones; the staff will happily talk you through the tasting notes of each beer. ✉ *#02–062 Chinatown Complex, Blk 335 Smith St., Chinatown* ✣ *Stall 62* ☎ *9430–2750* ⊕ *www.facebook.com/smithstreettaps* Ⓜ *Chinatown.*

🛍 Shopping

China Square Central

ANTIQUES/COLLECTIBLES | This mall is the best place in Singapore for vintage and designer toys. Here you can nerd out in more than ten shops that are packed with scores of action figures and collectibles, vintage video-game consoles, comic books, and much more. There is also a good selection of restaurants and cafés. ✉ *18 Cross St., Chinatown* ☎ *6327–4473* ⊕ *www.chinasquarecentral.com* Ⓜ *Chinatown.*

Chinatown's outdoor shops are a good spot to pick up souvenirs.

★ Chinatown Street Market

GIFTS/SOUVENIRS | This is one of the most popular spots in the city to souvenir shop. The stalls sprawl across Pagoda Street, Trengganu Street, Sago Lane, Smith Street, and Temple Street, so you just need to pick a starting point and get walking. You can buy everything from lacquerware and handmade fans to paintings and tacky T-shirts. Prices are usually fixed. ✉ *Pagoda St., Chinatown* Ⓜ *Chinatown.*

East Inspirations

ANTIQUES/COLLECTIBLES | At this family-run Chinese antiques shop, the treasure trove of ceramics, vases, furniture, and textiles could keep you entertained for hours. Each item has been curated by the shop's owner, Mr. Cheong, who fell in love with antiques more than 40 years ago and has been selling them ever since. He stocks all manner of elaborate items, from huge ornate wardrobes to tiny, intricately designed vases, while orange silks embroidered in dragons and flowers hang from the walls. ✉ *33 Pagoda St., Chinatown* ☎ *6224–2993* ⊕ *www.east-inspirations.com/find-us* Ⓜ *Chinatown.*

★ Wing Antiques & Collectibles

ANTIQUES/COLLECTIBLES | It's a shame that no photography is allowed at this dusty old antiques shop. Its remarkable groupings of vintage goods, arranged in what you might call haphazard symmetry, make for one of the more photogenic mishmashes of random items in Singapore. Then again, photos might sully the surprises an hour of treasure hunting might yield. It's a great shop if you like thrifting. ✉ *#03–27/28 Havelock II Retail, 02 Havelock Rd., Chinatown* ☎ *6438–0089* Ⓜ *Chinatown.*

Yue Hwa

DEPARTMENT STORES | Inside this aging, five-level, Chinese department store you'll find plenty of unique (and often pricey) products, including medicinal herbs, tea, silks, fashion, and home furnishings. Many of the items are from mainland China. ⊠ *70 Eu Tong Sen St., Chinatown* ☎ *6538–4222* ⊕ *www.yuehwa.com.sg* Ⓜ *Chinatown.*

Activities

Indie Singapore Tours

WALKING TOURS | This free, 3.5-hour walking tour of Chinatown runs every Tuesday and Friday morning. The guide points out local highlights and main attractions in addition to illustrating how this diverse part of Singapore is made up of a unique blend of cultures and religions. Bookings are essential and can be made up to four weeks in advance. Tips at the end are appreciated. ⊠ *151 New Bridge Rd., Chinatown* ⊕ *indiesingapore.com* Ⓜ *Chinatown Exit A.*

★ Monster Day Tours

WALKING TOURS | The free walking tour takes you on a 2.5-hour trip around the area, starting at the Chinatown MRT and ending at Telok Ayer. It's a great way to get your bearings and learn the history of the area as you tour the food streets, markets, and temples with a knowledgeable guide. At the end, tips are appreciated but not compulsory: the company recommends a S$10 tip if you thought your guide was professional, up to $30 if you really loved the tour. Tours are available Thursday and Sunday at 9:30 am and Tuesday and Friday at 4:30 pm. ⊠ *151 New Bridge Rd., Chinatown* ☎ *9231–3858* ⊕ *www.monsterdaytours.com* Ⓜ *Chinatown Exit A.*

The CBD

On weekdays, the Central Business District is packed with professionals traveling to and from work. High-rise office buildings and hotels fill the area next to Chinatown and many of its surrounding streets, but this is also the area where you'll find many heritage buildings and other reminders of Singapore's history.

Plan on spending at least a half-day here. The two-mile walk from Raffles Place to Gardens by the Bay will give you a good feel for this bustling, business-heavy part of town. Several of the city's biggest attractions will take up more of your time along the way.

Tanjong Pagar MRT station is a stop on the East West Line (green); Raffles Place MRT station is a stop on both the East West (green) and North South (red) lines. Several buses service the area, and taxi stands are fairly numerous.

Sights

Collyer Quay

PROMENADE | Land reclamation projects throughout the 19th century pushed the seafront several blocks away from Collyer Quay. At that time, the view from here would have been a virtual wall of anchored ships. Today, you look out onto Marina Bay. European traders once arrived by steamship and Chinese immigrants arrived by wind-dependent junks at **Clifford Pier,** a covered jetty with high, vaulted ceilings that ceased operations in 2006. Nearby, the **Customs House** building once facilitated the arrival of leisure seekers and traders. Now, the historical buildings host some of the trendiest restaurants and bars in town, with **The Fullerton Bay Hotel** nestled between. ⊠ *Collyer Quay, CBD* Ⓜ *Raffles Place*.

★ Lau Pa Sat

MARKET | This market is the largest Victorian cast-iron structure left in Southeast Asia. Already a thriving fish market in 1822, it was redesigned as an octagon by George Coleman in 1834 and again redesigned, as seen today, in 1894. It now serves as a food court, with hawker stalls that are busy during the day with office workers. After 7 pm, Boon Tat Street is closed to traffic, and the mood turns festive: hawkers wheel out their satay carts, and buskers often perform inside. ⊠ *18 Raffles Quay, CBD* ☎ *6220–2138* ⊕ *www.laupasat.biz* Ⓜ *Raffles Place*.

Merlion Park

PUBLIC ART | This waterfront space is where you will find two statues of the Merlion, a mythical beast and Singapore icon that symbolizes courage, strength, and excellence. Half lion, half fish, it's based on the national symbol, the lion (from which the name Singapore was derived), while its fish tail represents the country's past as a fishing town. The larger, 28-foot statue gushes water into the Singapore River through its mouth and looks even more dramatic after dark when it's floodlit and its eyes glow. The other statue, sometimes known as the "cub" for its smaller size, faces landward and is an equally unique photo opportunity. ⊠ *1 Fullerton Rd., CBD* ✛ *Opposite the Fullerton Hotel* ☎ *6736–6622* ⊕ *www. visitsingapore.com* Ⓜ *Raffles Place*.

Wak Hai Cheng Bio Temple

RELIGIOUS SITE | Built in 1826 by Teochew Chinese from Guangdong Province and dedicated to the goddess of the sea, this is one of Singapore's oldest Taoist temples. It's also known as Yueng Hai Ching Temple, which means Temple of the Calm Sea. Traders and travelers returning from China visited the temple on disembarking—believe it or not, Philip Street was then very close to the water—to offer their thanks for a safe journey. It has been maintained by the Ngee Ann Clan Association since 1845 and was rebuilt in 1895. Inside, there's an imperial signboard presented by Qing Dynasty Emperor Guang Xu in 1907. Each of the structure's twin wings can be accessed by its own entrance, each of which has different ornamental features. Besides dragons and pagodas, human figurines and scenes from Chinese operas are depicted on the temple's roof. ⊠ *30B Phillip St., CBD* ☎ *6533–8537* Ⓜ *Raffles Place.*

🍴 Restaurants

The Black Swan

$$$ | EUROPEAN | Join the bankers, brokers, and finance executives that swarm this opulent art deco—style bar and chophouse that stands out against its sleek concrete-and-metal neighbors. Indulge in a fine selection of beef cuts from America and Australia, and wash it all down with a tipple from the extensive list of wine, spirits, and cocktails. **Known for:** Great Gatsby-esque decor; no-waste cuisine; office crowd favorite. Ⓢ *Average main: S$50* ⊠ *19 Cecil St., CBD* ☎ *6438–3757* ⊕ *www.theblackswan.com.sg* Ⓜ *Raffles Place.*

★ Saint Pierre

$$$$ | FRENCH FUSION | FAMILY | At this intimate 30-seater run by celebrated chef Emmanuel Stroobant, you'll be served delicate, Asian-inflected French cuisine alongside a panoramic view of the Marina Bay waterfront. The chic, Michelin-starred establishment is a favorite among many not just for its fine food but also its inclusive offerings such as special menus for vegetarians and children. **Known for:** impeccable food and service; family-friendly fine dining; picturesque waterfront views. Ⓢ *Average main: S$70* ⊠ *One Fullerton, 1 Fullerton Rd., #02–02B, Singapore* ☎ *6438–0887* ⊕ *www.saintpierre.com.sg* ⊗ *Closed Mon.-Wed.* Ⓜ *Raffles Place.*

Shoukouwa

$$$$ | SUSHI | The two-Michelin-starred Shoukouwa offers perhaps the most intimate dining experience in all of Singapore, with just eight counter seats and a private room for six. Reservations are a must, but for your trouble, you get elegant omakase meals created with obsessive attention to detail—even the sushi rice is dressed in a meticulously crafted mix of artisanal vinegars. **Known for:** fastidiously fashioned sushi; attention to detail; intimate dining experience. ⑤ *Average main: S$380 ⊠ One Fullerton, 1 Fullerton Rd., #02–02A, CBD* ☎ *6423–9939* ⊕ *www.shoukouwa.com.sg* ⊘ *Closed Mon.-Tues.* Ⓜ *Raffles Place.*

Zafferano Italian Restaurant and Lounge

$$$ | **MODERN ITALIAN** | This corporate executive favorite encased by floor-to-ceiling windows serves up mod Italian food with a side of sweeping Marina Bay views. Wine aficionados can pair their meals with a selection from more than 200 premium Italian wines and collection of vintages. **Known for:** contemporary Italian cuisine; stunning views; personable service. ⑤ *Average main: S$50 ⊠ Ocean Financial Centre, 10 Collyer Quay, Level 43, CBD* ☎ *6509–1488* ⊕ *zafferano.sg* ⊘ *Closed Sun. No lunch Sat.* Ⓜ *Raffles Place.*

🛏 Hotels

★ The Fullerton Bay Hotel

$$$$ | **HOTEL** | Set along a historic pier, the Fullerton Bay Hotel is built completely over water, with a glass facade that sets it apart from the historic buildings nearby. **Pros:** great views; 24-hour gym; contemporary art. **Cons:** small lobby; breakfast buffet is cramped; expensive. ⑤ *Rooms from: S$590 ⊠ 80 Collyer Quay, CBD* ☎ *6333–8388* ⊕ *www.fullertonhotels.com/the-fullerton-bay-hotel* ⤴ *100 rooms* ⦿❙ *Free Breakfast* Ⓜ *Raffles Place.*

The Fullerton Hotel

$$$$ | **HOTEL** | **FAMILY** | Singapore's former General Post Office-turned-hotel has many historic details paying tribute to its past, making this an atmospheric setting to base yourself; plus, its central location means that you'll be within walking distance of many of the top sights. **Pros:** iconic building; award-winning restaurants; great city views. **Cons:** small pool with too-few deck chairs; small TVs; starting to show its age. ⑤ *Rooms from: S$500 ⊠ 1 Fullerton Sq., CBD* ☎ *6733–8388* ⊕ *www.fullertonhotels.com* ⤴ *400 rooms* ⦿❙ *Free Breakfast.*

M Hotel Singapore

$$ | **HOTEL** | The dull exterior makes the modern and stylish interior of this business hotel a bit of a surprise, and, though it's near the business district, it's removed from all the hurly-burly. **Pros:** central location; weekend deals; plenty of dining options in the area. **Cons:** can seem dull on weekends; small pool; impersonal

lobby. $ *Rooms from: S$200* ⊠ *81 Anson Rd., CBD* ☎ *6224–1133* ⊕ *www.millenniumhotels.com* ⇥ *415 rooms* ⏧ *Free Breakfast* Ⓜ *Tanjong Pagar.*

🍸 Nightlife

Lantern

BARS/PUBS | With a happy hour menu that starts at 11 am, any time is a good time to chill out with a drink on one of the sunbeds or cozy couches at this bar on the rooftop of The Fullerton Bay Hotel. To get seats with the best views, book well ahead. ⊠ *Fullerton Bay Hotel, 80 Collyer Quay, Level 8, CBD* ☎ *6597–5299* ⊕ *www. fullertonhotels.com* Ⓜ *Raffles Place.*

★ Tippling Club

BARS/PUBS | This outstanding mixology bar doubles as an award-winning restaurant where the cocktails are inspired by the food. There are two ways to experience it: the bar, which requires no reservations, or the restaurant, which requires a reservation. Get a dinner reservation if you can so you can try the innovative cocktails with their excellent modern cooking. ⊠ *38 Tanjong Pagar Rd., CBD* ☎ *6475–2217* ⊕ *www.tipplingclub.com* Ⓜ *Tanjong Pagar.*

🎭 Performing Arts

Singapore Chinese Orchestra

CONCERTS | Singapore's only professional Chinese orchestra is comprised of more than 80 musicians. It stages annual block-busters, both locally and internationally, that push the boundaries of traditional Chinese music, and it holds free performances to promote appreciation of the genre. ⊠ *Singapore Conference Hall, 7 Shenton Way, CBD* ☎ *6557–4034* ⊕ *www.sco.com.sg* Ⓜ *Tanjong Pagar.*

🛍 Shopping

CYC The Custom Shop

CLOTHING | Open since 1935, this upscale clothing store specializes in stylish men's and women's shirts, suits, and skirts custom-made from more than 1,000 different fabrics. A second branch is at Capitol Piazza. ⊠ *Fullerton Hotel, 1 Fullerton Sq., #01–06, CBD* ☎ *6538–0522* ⊕ *www.cyccompany.com* 🕒 *Closed Sun.* Ⓜ *Tanjong Pagar.*

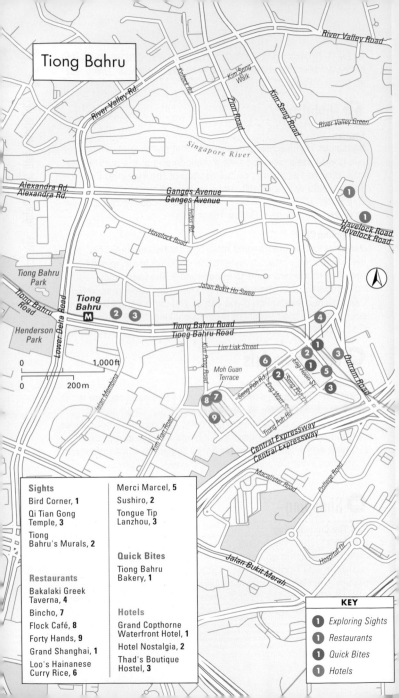

Tiong Bahru

Sights

Bird Corner, **1**

Qi Tian Gong Temple, **3**

Tiong Bahru's Murals, **2**

Restaurants

Bakalaki Greek Taverna, **4**

Bincho, **7**

Flock Café, **8**

Forty Hands, **9**

Grand Shanghai, **1**

Loo's Hainanese Curry Rice, **6**

Merci Marcel, **5**

Sushiro, **2**

Tongue Tip Lanzhou, **3**

Quick Bites

Tiong Bahru Bakery, **1**

Hotels

Grand Copthorne Waterfront Hotel, **1**

Hotel Nostalgia, **2**

Thad's Boutique Hostel, **3**

KEY

1 *Exploring Sights*

1 *Restaurants*

1 *Quick Bites*

1 *Hotels*

What's in a Name? 👁

The name Tiong Bahru combines the word "Tiong," meaning "to die" in the Hokkien dialect, and "Bahru" meaning "new" in Malay. It's thought the name refers to the Chinese burial ground that was here in the 1800s and that no longer exists. By the early 1900s, many of the bodies had already been exhumed to build the neighborhood you see today.

Tiong Bahru

Not far from Chinatown is one of Singapore's coolest neighborhoods, a trendy spot to relax at a café, sample craft suds at a bar, or shop at boutiques along mural-lined streets.

👁 Sights

Tiong Bahru isn't known for its sights, but the whole area is a living testament to Singapore's heritage and culture. Walk around the art deco buildings in search of murals, or follow the Heritage Trail to find places of historical significance.

Bird Corner
LOCAL INTEREST | Today, Bird Corner is nothing but a metal monument with cords drooping down where bird cages once hung—but in the 1980s, it was the site of Tiong Bahru's most loved coffeeshop, where locals could hang their bird cages while they sat and sipped coffee to the sounds of sweet song. The shopowner, Wah Heng, devised the concept after seeing how much attention a nearby pet shop was getting from its bird cages. It was an astute move: many bird owners made a beeline for the coffeeshop to show off their birds, and before long, the cacophony of song and colorful cages drew attention from locals, tourists, and journalists alike. This continued until the early 2000s, but eventually the shop was closed after buildings nearby needed renovating. Today, there isn't a huge amount left to see, but visiting the sight will still give you a glimpse of what Bird Corner must have once been like. ✉ *3 Seng Poh Rd., Tiong Bahru* Ⓜ *Tiong Bahru.*

Qi Tian Gong Temple

RELIGIOUS SITE | The small but elaborate Qi Tian Gong Temple, housed within a simple shophouse, is more popularly known as the Monkey God Temple due to its dedication to Sun Wu Kong, the Monkey King. The monkey, which comes from 16th-century fable *Journey to the West* by writer Wu Chenen, represents human caprice and genius. This temple was founded in 1920 in a small taro garden on Eng Hoon Street but was moved to its current location in 1938. There are more than 40 other Monkey God temples found in Singapore alone. ✉ *44 Eng Hoon St., Tiong Bahru* ☎ *6220–2469* ⊕ *qitiangong.com* Ⓜ *Outram.*

★ Tiong Bahru's Murals

PUBLIC ART | There isn't a map to guide you, but hunting for Tiong Bahru's murals is a fun way to spend a few hours. Local artist Yip Yew Chong has painted intricate pictures across the neighborhood: look out for *Pasar and the Fortune Teller* on Block 73 of Eng Watt Street; *Bird Singing Corner* on Block 71 of Seng Poh Lane; and *Home* on Block 74 of Tiong Poh Road. There are many more, though, so keep your eyes open and your camera ready. ✉ *Seng Poh Ln., Tiong Bahru* Ⓜ *Tiong Bahru.*

🍴 Restaurants

Bakalaki Greek Taverna

$$ | **GREEK** | The name Bakalaki comes from the Greek words *bakaliko*, meaning a colorful neighborhood eatery, and *meraki*, representing love, spirit, and soul. Both words apply to this Greek Taverna, where the dynamic dishes relate the stories, cultures, and flavors of Greece. **Known for:** sharing plates of tzatziki and pitas; Greek wine; convivial outside dining. ⑤ *Average main: S$20* ✉ *3 Seng Poh Rd., Tiong Bahru* ☎ *6836–3688* ⊕ *bakalaki.com* ⊗ *No lunch Mon.–Thurs.* Ⓜ *Tiong Bahru.*

★ Bincho

$$$ | **JAPANESE** | This might be the coolest dinner spot in Singapore. Tucked inside a traditional Singaporean shophouse, this place transforms every night into a dark and mysterious Japanese *yakitori*, where dishes are served in a cloak of dry ice; the alluring smell of charcoal fills the air, and chalk-board menus list the small plates, which are always colorful, intriguing, and based on what's fresh that day. **Known for:** meat and veggies grilled over charcoal; delicious tasting menus; extensive sake list. ⑤ *Average main: S$30* ✉ *78 Moh Guan Terr., Tiong Bahru* ☎ *6438–4567* ⊕ *www.bincho.com.sg/hua-bee* ⊗ *Closed Mon.* Ⓜ *Tiong Bahru.*

Flock Café

$$ | EUROPEAN | Modern and moodily-lit, this cool little café attracts a young and artsy crowd. The flat whites are excellent—rare in country where the norm is either strong and black or sugary sweet—the all-day breakfasts feature piles of eggs, sausage, and bacon; and the lunch options include pastas, salads, and burgers. **Known for:** great coffee; all-day breakfast; people-watching from outdoor seating. $ *Average main: S$15* ✉ *#01–25 Tiong Bahru Estate, 78 Moh Guan Terr., Tiong Bahru* ☎ *6536–3938* ⊕ *flockcafe. com.sg* Ⓜ *Tiong Bahru.*

Forty Hands

$$ | CAFÉ | Head to one of Tiong Bahru's hippest cafés for upscale hot dogs, toasted sandwiches, and artisanal coffees served to the sounds of booming indie rock and hip-hop. During the week, Forty Hands is filled with young creative types sipping cappuccinos and snacking on truffle fries, oversized cookies, and dogs smothered in chutney; weekends bring out the brunchers, who come to sop up the previous night's indulgences with a small menu of classic morning platters. **Known for:** Australian-style brunch; bean-to-cup coffee; great Croque Monsieurs. $ *Average main: S$17* ✉ *#01–12, 78 Yong Siak St., Tiong Bahru* ☎ *6225–8545* ⊕ *www.40hand-scoffee.com* ۞ *Closed Mon.* Ⓜ *Tiong Bahru.*

Grand Shanghai

$$$ | CHINESE | Featuring a sumptuous interior inspired by the glamour of 1930s Shanghai, this lively restaurant offers a near-encyclopedic menu of Shanghainese classics: there are multiple varieties of soups, noodles, seafood, meats, and dim sum. Some selections, such as the suckling pig, must be ordered at least a day in advance, so call ahead if you have a taste for a specific delicacy and want to make sure it's available. **Known for:** the freshest and finest ingredients; traditional 1930s decor; crispy smoked duck in hoisin sauce. $ *Average main: S$45* ✉ *#01–01 Kings Centre, 392 Havelock Rd., Chinatown* ☎ *6836–6866* ⊕ *www.grandshanghai.com.sg* ۞ *Closed Mon. No lunch Sat.* Ⓜ *Tiong Bahru or Outram Park.*

★ Loo's Hainanese Curry Rice

$ | CHINESE | Established in 1946, this might be one of the best-known Hainanese curry rice outlets in Singapore. There is almost always a line of people, all waiting to try Loo's famous coconut milk pork cutlet curry, which (according to the sign outside) takes days to cook. **Known for:** casual, canteen-like aesthetic; slow-cooked pork cutlet curry; long lines of people. $ *Average main: S$6* ✉ *71 Seng Poh Rd., Tiong Bahru* ☎ *6225–3762* ۞ *Closed Thurs. No dinner* ▭ *No credit cards* Ⓜ *Tiong Bahru.*

Table Manners in Singapore

Thanks to their nation's multiculturalism, Singaporeans are accepting of variations in etiquette, but there are a few things to keep in mind. Traditionally, your food is served family style—placed all at once on the table so everyone can dig in—or, for more formal meals, served a course at a time, again with diners sharing from a single dish. If you're with friends, you can use your chopsticks to serve yourself from the communal dishes, but it's more polite to use a fresh pair of chopsticks if possible. Never leave your chopsticks upright in a rice bowl—this resembles the joss sticks left in incense bowls at graves which is considered a bad omen. It's a sign of respect for a Singaporean to serve you during a family-style meal. It's polite to reciprocate the gesture when their bowl is nearing empty. If you want to be respectful, you should wait for the host or any older people to start eating before you tuck in. Many locals may have religion-based dietary restrictions, such as only eating vegetarian or *halal* (Muslim) food. If you're arranging a meal with Singaporeans be sure to clarify their eating habits before deciding on a restaurant. Smoking is banned in air-conditioned restaurants and banquet/meeting rooms, but many establishments have outdoor patios and seating areas for smokers.

★ Merci Marcel

$$ | FRENCH FUSION | Rendezvous over a morning coffee, tuck into a light lunch, or sip chilled rosé in the evening breeze at this French-style café. The Parisian decor is complete with cozy sofas, plenty of plants, and a lovely outside space strung with fairy lights and cute lanterns. **Known for:** a cheese bar full of European farm selections; wide variety of French wines; lovely outside seating area. ⑤ *Average main: S$20* ⌧ *#01–68, 56 Eng Hoon St., Tiong Bahru* ☎ *65/6224–0113* ⊕ *mercimarcel.com* Ⓜ *Tiong Bahru.*

★ Sushiro

$ | JAPANESE | Hailing from Japan, this popular *kaiten* sushi restaurant features delicious plates rotating around the room on a conveyor belt, ready for you to pluck them off when they pass by. You can also order dishes from the electronic tablet in front of you. **Known for:** conveyor-belt system; fresh sushi; long wait times. ⑤ *Average main: S$3* ⌧ *#02–118 Tiong Bahru Plaza, 302 Tiong Bahru Rd., Tiong Bahru* ☎ *6970–2293* ⊕ *www.sushiroglobalhold-ings.com/singapore* Ⓜ *Tiong Bahru.*

Tongue Tip Lanzhou

$ | **CHINESE** | This casual restaurant, which originated in Lanzhou, in the Gansu province of China, specializes in piping hot bowls of noodles. You can create a bowl to your preference, choosing thickness and texture, toppings, and side dishes. **Known for:** noodles on the go; affordability; casual atmosphere. $ *Average main: S$10* ⊠ *#02–107 Tiong Bahru Plaza, 302 Tiong Bahru Rd., Tiong Bahru* ⊕ *www.facebook.com/Tonguetipbeefnoodles* Ⓜ *Tiong Bahru.*

Coffee and Quick Bites

Tiong Bahru Bakery

$ | **BAKERY** | Sandwiches, freshly baked breads, quiches, and a variety of sweet and savory pastries make up the menu at this popular café, the perfect spot to grab a quick bite and caffeinate while shopping the area's boutiques. The lighting mounted in wooden boards suspended from the ceiling by rope, the exposed brick and white-washed walls, and the soft, down-tempo beats all make for a relaxing interior. **Known for:** excellent coffee; Kouign-amann pastries; freshly baked bread. $ *Average main: S$14* ⊠ *#01–70, 56 Eng Hoon St., Tiong Bahru* ☎ *6220–3430* ⊕ *www.tiongbahrubakery.com* Ⓜ *Tiong Bahru.*

🛏 Hotels

Tiong Bahru is a lovely place to stay if you're looking for somewhere quiet and laid-back. The MRT is within walking distance of most of the hotels, connecting you to Chinatown and the Downtown area in a matter of minutes.

Grand Copthorne Waterfront Hotel

$$$ | **HOTEL** | Large windows throughout this hotel give full focus to the Singapore River, and the rooms bring to mind those of a resort, with parquet floors and rattan furniture. **Pros:** family-friendly; business services; central location. **Cons:** small pool for such a large hotel; bathrooms have no tubs; rooms could be bigger. $ *Rooms from: S$310* ⊠ *392 Havelock Rd., Tiong Bahru* ☎ *6733–0880* ⊕ *www.millenniumhotels.com* ⇌ *574 rooms* ⏁❘ *No meals.*

Hotel Nostalgia

$$ | **HOTEL** | This boutique-style hotel is furnished to reflect Singapore's colonial heritage, with rooms that are clean, comfortable, and well designed. **Pros:** great value; outdoor pool; heart of the neighborhood near Bird's Corner. **Cons:** some rooms don't have windows; no parking; rooms are quite small. $ *Rooms from: S$150* ⊠ *77 Tiong Bahru Rd., Tiong Bahru* ☎ *6808–1818* ⊕ *www.hotelnostalgia.com.sg* ⇌ *50 rooms* ⏁❘ *No meals.* Ⓜ *Tiong Bahru.*

Thad's Boutique Hostel

$ | **B&B/INN** | Just off Outram Road, this hostel is a cheap and cheerful place to lay your head for a few nights. **Pros:** cheap, clean, and comfortable; shared kitchen available; beds feel private despite dorm setting. **Cons:** breakfast is bland; bathrooms are shared; sharing a room can be difficult. ⑤ *Rooms from: S$40* ✉ *259 Outram Rd., Tiong Bahru* ☎ *6221–5060* ⊕ *www.thadsboutiquehostel.com* ⤴ *9 rooms* ⦿ *Free Breakfast.*

Nightlife

Don't come to Tiong Bahru looking for a loud and lively night out. But if you're in the mood for a relaxed drink, there are plenty of good bars to choose one, each one serving up locally made craft beer or chilled glasses of wine.

★ Canjob Taproom

BREWPUBS/BEER GARDENS | This tiny bar specializes in craft beers on tap, including Czech pilsners, pale ales, and IPAs. The decor is very cool, with overturned barrels for tables and enormous fridges full of beer you can buy to takeaway. There's also a range of bar snacks, including salted eggs, "porky brat" bratwurst hotdogs, and spam fries. ✉ *50 Tiong Bahru Rd., Tiong Bahru* ⊕ *www.facebook.com/canjobtaproom* Ⓜ *Tiong Bahru.*

Coq & Balls

BARS/PUBS | Popular with the hipster crowd, this cheekily-named bar is often busy on a Saturday night with revelers piling in for their draft beers, ciders, and ales. The daily happy hour runs until 8 pm, and the menu of bar bites includes grilled cheese sandwiches, truffle fries, and popcorn chicken. ✉ *6 Kim Tian Rd., Tiong Bahru* ☎ *6276–6609* ⊕ *www.coqnballs.com* Ⓜ *Tiong Bahru.*

Hops n Malt

BARS/PUBS | This quirky bar, decked out in red and green mosaics, is popular on weekends for its extensive beer list. It also serves comfort foods such as beef and Guinness stew and chicken nachos. ✉ *16 Kim Tian Rd., Tiong Bahru* ☎ *6681–6555* ⊕ *chilli.com.sg/local-ventures/hopsnmalt* Ⓜ *Tiong Bahru.*

★ Lin Rooftop Bar

WINE BARS—NIGHTLIFE | On the rooftop of the Link Hotel, this open-air bar is decked out in twinkling fairy lights and has great views of the neighborhood. The drink menu is fairly standard—wine, beer, and a selection of signature cocktails—but most people come for the bird's eye location. Two Terracotta Army–style warrior statues greet you at the entrance. The bar is not well sign-posted: to reach it, go into the Link Hotel lobby, and take the elevator to the roof.

✉ *50 Tiong Bahru Rd., Tiong Bahru* ☎ *8699–9866* ⊕ *www.lin.com. sg* Ⓜ *Tiong Bahru.*

👜 Shopping

★ BooksActually

ANTIQUES/COLLECTIBLES | Wooden planks painted like piano keys mark the entrance to BooksActually, a vintage bookstore on hip Yong Siak Street. Here you can browse an excellent selection of fiction, nonfiction, and poetry to the sound of light indie-pop tunes. The back room has interesting bric-a-brac, and there's selection of book-vending machines out front, where you can purchase a "mystery" book wrapped in white paper for S$10. ✉ *9 Yong Siak St., Tiong Bahru* ☎ *6222–9195* ⊕ *www.booksactually-shop.com* Ⓜ *Tiong Bahru.*

Curated Records

MUSIC STORES | This indie vinyl record shop is full of nostalgia, selling more than 2,000 records in a range of genres from rock to jazz. The shop is small, but it's often very busy with locals who pop by to check out the new arrivals each week. ✉ *55 Tiong Bahru Rd., Block 55, Tiong Bahru* ☎ *6438–3644* ⊕ *www.curatedrecords. com* Ⓜ *Tiong Bahru.*

Echo of Nature

CLOTHING | True to its name, Echo of Nature uses fabrics and designs that reflect the natural world. There are a number of branches across Singapore catering to women of all walks of life. ✉ *#01–139 Tiong Bahru Plaza, 302 Tiong Bahru Rd., Tiong Bahru* ☎ *6352–2053* ⊕ *www.echoofnature.com.sg* Ⓜ *Tiong Bahru.*

Jehan Gallery

HOUSEHOLD ITEMS/FURNITURE | Owned and operated by a family whose history in the business dates back hundreds of years, Jehan Gallery specializes in exquisite, custom Oriental carpets and rugs, and also offers a good selection of indoor and outdoor home furnishings. ✉ *Tan Boon Liat Building, #03-08, 315 Outram Rd., Tiong Bahru* ☎ *6334–4333* ⊕ *www.jehangallery.com* Ⓜ *Tiong Bahru.*

Journey East

ANTIQUES/COLLECTIBLES | Funky, refurbished vintage furniture is the highlight of the fun indoor and outdoor housewares at Journey East. Such a store is best for those living in or moving to Singapore, but the staff can also arrange for purchases to be shipped worldwide. ✉ *Tan Boon Liat Building, 315 Outram Rd., #03–02, Tiong Bahru* ☎ *6473–1693* ⊕ *www.journeyeast.com* Ⓜ *Tiong Bahru.*

Nana & Bird

CLOTHING | Stepping into this independent women's clothing boutique is like stepping inside the wardrobe you've always wanted. It's no wonder, as the store was set up by two school friends whose aim was to sell only clothes they would want to buy themselves. Colorful, bold patterns are their style, with both local and international brands for sale. ⊠ *1M Yong Siak St., Tiong Bahru* ☎ *9117–0430* ⊕ *shop.nanaandbird.com* Ⓜ *Tiong Bahru.*

The Orientalist Carpets Showroom

SPECIALTY STORES | The showroom here is filled with magnificent Persian carpets and rugs, and you can learn about their history and manufacture by attending one of the shop's "carpet-appreciation" workshops. Custom-made carpets can also be arranged. ⊠ *#12–03 Tan Boon Liat Building, 315 Outram Rd., Tiong Bahru* ☎ *6732–0880* ⊕ *www.theorientalist.com* Ⓜ *Tiong Bahru.*

★ Tiong Bahru Plaza

SHOPPING CENTERS/MALLS | Conveniently located around the Tiong Bahru MRT station, this six-level mall has more than 160 stores selling everything from fashion to kitchenware. There's a number of great places to eat, with a food court in the basement and a selection of slick restaurants on level two. ⊠ *302 Tiong Bahru Rd., Tiong Bahru* ⊕ *www.tiongbahruplaza.com.sg* Ⓜ *Tiong Bahru.*

🏃 Activities

Heritage Tour

SELF-GUIDED | Take yourself on a heritage tour around Tiong Bahru using the National Heritage Board's map that you can download to your phone. Ten informative signs throughout the neighborhood help to guide you along as you learn about the area's history, including how it once used to be a swampy cemetery. The full trail is around 2.5 km (1.5 miles). ⊠ *Tiong Bahru Food Centre, 30 Seng Poh Rd., Tiong Bahru* ⊕ *www.roots.sg.*

Hipster "Old Town" Heartland Tour

WALKING TOURS | This three-hour tour from Monster Day Tours takes you on a deep dive through Tiong Bahru's history, culinary scene, and local flavor. You can enjoy coffee tastings, visit a Singaporean home, and sample hawker foods as the knowledgeable guide shares anecdotes about the neighborhood. ⊠ *300 Tiong Bahru Rd., Tiong Bahru* ✛ *Meet at Tiong Bahru MRT Station, Exit B* ☎ *9231–3858* ⊕ *www.monsterdaytours.com* 🎫 *Adults S$130; Children S$60.*

LITTLE INDIA AND KAMPONG GLAM

Updated by
Charlene Fang

◉ Sights 🍴 Restaurants 🛏 Hotels 🛍 Shopping 🍸 Nightlife
★★★★☆   ★★★☆☆   ★★☆☆☆   ★★★☆☆   ★★★☆☆

NEIGHBORHOOD SNAPSHOT

TOP EXPERIENCES

■ **Explore Tekka Market:** Take in the sights, sounds, and aromas of Little India's vibrant market full of food stalls.

■ **See the Sultan Mosque:** Learn more about this magnificent mosque (the largest in Singapore), built in 1824.

■ **Search for colorful murals:** Snap some photos against the backdrop of Little India's colorful masterpieces or of Kampong Glam's Gelam Gallery.

■ **Shop the boutiques:** Away from Singapore's splashy shopping malls, this area offers a more personal experience, where you can buy local textiles or make your own perfume.

■ **Have a night out:** Kampong Glam is home to some of the coolest bars in Singapore, including the famed Atlas.

GETTING HERE

Kampong Glam and Little India are north and east of the Singapore River and conveniently situated close to MRT stations—Bugis and Jalan Besar for Kampong Glam, Little India and Farrer Park for Little India. Both neighborhoods are best explored on foot; however, hailing down a taxi or ordering a ride share is easy. Note that Little India is particularly crowded on Sunday.

PLANNING YOUR TIME

The area can be covered in one day. Spend the morning in Little India, exploring its colorful streets and temples at leisure. In the mid-afternoon, make your way to Kampong Glam via taxi or MRT. Reach the Sultan Mosque by sunset for a breathtaking view of the golden dome.

QUICK BITES

■ **Bhai Sarbat Stall.** This famous *sarbat* (sweet drink) stall serves hot cups of expertly pulled tea full of milky, gingery goodness. ⊠ *21 Bussorah St., Kampong Glam* ⊕ *www.facebook. com/bhaisarbatsg* Ⓜ *Bugis*

■ **The Malayan Council.** Stop at this halal cafe known for its fluffy *ondeh ondeh* cake made with coconut chantilly cream and *gula melaka* (palm sugar). ⊠ *22 Dunlop St., Little India* ⊕ *www.ins-tagram.com/the-malayancouncil* Ⓜ *Little India*

■ **Moghul Sweet Shop.** If you have a sweet tooth, swing by this casual establishment selling traditional Indian confections. ⊠ *48 Serangoon Rd. #01–16, Little India* Ⓜ *Little India*

The culturally rich and historically significant neighborhoods of Little India and Kampong Glam, with their charming mix of old and new, are well worth exploring. Here, the vibrant streets are never quiet, hip cafes sit next to religious monuments, and chic watering holes and century-old eateries can be enjoyed in a single visit.

One of the most easily recognized parts of the city, Little India—designated as such during colonial rule—is the area east of the Singapore River and across from Chinatown. What is still the cultural center for Singapore's large Indian community is also one of the most vibrant parts of the city. You'll find shops selling saris, flower garlands, and all the necessary ingredients for an Indian meal; hip restaurants and bars sharing space with traditional eateries; locals off to visit temples; and streets just generally bustling with people. Many backpackers stay in the budget hostels along Dunlop Road. Recently, boutique hotels have also began to appear in the area.

The Kampong Glam neighborhood was the home of Malay groups before British colonization began in the early 1800s. Following the reallocation of ethnic groups, Kampong Glam was designated for the sultan, along with other Malays, as well as Arabs. Over the years, it served as a gathering point for local Muslims as well as Muslim immigrants from Malaysia, Indonesia, and the Middle East. Some street names, such as Arab Street, Baghdad Street, and Kandahar Street, reflect that history.

These days, this area north of the Singapore River remains composed of ethnic Malays, Arabs, Chinese, and Indians. "Glam" prononunced "glum" refers to a tree that grew in abundance in the area in early Singapore and was used for boat-making, as a seasoning, and as medicine. "Kampong" just means "village." Now a lively shopping and lifestyle destination, Kampong Glam has standout streets like Haji Lane and Khandahar Street, which is a good place to pick up local designs or to grab a bite. Bordering Kampong Glam is the Bugis area, once a red-light district and now a thriving retail area.

Little India

A wander around the streets of Little India should probably
include a stop at one of the restaurants or Tekka Market for a bite.
Make time to visit to one of its temples. The Mustafa Centre,
which should also be on the itinerary, is open 24 hours, seven
days a week. The neighborhood gets very crowded on Sundays,
so that's not the best day if you don't like crowds. A visit of a few
hours should suffice.

◉ Sights

Abdul Gaffoor Mosque

RELIGIOUS SITE | This mosque was completed in 1910 and has
recently been restored. Though it has none of the exotic, multi-
color statuary of the Hindu temples, it still woos you with its intricately detailed Moorish facade in the Muslim colors of green and
gold and its unusual architectural symmetry. When entering, make
sure your legs are covered to the ankles, and remember to take
off your shoes. Only worshipers are allowed into the prayer hall.
Out of respect, you shouldn't enter during evening prayer sessions
or at any time on Friday. ✉ *41 Dunlop St., Little India* ☎ *65/6295–
4209* ⊕ *www.abdulgafoormosque.sg* ✉ *Free* Ⓜ *Little India.*

★ Indian Heritage Centre

MUSEUM | Following the colonization of Singapore in 1819, Indians
began to make their way over to Singapore, and today they form
the third largest ethnic group. Inside the stunning Indian Heritage
Centre, the history of the Indian and South Asian communities
are detailed through five permanent exhibitions. Other showcases
include opulent gold jewelery from the Saigon Chettiars' Temple
Trust, personal heirlooms, and intricately carved doorways and
frames, one holding as many as 5,000 carvings. Free guided tours
in English, Tamil, and Chinese are offered. Before leaving, take
time to admire the building, modeled after a *baoli* (Indian step-
well)—it's especially eye-catching at sunset. ✉ *5 Campbell Ln.,
Little India* ☎ *6291–1601* ⊕ *www.indianheritage.org.sg/en* ✉ *$4*
⊗ *Closed Mon.* Ⓜ *Little India.*

Leong San See Temple

RELIGIOUS SITE | This temple's main altar is dedicated to Kuan Yin
(Goddess of Mercy)—also known as Bodhisattva Avalokitesvara—
and is framed by beautiful, ornate carvings of flowers, a phoenix,
and other birds. The temple, also called Dragon Mountain Temple,
was built in the late 19th century. To the right of the main altar is
an image of Confucius to which many parents bring their children

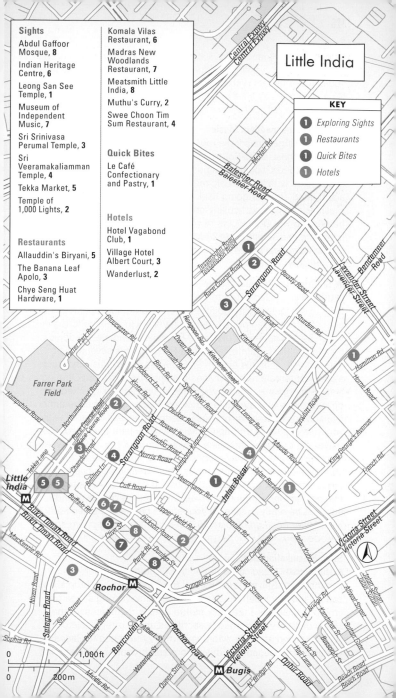

to pray for intelligence and filial piety. If you enter from the prayer hall's side doors, you'll reach the ancestral hall in the rear, where you can see tablets with the names of deceased worshippers. When you visit, be sure to observe a modest dress code. ⊠ *371 Race Course Rd., Little India* ☎ *6298–9371* Ⓜ *Farrer Park.*

Museum of Independent Music

MUSEUM | Singapore's indie music scene may not be as well known as those of its Southeast Asian neighbors, but it's still one worth exploring. Located on bustling Madras Street is this archival space filled with local music memorabilia, video documentaries, and related artifacts going back to the 1960s (when the Singapore music scene was particularly prominent). It also features indie heroes like The Oddfellows from the '90s and obscure genres like grindcore and screamo. ⊠ *23 Madras St., Little India* ☎ *8607–3534* ⊕ *www.cargocollective.com/moimsg* ▣ *$5* ⊗ *Closed Sat. and Sun.* Ⓜ *Jalan Besar.*

★ Sri Srinivasa Perumal Temple

RELIGIOUS SITE | Dedicated to Vishnu the Preserver, the temple is easy to recognize by its 60-foot-high monumental gopuram, with tiers of intricate sculptures depicting Vishnu in the nine forms in which he has appeared on Earth. Especially vivid are the depictions of Vishnu's manifestations as Rama, on his seventh visit, and as Krishna, on his eighth. Sri Srinivasa Perumal is very much a people's temple, with services that include Prasadam Offering and Term Archanai. Inside, you'll find devotees making offerings of fruit to one of the manifestations of Vishnu. This is done either by handing coconuts or bananas, along with a slip of paper with your name on it, to a temple official, who'll chant the appropriate prayers to the deity and place holy ash on your head, or by walking clockwise while praying, coconut in hand, around one of the shrines a certain number of times, then breaking the coconut (a successful break symbolizes that Vishnu has been receptive to the incantation). Dress conservatively—shawls can be provided—and be ready to take off your shoes before you enter. ⊠ *397 Serangoon Rd., Little India* ☎ *6298–5771* ⊕ *www.sspt.org.sg* Ⓜ *Farrer Park.*

Sri Veeramakaliamman Temple

RELIGIOUS SITE | Dedicated to Kali the Courageous, a ferocious incarnation of Shiva's wife, Parvati the Beautiful, this temple was built in 1881 by indentured Bengali laborers working at nearby lime pits. Inside is a jet-black statue of Kali, the fiercest of the Hindu deities, who demands sacrifices and is often depicted with a garland of skulls. More cheerful is the shrine to Ganesh, the elephant-headed god of wisdom and prosperity. Perhaps the

Little India's Murals 👁

Little India's colorful murals can be used as markers on your own informal tour of this vibrant neighborhood. Located sporadically on Clive Street, Upper Dickson Road, Starlight Road, Serangoon Road, Kerbau Road, Hindoo Road, and Dunlop Street, the murals depict everything from cheeky cows on bicycles to parrot astrologers to traditional Indian dancers. You'll have to keep an eye out as some are plastered on the sides of buildings while others are located along narrow alleyways.

A good resource to use when planning your walk is Art Walk Little India, ⊕ *www. artwalklittleindia.sg*, which hosts an annual art walk in January. Their map marks 18 murals in the neighborhood using top sights like Tekka Market, the Indian Heritage Centre, and the House of Tan Teng Niah as landmarks to guide you. Try to spot "A Ride Through Race Course Road" on 74 Race Course Road to reflect on the neighborhood's beginnings in the 1840s as a hub for horse racing.

most popular Hindu deity, Ganesh is the child of Shiva and Parvati. During the temple's opening hours you will see Hindus going in to receive blessings: the priests streak devotees' foreheads with *vibhuti,* the white ash from burned cow dung. ✉ *141 Serangoon Rd., Little India* ☎ *6295–4538* ⊕ *www.srivkt.org* Ⓜ *Farrer Park.*

★ Tekka Market

MARKET | One of the city's largest wet markets (where meat and fish are sold), Tekka also has a staggering array of fruits, vegetables, herbs, and spices for sale. On the Sungei Road side of the ground floor are stalls selling Chinese, Indian, Malay, and Western foods. Many of the stalls are run by second or third generation hawkers, making this an excellent place to sample Singapore's famed hawker food. Upstairs shops sell hardware, shoes, luggage, textiles, and Indian clothing. ✉ *665 Buffalo Rd., Little India* ⊕ *www.singapore-guide.com/food-dining/tekka-centre.htm* Ⓜ *Little India.*

Temple of 1,000 Lights

RELIGIOUS SITE | The Sakya Muni Buddha Gaya is better known by its popular name because of its lightbulbs surrounding a 50-foot Buddha. Sporting a fusion of Indian, Thai, and Chinese influences, the entire temple as well as the Buddha statue, was built by the Thai monk Vutthisasala. Until he died at the age of 94, he was always in the temple, ready to explain Buddhist philosophy to anyone who wanted to listen. The monk also managed to procure

Locals shop for fruits and veggies at the famous Tekka Market.

relics for the temple: a mother-of-pearl-inlaid cast of the Buddha's footprint and a piece of bark from the bodhi tree under which the Buddha is believed to have received enlightenment. Around the pedestal supporting the great Buddha statue is a series of scenes depicting the story of his search for enlightenment; inside a hollow chamber at the back is a re-creation of the scene of the Buddha's last sermon. ⊠ *336 Race Course Rd., Little India* ☎ *6294–0714* Ⓜ *Farrer Park.*

🍴 Restaurants

★ Allauddin's Briyani

$ | **INDIAN** | Of the Tekka Market's many tantalizing eateries, this spot, in business since the 1950s, comes highly recommended—as evidenced by lines that are particularly long at lunchtime. It's worth the wait, though, to enjoy a comfort meal of aromatic biryani rice combined with fork-tender chicken or mutton chunks, and all the orders come with a side of vegetable dhal and pickled vegetables. **Known for:** mutton biryani; fluffy rice; affordable local favorite. ⑤ *Average main: S$5* ⊠ *666 Buffalo Rd. , #01–232 Tekka Market and Food Centre, Little India* ☎ *6296–6786* ▭ *No credit cards* Ⓜ *Little India.*

★ The Banana Leaf Apolo

$$ | **INDIAN** | This casual, cafeteria-style, Indian restaurant is one of the best (and busiest) of its kind in Little India. Standout dishes include the signature fish-head curry, as well as the fish tikka, mutton mysore, and prawn masala, but choose whatever sounds good, and you'll still do well. **Known for:** authentic Indian served on banana leaves; low prices; fish-head curry. $ *Average main: S$16* ⊠ *54 Race Course Rd., Little India* ☎ *6293–8682* ⊕ *www. thebananaleafapolo.com* Ⓜ *Little India.*

Chye Seng Huat Hardware

$ | CAFÉ | Singapore's third-wave coffee scene is surprisingly vibrant thanks to Chye Seng Huat Hardware, one of the first specialty coffee spots in the area. The former hardware store turned hip coffee space is rarely empty, and regulars swear by both the brews and the robust brunch menu. **Known for:** flat white; lively weekend brunch crowd; ethically sourced coffee beans. $ *Average main: S$6* ⊠ *150 Tyrwhitt Rd., Little India* ☎ *6396–0609* ⊕ *www.cshhcoffee.com* ⊗ *Closed Mon.* Ⓜ *Farrer Park.*

Komala Vilas Restaurant

$ | INDIAN | In operation since 1947, this is one of Little India's best-known stops for northern and southern Indian vegetarian cuisine. Most plates come with curries, rice, dhal, condiments, Indian breads, or special sauces; for dessert there's a well-stocked counter of sweets. **Known for:** paper thin dosais (lentil and rice flour pancakes); Indian sweets; busy downstairs, quieter upstairs. $ *Average main: S$7* ⊠ *76–78 Serangoon Rd., Little India* ☎ *6293–6980* ⊕ *www.komalavilas.com.sg* Ⓜ *Little India.*

Madras New Woodlands Restaurant

$ | SOUTH INDIAN | This no-frills vegetarian restaurant is a long-running local favorite and one of the better south Indian restaurants in vibrant Little India. Opt for the *thali* if you're hungry: it's a large platter of *dosai* (pancakes) with three spiced vegetables, curd, dhal, *rasam* (hot and sour soup), papadam, and Indian-style condiments. **Known for:** south Indian cuisine; paper dosai; masala tea. $ *Average main: S$6* ⊠ *12–14 Upper Dickson Rd., Little India* ☎ *6297–1594* ▬ *No credit cards* Ⓜ *Little India.*

★ Meatsmith Little India

$$ | INDIAN | Give into the heady aromas wafting out of this Indian-influenced barbecue joint, and you won't regret it. Although a meal here is pricier than those at its more casual neighbors, the cost difference is easily justified by the intense, mouthwatering flavors and creative menu. **Known for:** juicy suckling pig biryani; spice-heavy meats; cool, grungy spot for a meal. $ *Average main: S$26* ⊠ *21 Campbell Ln., Little India* ☎ *6298–1188* ⊕ *www. meatsmith.com.sg* ⊗ *Closed Mon.* Ⓜ *Jalan Besar.*

Muthu's Curry

$ | INDIAN | You'll be spoiled for choice when it comes to Indian food on Race Course Road, but Muthu's Curry, along with the similarly popular Banana Leaf Apolo a few blocks down, is widely considered the best of the lot. There's a full range of North and South Indian options here, but the fish-head curry with okra and pineapple, the *milagu kozhi varuval* (chicken with pepper and coriander seeds), and the masala prawns are some of the standouts. **Known for:** wide variety of Indian dishes; fish-head curry; contemporary space. $ *Average main: S$12* ⊠ *#01–01, 138 Race Course Rd., Little India* ☎ *6392–1722* ⊕ *www.muthuscurry.com* Ⓜ *Little India.*

Swee Choon Tim Sum Restaurant

$ | CANTONESE | A local favorite for late night dim sum, this low-frills supper spot has been known to have a line well into the wee hours of the morning. Order the usual suspects—siew mai, bean-curd prawn roll, or pork congee with century egg—but save space for signature dishes like the *mee sua kueh*, a deep-fried vermicelli cake, and Shanghainese favorites like the Sichuan chilli wantons and juicy xiao long bao. **Known for:** affordable dim sum; deep-fried vermicelli cake; mouthwatering chilli wantons. $ *Average main: S$7* ⊠ *183–193 Jalan Besar, Little India* ☎ *6225–7788* ⊕ *www. sweechoon.com* ☉ *Closed Tues.* Ⓜ *Jalan Besar.*

☕ Coffee and Quick Bites

★ Le Café Confectionary and Pastry

$ | BAKERY | Le Café's trademark shortbread-like crust, which has a light almond flavor, puts its pastries a class above those made elsewhere; it's also why the shop's buttery, golf ball–sized pineapple tarts and silky smooth bean curd tarts are often sold out. Luckily, Le Café sells a bunch of other goodies, including traditional moon-pie pastries filled with lotus-seed paste and prawn-roll snacks that are downright addictive. **Known for:** arguably the best pineapple tarts in Singapore; traditional moon pies; silky smooth bean-curd tarts. $ *Average main: S$7* ⊠ *Blk 637 Veerasamy Rd., #01–111, Little India* ☎ *6294–8813* ⊕ *www.lecafe.com.sg* ☉ *No dinner* Ⓜ *Jalan Besar.*

Hotels

Hotel Vagabond Club

$$$ | **HOTEL** | Designed by French designer Jacques Garcia, this small boutique hotel stands out with its velvet furnishings, opulent decor, and rotational Artist-in-Residence program. **Pros:** tasteful decor and art; personalized service; club lounge privileges. **Cons:** standard rooms are on the small side; a bit far from the MRT station; street noise. $ *Rooms from: S$280 ⊠ 39 Syed Alwi Rd., Little India* ☎ *6291–6677* ⊕ *www.hotelvagabondsingapore. com* ⇄ *41 rooms* ⦿ *No meals* Ⓜ *Jalan Besar.*

Village Hotel Albert Court

$$$ | **HOTEL** | Located just minutes from the heart of Little India, this hotel, while not new, has worn its years well and features rooms tastefully decorated with charming Peranakan motifs and traditional Indian carvings. **Pros:** friendly staff; walking distance to Little India; whirlpool-tub area. **Cons:** no swimming pool; older property; breakfast could be improved. $ *Rooms from: S$275 ⊠ 180 Albert St., Little India* ☎ *6339–3939* ⊕ *www.villagehotels. com.sg* ⇄ *210 rooms* ⦿ *No meals* Ⓜ *Little India.*

Wanderlust

$$ | **HOTEL** | Located minutes away from the Downtown MRT line, this newly refurbished hotel, housed in a 1920s art deco building, has some rooms equipped with a kitchenette. **Pros:** slick, modern design; hip on-site restaurant Kotuwa; loft rooms. **Cons:** some rooms are small; no swimming pool; not all rooms have kitchenettes. $ *Rooms from: S$200 ⊠ 2 Dickson Rd., Little India* ☎ *6396–3322* ⊕ *www.8mcollective.com/wanderlust* ⇄ *29 rooms* ⦿ *No meals* Ⓜ *Jalan Besar.*

 Nightlife

Rogue Trader

BARS/PUBS | While there's a movie of the same name about the real life of Singapore-based rogue trader Nick Leeson, that's where the similarities end. This British colonial–style cocktail bar is known for its menu of Indian-inspired tipples and its wide selection of whiskies. Expect your taste buds to be challenged—the bartenders are known to experiment with unusual ingredients like goji berries and sumac. And since it's located above Meatsmith Little India, expect the bar food to be a cut above the usual pub grub. ⊠ *21 Campbell Ln., Level 2, Little India* ☎ *9625–9056* ⊕ *www.facebook.com/roguetrader.sg* ☞ *Closed Mon.* Ⓜ *Little India.*

The Whiskey Library

WINE BARS—NIGHTLIFE | Hidden in a corner of the Hotel Vagabond Club, this bar houses a collection of 1,000 rare, single-cask, limited-edition whiskies that would impress even the most seasoned connoisseur. It's styled like a typical whiskey den, with lots of wood, velvet, and a glass showcase. The cigar menu is up to par, and entertainment varies depending on the night. ⊠ *Hotel Vagabond Club, 39 Syed Alwi Rd., Little India* ☎ *6291–6677* ⊕ *www.hotelvagabondsingapore.com* Ⓜ *Jalan Besar.*

☺ Performing Arts

Sri Warisan Som Said Performing Arts

DANCE | This popular troupe has traditional Malay performances in town several times a year. ⊠ *47 Kerbau Rd., Little India* ☎ *6225–6070* ⊕ *www.sriwarisan.com* Ⓜ *Little India.*

⬤ Shopping

Haniffa Textiles

TEXTILES/SEWING | Spread across eight shop spaces, Haniffa Textiles has made a name for itself with its stock of sarees. Try this silk shop for a cornucopia of richly colored and ornamented fabrics, scarves, bedspreads, and the like, often at surprisingly affordable prices. ⊠ *60 Serangoon Rd., Little India* ☎ *6392–7655* ⊕ *www.haniffa.com.sg* Ⓜ *Little India.*

Jothi Store & Flower Shop

FLOWERS | Around since 1963, this bustling, family-owned shop is hard to miss, thanks to the dozens of fragrant garlands decorating the store front. Inside, the shelves stock Indian household goods (prayer items, cosmetics, copperware, henna), so even if you don't end up buying anything, you'll leave with a better understanding of Indian culture. ⊠ *1 Campbell Ln., Little India* ☎ *6338–7008* ⊕ *www.jothi.com.sg* Ⓜ *Little India.*

Little India Arcade

SHOPPING NEIGHBORHOODS | You'll find plenty of colorful eye candy at this cluster of shops near the Little India MRT. Jewelry, music, Indian-style sweets and snacks, and fabrics are all available. Across the street at the Tekka Market, you can also walk through a bustling food market and feast on cheap Indian eats at the hawker stalls. ⊠ *#02–07, 48 Serangoon Rd., between Campbell La. and Hastings Rd., Little India* ☎ *6295–5998* ⊕ *www.littleindiaarcade.com.sg* Ⓜ *Little India.*

Shop for everything from jewelry to perfume to chocolate on a trip to the Mustafa Centre.

Mud Rock Ceramics

CERAMICS/GLASSWARE | Handmade and beautifully imperfect, the ceramics from this shop make perfect mementos. The bowls, plates, vases, and other items are so popular that even local eateries—including The Coconut Club, Le Binchotan, The Ottomani—use them. You can plan ahead to attend one of their classes (by appointment only), or get a piece delivered to your hotel. Custom orders are accepted. ⊠ *85 Maude Rd., Little India* ☏ *6291–1186* ⊕ *www.mudrockceramics.com* Ⓜ *Jalan Besar.*

★ Mustafa Centre

SHOPPING CENTERS/MALLS | This used to be a humble store frequented only by local shoppers—until word spread about its low prices and mind-boggling variety of goods. A visit to this sprawling, 24/7 complex just might be your most memorable Singapore shopping experience, provided you don't mind patiently navigating the sometimes overwhelming crowds. Surrounded by scores of Indian restaurants, some of which are similarly open all day and night, Mustafa Centre carries just about any manufactured product you can imagine—and they're often sold at cut-rate prices. It's great fun to wander and see what kind of treasures you can turn up. Be sure to check out the massive supermarket, and, if you have spare money to change, do it here as the foreign-exchange rates are competitive. ⊠ *Mustafa Centre, 145 Syed Alwi Rd., Little India* ☏ *6295–5855* ⊕ *www.mustafa.com.sg* Ⓜ *Farrer Park.*

🏃 Activities

The Original Singapore Walks

WALKING TOURS | This 2½-hour walking tour gives a good overview of the bustling Little India district. Meet traditional vendors selling garlands and temple offerings, buy spices at the Tekka Market, have a meal at Singapore's oldest Indian restaurant, and visit Sri Veeramakaliamman Temple, where a professional guide will help decode the carvings and statues. End the day learning how to tie a sari properly. Comfortable shoes are recommended. The tour is offered on Tuesdays and departs from Little India MRT station at 9:30 am. ✉ *Little India* ☎ *6325–1631* ⊕ *www.journeys.com.sg/ tosw* 🖺 *S$38* Ⓜ *Little India*.

Yoga in Common

AEROBICS/YOGA | Drop into this peaceful shala for some down time on the mat. Located in a conservation shophouse on the fringe of Little India, it offers classic Hatha, Vinyasa, and Ashtanga classes; slower yin–yang and yin-by-candlelight sessions; and Kundalini and yin sound baths. Single classes are available as is a "Travelling Yogi's Pass 3" pass that's valid for seven days. Private sessions can be organized. ✉ *22 Petain Rd., Level 2, Little India* ☎ *9698– 5771* ⊕ *www.yoga-incommon.com* Ⓜ *Farrer Park*.

Kampong Glam

The Sultan Mosque serves as the unofficial center of the neighborhood, with the many shops of Arab Street a short walk away. A visit here would pair well with one to Little India, a few blocks to the north. With so many shops worth exploring, you'll probably want to come during business hours. A couple of hours is probably enough time to explore and to have a bite at one of the restaurants in the area toward the evening when things comes alive.

👁 Sights

Arab Street

NEIGHBORHOOD | On this street of specialty shops, you'll find baskets of every description—stacked on the floor or suspended from the ceiling. Farther along, the road is dominated by shops that sell fabrics: batiks, embroidered table linens, rich silks, and velvets. Some restaurants and cafes break up the mix. ✉ *Arab St., Kampong Glam* Ⓜ *Bugis*.

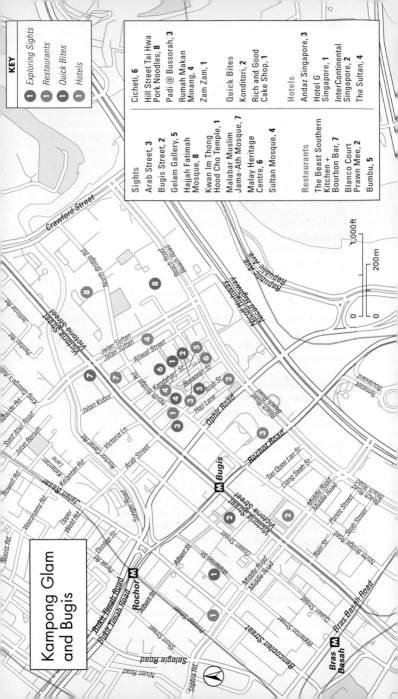

Kampong Glam and Bugis

KEY

- Exploring Sights
- Restaurants
- Quick Bites
- Hotels

Sights

Arab Street, 3
Bugis Street, 2
Gelam Gallery, 5
Hajah Fatimah
Mosque, 8
Kwan Im Thong
Hood Cho Temple, 1
Malabar Muslim
Jama-Ath Mosque, 7
Malay Heritage
Centre, 6
Sultan Mosque, 4

Restaurants

The Beast Southern
Kitchen +
Bourbon Bar, 7
Blanco Court
Prawn Mee, 2
Bumbu, 5

Cicheti, 6
Hill Street Tai Hwa
Pork Noodles, 8
Padi @ Bussorah, 3
Rumah Makan
Minang, 4
Zam Zam, 1

Quick Bites

Konditori, 2
Rich and Good
Cake Shop, 1

Hotels

Andaz Singapore, 3
Hotel G
Singapore, 1
InterContinental
Singapore, 2
The Sultan, 4

Gelam Gallery

ART GALLERIES—ARTS | Singapore's "outdoor art gallery" is open 24/7 amid the back alleyways off Muscat Street. Here, more than 30 colorful murals have been drawn by artists like local graffiti pioneer Slacsatu and graduates from Singapore's LASALLE College of the Arts and the Nanyang Academy of Fine Arts. ⊠ *80 Arab St., Kampong Glam* ⊕ *www.facebook.com/OneKampongGelam* Ⓜ *Bugis.*

Hajjah Fatimah Mosque

RELIGIOUS SITE | In 1845, Hajjah Fatimah, a wealthy Muslim woman married to a Bugis trader, commissioned a British architect to build this mosque (hajjah is the title given to a woman who has made the pilgrimage to Mecca). The minaret is reputedly modeled on the spire of the original St. Andrew's Church in the Civic District, but it leans at a six-degree angle. No one knows whether this was intentional or accidental, and engineers brought in to see if the minaret could be straightened have walked away shaking their heads. Islam forbids carved images of Allah. Usually, the only decorative element employed is the beautiful flowing Arabic script in which quotations from the Qur'an (Koran) are written across the walls. This relatively small mosque is an intimate oasis amid all the bustle. It's extremely relaxing to enter the prayer hall (remember to take your shoes off), sit in the shade of its dome, and admire the 12 lancet windows with yellow and green stained glass. French contractors and Malay artisans rebuilt the mosque in the 1930s. Hajjah Fatimah and her daughter and son-in-law are buried in an enclosure behind the mosque. ⊠ *4001 Beach Rd., Kampong Glam* ☎ *6297–2774* Ⓜ *Bugis.*

Malabar Muslim Jama-Ath Mosque

RELIGIOUS SITE | The only mosque in Singapore built and managed by the Malabar Muslim community (immigrants to Singapore from Kerala) was rebuilt in 1962 and has striking blue geometric tiles and a golden dome. Friday prayers are conducted in Arabic and translated into several languages including Malayalam and Urdu. Note that photographs shouldn't be taken here after 1 pm. ⊠ *471 Victoria St., Kampong Glam* ☎ *6294–3862* ⊕ *www.malabar.org.sg* Ⓜ *Bugis.*

Malay Heritage Centre

CASTLE/PALACE | This large cultural center is in what was once the home of Malay royalty. The Malay-style mansion, which was built in the 1840s on the site of an even simpler thatched building, may have been designed by George Coleman. Next door is another grand royal bungalow: the home of the sultan's first minister. Notice its gateposts surmounted by green eagles. The center serves as a heritage institution for the local Malay community and offers free guided tours in English and Mandarin. ☒ *85 Sultan Gate, Kampong Glam* ☎ *6391–0450* ⊕ *www.malayheritage.org.sg* Ⓜ *Bugis*.

★ Sultan Mosque

RELIGIOUS SITE | The first mosque on this site was built in the early 1820s with a S$3,000 grant from the East India Company. The current structure, built in 1928 by Denis Santry of Swan & Maclaren—the architect who designed the Victoria Memorial Hall—is a dramatic building with golden domes and minarets that glisten in the sun. The walls of the vast prayer hall are adorned with green and gold mosaic tiles on which passages from the Koran are written in Arabic. The main dome has an odd architectural feature: hundreds of bottle ends are jammed in between the dome and base. This unusual feature originated as a way for lower-income Muslims to donate during the mosque's construction so that all could contribute. Five times a day—at dawn, 12:30, 4, sunset, and 8:15—the sound of the muezzin, or crier, calls the faithful to prayer. At midday on Friday, the Islamic Sabbath, Muslims from all over Singapore enter through one of the Sultan Mosque's 14 portals to recite the Koran. During Ramadan, the month of fasting, the nearby streets, especially Bussorah, and the square in front of mosque are lined with hundreds of stalls selling curries, cakes, and candy; at dusk Muslims break their day's fast in this square. Non-Muslims, too, come to enjoy the rich array of Muslim foods and the festive atmosphere. The best view of the Sultan Mosque is at the junction of Bussorah Street and Beach Road. ■**TIP**→ **Walk-ins are welcome Saturday through Thursday from 10 am to 12 pm and from 2 pm to 4 pm, as well as on Friday from 2:30 pm to 4 pm.** ☒ *3 Muscat St., Kampong Glam* ☎ *6293–4405* ⊕ *www. sultanmosque.sg* ⊘ *Closed Sun.* Ⓜ *Bugis*.

🍴 Restaurants

The Beast Southern Kitchen + Bourbon Bar

$$ | **AMERICAN** | Lending Singapore's food scene a charming dose of Southern comfort, The Beast serves staples like country fried steak, chicken and waffles, and cheesy grits in a laid-back setting of rusted oil drums and wood counter tops. If you have the stomach, try the Beast Burger, a 1.6-pound beef patty with a pound each of pulled pork and buttermilk fried chicken—it's free if you finish it in 60 minutes. **Known for:** sizable burgers; bourbon tastings; full flavors. ⑤ *Average main: S$20* ☒ *17 Jalan Klapa, Kampong Glam* ☎ *6295–0017* ⊕ *www.thebeast.sg* Ⓜ *Jalan Besar*.

Blanco Court Prawn Mee

$ | **ASIAN** | Arguably one of Singapore best spots for a bowl of prawn noodles, this humble establishment draws regulars who love its slow-simmered umami broth with fresh prawns and fork-tender pork ribs. The line for a bowl can be long, so come early to avoid an unnecessary wait. **Known for:** prawn noodles in a hearty broth; jumbo option; flavorful chilli. ⑤ *Average main: S$5* ✉ *243 Beach Rd., #01–01, Kampong Glam* ☎ *9626–4410* ⊘ *Closed Tues.* 🚫 *No credit cards* Ⓜ *Bugis.*

Bumbu

$ | **INDONESIAN** | Coffee chicken, butter-oat soft-shell crab, and beef green curry are among the Halal Thai–Indo fusion dishes at this homey shophouse. Salads, particularly the Thai-style pomelo, are great sides, and portions are generally small, so this is an easy place to taste a number of different dishes. **Known for:** pretty Peranakan decor; affordable buffet; butter-oat soft-shell crab. ⑤ *Average main: S$12* ✉ *44 Kandahar St., Kampong Glam* ☎ *6392–8628* 🌐 *www.bumbu.com.sg* ⊘ *Closed Mon.* Ⓜ *Bugis.*

★ Cicheti

$$ | **ITALIAN** | Expect good vibes and authentic food at this hip Italian eatery, known for its pizzas baked in a signature wood-fired oven imported from Naples itself. The 10-inch Neopolitan pies are a favorite, but for a well-rounded meal, don't ignore the handmade pastas and small selection of desserts. **Known for:** 10-inch Neopolitan pies; handmade pastas; cool vibe. ⑤ *Average main: S$24* ✉ *52 Kandahar St., Kampong Glam* ☎ *6292–5012* 🌐 *www.cicheti.com* Ⓜ *Bugis.*

★ Hill Street Tai Hwa Pork Noodles

$ | **CHINESE** | Be warned: The line for this one-Michelin-star eatery rarely lets up, but the wait is worth it. After just one spoonful of the juicy minced meat and springy egg noodles dressed in a secret recipe of chilli and black vinegar, you'll understand why locals have kept this no-frills eatery a well-guarded secret for years. **Known for:** one-Michelin-star eatery; long lines, but it's just $5; heritage hawker. ⑤ *Average main: S$5* ✉ *466 Crawford Ln., #01–12, Kampong Glam* ⊘ *Closed every first and third Mon.* 🚫 *No credit cards* Ⓜ *Lavender.*

Padi @ Bussorah

$$ | **INDONESIAN** | Tuck into a communal meal of *nasi ambeng* (a Javanese rice dish with meat and vegetables) at this popular Kampong Glam eatery. The celebratory dish, commonly served during festive occasions, can be customized to fit the size of your dining party (from two onwards). **Known for:** full flavored nasi ambeng, a

Javanese rice dish; group dining; tender beef rendang. $ *Average main: S$15* ✉ *53 Bussorah St., Kampong Glam* ☎ *6291–3921* ⊕ *www.padibussorah.com* Ⓜ *Bugis.*

★ Rumah Makan Minang

$ | **INDONESIAN** | **FAMILY** | A second generation business that started out as a wooden stall, this authentic *nasi padang* (Padang steamed rice served with various pre-cooked dishes) eatery's star dish is fork-tender *beef rendang* (Indonesian dry beef curry) slow cooked over charcoal. Other dishes include the *ayam belado hijau* (chicken in a secret green chilli marinade) and the crispy *tahu telur* (fried tofu mixed with blanched bean sprouts, peanuts, and a dark sweet soy sauce) and order a serving of the house-made *sambal balado merah* (hot and spicy chilli)—it packs a punch, so go easy. **Known for:** its status as a Kampong Glam institution; traditional Indonesian Minangkabau (from West Sumatra) recipes; famous beef rendang cooked over charcoal. $ *Average main: S$8* ✉, *18 & 18A Kandahar St., Kampong Glam* ☎ *6294-4805* ⊕ *www.minang. sg* ▭ *No credit cards* Ⓜ *Bugis.*

★ Zam Zam

$ | **ASIAN** | In business for more than a century, this hole-in-the-wall eatery serves what's arguably Singapore's best *murtabak*. Stuffed with mutton, chicken, or beef, it's a bit like a folded dough omelette with egg mixed in, *roti prata* (a fried flat bread), onions, and spices, all of it grilled together and served with a side of curry sauce. **Known for:** Singapore's best murtabak; casual and cheap local street food; late-night eatery. $ *Average main: S$5* ✉ *697 North Bridge Rd., Kampong Glam* ☎ *6298–6320* ⊕ *www. zamzamsingapore.com* ▭ *No credit cards.*

☕ Coffee and Quick Bites

Konditori

$ | **CAFÉ** | This cute Swedish cafe's halal bakes are slightly pricey, but they're favored by local cafe aficionados. Stick to signature items like the strawberry cream cheese Danish and traditional semla bun, available year round. **Known for:** creative baked goods; traditional semla bun; halal-certified pastries and breads. $ *Average main: S$5* ✉ *33 Bussorah St., Kampong Glam* ☎ *6209–8580* ⊕ *www.konditori.sg* Ⓜ *Bugis.*

Rich and Good Cake Shop

$ | **BAKERY** | Blink and you might miss this nondescript, old-school bakery famous for its pillow-soft Swiss rolls. Every morning sees 10 freshly baked varieties, including mango, strawberry, and blueberry, but distinctive local flavors like durian and kaya (coconut jam) are the true standouts. **Known for:** fresh Swiss rolls; old-school vibes; unusual local flavors. ⑤ *Average main: S$9* ✉ *24 Kandahar St., Kampong Glam* ☎ *6294–3324* ⊕ *www.facebook. com/richandgoodcakeshop* ⊘ *Closed Sun.* ⊟ *No credit cards* Ⓜ *Bugis.*

Hotels

Hotel G Singapore

$$$ | **HOTEL** | This urban hotel with slick decor and tech-outfitted rooms fits right in with its buzzy location minutes away from Bugis Village and Kampong Glam. **Pros:** burger bar and fitness center on site; good location; eco- and tech-friendly. **Cons:** no pool; if you're traveling with infants, rooms can't accommodate a crib; small rooms. ⑤ *Rooms from: S$280* ✉ *200 Middle Rd., Kampong Glam* ☎ *6809–7988* ⊕ *www.hotels-g.com* ⇆ *308 rooms* ⊘ *No meals* Ⓜ *Bugis.*

The Sultan

$$ | **HOTEL** | Just a five-minute walk from Sultan Mosque, this small boutique hotel spread across 10 heritage shophouses is an affordable option for short stays. **Pros:** convenient location; charming design details; rooftop terrace. **Cons:** thin walls; street noise; some rooms do not have windows. ⑤ *Rooms from: S$150* ✉ *101 Jalan Sultan , #01–01 The Sultan, Kampong Glam* ☎ *6723–7101* ⇆ *64 rooms* ⊘ *Free Breakfast* Ⓜ *Bugis.*

🍸 Nightlife

★ Atlas

PIANO BARS/LOUNGES | Truly one of a kind, this grandiose bar with a high, ornate ceiling is mesmerizing—and one of the most buzzed-about lounges in Singapore. It holds more than 1,000 gins and 250 Champagnes, including a rare bubbly that was served on the Titanic (yes, the *actual* Titanic). Helmed by head bartender Jesse Vida, the tipples are inspired by the 1930s with a strong focus on (you guessed it) gin and Champagne. For a splurge, any cocktail can be made with your Champagne of choice. ✉ *Parkview Square, 600 North Bridge Rd., Kampong Glam* ☎ *6396–4466* ⊕ *www. atlasbar.sg* Ⓜ *Bugis.*

Bar Stories

BARS/PUBS | One of the first mixology bars in Singapore, this hole-in-the-wall still turns out some of the more surprising concoctions on the island. While there's no formal menu—a bespoke cocktail is created based on your flavor profile—you can rest assured that your drink will be to your liking. Reservations are highly recommended as it is a small space. ⊠ *57A Haji Ln., Bugis* ☎ *6298–0838* ⊕ *www.barstories.sg* Ⓜ *Bugis.*

BluJaz Cafe

BARS/PUBS | An institution of the Kampong Glam area and Singapore's live music scene, this lounge-bar fills three floors and has a spacious outdoor seating area. Known as a hub for stand-up comedy acts, live music (especially jazz), and international DJs, a lively vibe is always expected. The bar menu is a mix of Eastern and Western dishes. The owners have branched out by opening a nearby Mexican restaurant, Piedra Niegra, on the corner of Beach Road and Haji Lane. ⊠ *11 Bali Ln., Kampong Glam* ☎ *8126–2936* ⊕ *www.blujazcafe.net* Ⓜ *Bugis.*

Ginett Singapore

WINE BARS—NIGHTLIFE | Drinking isn't a cheap affair in Singapore unless you plan to guzzle beers at a hawker center, and sometimes not even then. That's exactly why Ginett deserves special mention for its extensive wine menu with affordable pours from as low as S$6 for a glass to S$30 for a bottle. There's also a full (mainly French) food menu—items from the charcoal grill are recommended—with a popular "1 Meter Board" (S$50) of five different types of cheese and cold cuts or a "Pâté and Terrines" board (S$35). ⊠ *Hotel G Singapore, 200 Middle Rd., Kampong Glam* ☎ *6809–7989* ⊕ *www.randblab.com/ginett-sg* Ⓜ *Bugis.*

Going Om

BARS/PUBS | Inspired by the Himalayas, Going Om is a bit of a spiritual haven for the hippie community. Live music is often performed in front of the bar by buskers who show up most nights around 9 pm; small tables are set up for people to soak up the easy-going surroundings. You can tuck into standard bar staples like popcorn chicken and Parmesan fries, but even more interesting are the in-house services like card readings, holistic healing, and yoga or meditation classes. ⊠ *63 Haji Ln., Kampong Glam* ☎ *6396–3592* ⊕ *www.going-om.com* Ⓜ *Bugis.*

IB HQ | A Cocktail Bar

BARS/PUBS | This small, 30-seat, shophouse is part bar, part research facility. The research is really about husband and wife team Kamil Foltan and Zurina Bryant exploring locally sourced ingredients like betel leaf and lemongrass, and showcasing them in a tightly curated (and revolving) menu of tipples (S$24+ unless otherwise stated). Expect a chill, laid-back vibe and unconventional concoctions like the Pandan Szaerac, in which pandan-infused whisky gives a twist to the beloved bar classic. While waiting, ask them how they use the rotary evaporator and sous vide machine to construct their concoctions. ⊠ *774A North Bridge Rd., Bugis* ☎ *9152–4550 WhatsApp for reservations after 8 pm and groups larger than 6* ⊕ *www.ibhqsingapore.com* ☞ *Closed Sun. and Mon.* Ⓜ *Bugis*.

🎭 Performing Arts

Aliwal Arts Centre

ARTS CENTERS | This multidisciplinary arts center is home to a number of local performing groups, including groundbreaking collectives like Teater Ekamatra and New Opera Singapore. Check the website for what's going on (workshops, performances, classes), and keep an eye out for the annual Aliwal Urban Art Festival and Aliwal Arts Night Crawl. ⊠ *28 Aliwal St., Kampong Glam* ☎ *6435–0131* ⊕ *www.aliwalartscentre.sg* Ⓜ *Bugis*.

★ The Projector

FILM | What was once Singapore's historic Golden Theatre has been transformed into The Projector, an indie theater space and hangout spot for Singapore's creative talents. There's always something going on, thanks to an eclectic rotation of films, documentaries, festivals, and themed screenings. A lobby bar enables you to enjoy a glass of wine or a cold beer during a show. ⊠ *Golden Mile Tower, 6001 Beach Rd., Level 5, Kampong Glam* ⊕ *www.theprojector.sg* Ⓜ *Bugis*.

🛍 Shopping

★ Haji Lane

CLOTHING | Need a break from Singapore's fun but sometimes suffocating mall culture? Head to the open air and this strip of restored shophouses, which stretches from Beach Road to North Bridge Road in Kampong Glam. Among the numerous indie fashion and lifestyle shops are Sup (trendy streetwear and limited-edition sneakers), Victoria Jomo (handbags, vintage jewelry, designer women's clothing), The Salad Shop (imported housewares and fashions), and The Nail Social (which uses nontoxic, eco-friendly, fair-trade, and cruelty-free nail products). The best way to tackle Haji Lane is to simply give yourself a few hours to wander and window-shop at random. ⊠ *between Beach Rd. and North Bridge Rd., Kampong Glam* Ⓜ *Bugis*.

★ Jamal Kazura Aromatics

PERFUME/COSMETICS | Locals flock to Jamal Kazura Aromatics for high-quality perfumes and essential oils. Allow about 30 minutes for a consultation with one of the shop's staff members, who'll ask you a few questions about your lifestyle and favorite smells before concocting your personalized take-home fragrance. Call ahead to make an appointment. There are two other nearby outlets: one at 27 Arab Street and another at 21 Bussorah Street. ✉ *21 Bussorah Street, Kampong Glam* ☎ *6293–2350* ⊕ *www.jamalkazura.com.*

Life By Design

SPECIALTY STORES | It's unlikely you'll be in the market for a oujia board while on the road, but even so, this one-stop shop of spiritual curios makes for a fun distraction. It sells tarot cards, sage smudge sticks, oracle decks, and healing crystals, and it offers services like vibrational healing and spiritual counseling, which you need to arrange ahead of time. ✉ *43 Haji Ln., Kampong Glam* ☎ *6884–9968* ⊕ *www.designyourlifecm.com* Ⓜ *Bugis.*

Scene Shang

HOUSEHOLD ITEMS/FURNITURE | Inside this light-filled furniture shop, you'll find refreshingly modern tables and consoles that nod to traditional Chinese design. Look for the HANG system of stackable, hand-carved drawers and trays inspired by the Ming dynasty—it was the 2014 winner of the President's Design Award, Singapore's highest such honor. Small items like jewelery boxes and tea pets (ornamental symbols for good luck, fortune, and happiness) can be easily transported home. ✉ *63 Beach Rd., Kampong Glam* ☎ *6291–9629* ⊕ *www.shop.sceneshang.com* Ⓜ *Bugis.*

Sifr Aromatics

PERFUME/COSMETICS | The hip offshoot of local perfumer Jamal Kazura Aromatics offers a more bespoke experience than its parent store. Drop in to custom blend a scent (reservations required; put aside at least 90 minutes) at the elaborate perfume organ. Aside from the sweet, woody base note of oud, unusual ingredients like ambergris, agarwood chips, and white amber can be incorporated. There are also pre-made scents, soy-based candles, and vials of essential oil for sale. ✉ *42 Arab St., Kampong Glam* ☎ *6392–1966* ⊕ *www.sifr.sg* Ⓜ *Bugis.*

★ Supermama

CERAMICS/GLASSWARE | Perhaps the best way to bring home a piece of Singapore is to buy from this local brand helmed by husband and wife Edwin and Mei Ling. They design and produce meaningful *omiyage* (contemporary gift ware) using Singapore's rich culture as inspiration. Plates, cups, and bowls are emblazoned with uniquely local icons like the Merlion, the Singapore Flyer, and Jewel Changi's Vortex (that jaw-dropping airport waterfall you've been hearing about). Their Supermama Porcelain line is made in collaboration with Kihara, a well-known Japanese porcelain label. ⊠ *265 Beach Rd., Kampong Glam* ☏ *6291–1946* ⊕ *www.superma-ma.sg* Ⓜ *Bugis.*

Toko Aljunied

CLOTHING | Since 1940, this heritage business has sold authentic batik (traditional hand-dyed textiles originating from Java, Indonesia) either by the meter or as pre-made pieces to bring home. They also sell small gifts, tablecloths, and napkins. Store assistants can help with sizing and pairing matching accessories. ⊠ *91 Arab St., Kampong Glam* ☏ *6294–6897* Ⓜ *Bugis.*

🏃 Activities

Green Apple Spa

SPA/BEAUTY | When you're fatigued from exploring the city, head to this trusted spa for a foot massage (from $30 for 30 minutes) that takes place in a mini movie theater setting, complete with comfortable recliner chairs. It's open until 4 am, and the treatment menu includes other services like tui na and deep-tissue massages. There's always a special promotion going on, so you might just stay longer than intended. ⊠ *765 North Bridge Rd., Kampong Glam* ☏ *6299–1555* ⊕ *www.greenapple.sg* Ⓜ *Bugis.*

Bugis

A great base from which to explore the historic Kampong Glam area, which is within walking distance, Bugis buzzes with a youthful energy that gives it the vibe of a university town. It's also a shopping hub known for its youth-friendly stores, where you can find everything from costumes to game arcades. The area has come a long way: it was Singapore's red light district until the 1980s, when the government transformed into the flourishing retail precinct it is today.

👁 Sights

Bugis Street

NEIGHBORHOOD | In its younger years, Bugis Street was the epitome of Singapore's seedy, but colorful nightlife, famous for the skimpily garbed cross-dressers who paraded its sidewalks. The government wasn't delighted, though, and the area was razed to make way for the Bugis MRT station. So strong was the outcry that Bugis Street has been re-created (but not really) just steps from its original site, between Victoria and Queen streets, Rochor Road, and Cheng Yan Place. The shophouses have been resurrected, and hawker food stands compete with casual-dining restaurants. Closed to traffic, the streets in the center of the block are a haven for bargain hunters after fast fashion or made-in-China trinkets. Across the road is Bugis Junction, a shopping center packed with mid-range dining options and clothing stores. ☒ *Bugis St., Bugis* ☎ *65/6338–9513* ⊕ *www.bugisstreet.com.sg* Ⓜ *Bugis.*

Kwan Im Thong Hood Cho Temple

RELIGIOUS SITE | The dusty, incense-filled interior of this popular temple has altars heaped with hundreds of small statues of gods from the Chinese pantheon. Of the hundreds of Chinese deities, Kwan Im, more often known as Kuan Yin, is perhaps most dear to the hearts of Buddhist Singaporeans. Legend has it that just as she was about to enter Nirvana, she heard a plaintive cry from Earth. Filled with compassion, she gave up her place in paradise to devote herself to alleviating the pain of those on Earth; thereupon, she took the name Kuan Yin, meaning "to see and hear all." People in search of advice on anything from an auspicious date for a marriage to possible solutions for domestic or work crises come to the Kwan Im temple, shake *cham si* (bamboo fortune sticks), and wait for an answer. The gods are most receptive on days of a new or full moon. ☒ *178 Waterloo St., Bugis* ⊕ *www.kuanimtng. org.sg* Ⓜ *Bugis.*

🛏 Hotels

Andaz Singapore

$$$ | **HOTEL** | This energetic five-star hotel by the Hyatt group features locally inspired decor, communal spaces with all-day refreshments, an infinity pool, and a popular rooftop bar with 360-degree skyline views (and tepees for you to stargaze from). **Pros:** warm, inviting rooms; floor-to-ceiling windows; complimentary minibar and all-day refreshments in the Sunroom lounge. **Cons:** reception is on the 25th floor; no porters; hotel is located within an office building. Ⓢ *Rooms from: S$290* ☒ *DUO Tower, 5 Fraser St., Level 25, Bugis* ☎ *6408–1234* ⊕ *www.hyatt.com* ⇥ *342 rooms* ⦿ *No meals* Ⓜ *Bugis.*

InterContinental Singapore

$$$$ | **HOTEL** | **FAMILY** | With its gorgeous Peranakan-style furnishings, silk wall coverings, elegant chandeliers, and rooms styled after 1920s heritage shophouses, this Bugis Junction hotel is luxuriously local. **Pros:** connected to the Bugis MRT station;

family-friendly; 24-hour fitness center. **Cons:** neighborhood gets busy on weekends; a distance from the main business and shopping areas; rooms feel slightly closed in. $ *Rooms from: S$415* ✉ *80 Middle Rd., Bugis* ☎ *6338–7600, 6338–7366* ⊕ *www.singapore.intercontinental.com* ⤳ *403 rooms* ○ *No meals* Ⓜ *Bugis.*

⭐ Performing Arts

Singapore Dance Theatre
DANCE | **FAMILY** | Founded in 1988, this dance company has a repertoire that ranges from classical to contemporary ballet. Periodic performances are held at the Esplanade Theatre, as well as on outdoor stages in Fort Canning Park. It also offers 90-minute dance classes in a variety of genres. ✉ *Bugis +, 201 Victoria St., #07–02/03, Bugis* ☎ *6338–0611* ⊕ *www.singaporedancetheatre.com.*

👜 Shopping

Bugis Junction
SHOPPING CENTERS/MALLS | **FAMILY** | This unique shopping complex is worth visiting just to see its shophouse facades, all enclosed under glass domes and cooled with arctic-strength air-conditioning. While you're here, look for affordable streetwear boutiques, a movie theater, cafés and restaurants, and the Kinokuniya bookstore . The center of Bugis Junction connects to the InterContinental Singapore hotel and Bugis MRT station. ✉ *200 Victoria St., Bugis* ☎ *6557–6557* ⊕ *www.capitaland.com/sg/malls/bugisjunction/en.html* Ⓜ *Bugis.*

Chapter 6

ORCHARD ROAD

WITH THE BOTANIC GARDENS

Updated by
Olivia Lee

⦿ Sights	🍴 Restaurants	🛏 Hotels	🛍 Shopping	🍸 Nightlife
★★★★☆	★★★★★	★★★★★	★★★★★	★★★★★

NEIGHBORHOOD SNAPSHOT

TOP EXPERIENCES

■ **Shop 'til you drop:** Orchard Road is right up there with New York's Madison Avenue or London's Oxford Street when it comes to shopping, so leave space in your suitcase.

■ **The Botanic Gardens:** You could spend days walking around these world-class tropical gardens, but if time is short, make a beeline for the Orchid Garden.

■ **Emerald Hill:** This pretty street, full of colorful Peranakan-style houses that have been turned into bars, makes for a welcome break after a busy day shopping.

■ **Sky-high views:** Immerse yourself in 360-degree views of the city from the 56th floor of a mall in the ION Sky observation area.

■ **Local hidden gems:** Almost every mall on Orchard Road has a food court in the basement. Just look for the stalls with the longest lines and join them.

GETTING HERE

Orchard Road stretches for just over 2 km (1.25 miles), served by the Orchard, Somerset, and Dhoby Ghaut MRT stations, all of which are on the North South Line (red). Bus stops line Orchard and Scotts roads, but the one-way system can be a little confusing. To go east, you can use any of the Orchard Road stops, but you have to cross behind the street to Orchard Boulevard for buses heading towards the west.

PLANNING YOUR TIME

Set aside a few hours to peruse the malls and watch the flood of pedestrians strolling down the wide sidewalks, then return at night for dinner and drinks.

QUICK BITES

■ **Maddie's Kitchen.** This canteen is loved for its cheap and tasty seafood soups packed with jumbo shrimp and noodles. ⊠ *Level 2, lot 10-13, Far East Plaza, 14 Scotts Rd., 228213* ⊕ *www.facebook.com/kitchenmaddies* Ⓜ *Orchard MRT*

■ **Orchard Towers Food Court.** It might look dingy, but in its basement you will find a great lunchtime food court full of stalls serving quick and cheap Singaporean dishes like *pork congee (savory porridge).* ⊠ *B1, 400 Orchard Rd., 238875* Ⓜ *Orchard MRT*

■ **Watanabe Coffee.** This Japanese coffee shop serves specialty brews alongside an eclectic menu including rice omelets, hamburger steaks, and spaghetti. ⊠ *350 Orchard Road Shaw House, Isetan Scotts #01–00, 238868* ⊕ *www.w-coffee.net* Ⓜ *Orchard MRT*

Orchard Road, Singapore's bustling shopping drag, is a three-lane-wide, one-way street flanked by tree-lined walkways. The road was named for the fruit plantations found here in the 19th century. The first malls made their debut back in the 1970s, and it's been under nonstop development ever since.

The road is a true shopper's paradise. Instead of being lined with traditional shops, it's lined with enormous malls, each one housing countless fashion, retail, and food outlets, and each one providing a cooling escape from Singapore's sweat-inducing outside world. In fact, wide underground tunnels connect the various shopping centers, so you never really have to leave the air-conditioning.

Orchard Road's ION and Somerset 313 malls are among the two most popular, packed with top fashion labels across multiple floors. The Shaw Centre is another good choice, loved for its IMAX cinema and excellent basement food court. Because of Orchard's convenient location—a central point between the east, west, and downtown districts—you can find a number of the city's best hotels here. It's also a foodie paradise, with restaurants of all kinds crammed into every mall on every street.

In the evening, the street transforms from a shopping domain to a nightlife destination. This is where you will find the infamous Orchard Towers, a large entertainment complex with several bars where pole dancers and racy performers are often part of the show. For a slightly more serene experience, there's colorful Emerald Hill, a lane filled with restored, traditional, bright red and green shophouses offering several laid-back bars for a relaxing drink. And just one stop on the MRT brings you to Newton Circus, a hawker center that is always packed at night thanks to its great (albeit a little overpriced) seafood and local treats.

◉ Sights

Orchard Road isn't especially known for its sights; people mainly come here to eat and shop. Still, there are several places of interest worth checking out—provided your hands aren't too full of shopping bags. Of note are the nearby Botanic Gardens, as well as a number of independent galleries and theaters that showcase work from local and international artists.

Art Forum

ART GALLERIES—ARTS | Owned by the Shanghai-born art dealer and author Marjorie Chu, Art Forum is a beautiful contemporary art gallery with a focus on Southeast Asia. Paintings and sculptures from more than 150 local and international artists are on display within this restored, whitewashed terrace house, and Chu herself is a wonderful resource for learning about the region's evolving arts scene. The art collection is displayed on a rotating basis. ✉ 82 Cairnhill Rd., Orchard ☎ 6737–3448 ⊕ www.artforum.com.sg Ⓜ Newton.

Bruno Gallery

ART GALLERIES—ARTS | The international art group Bruno has a wonderful little studio on Tanglin Road, near the top of Orchard Road. The gallery chain is one of the few to focus on Israeli art. You can walk in to simply admire the art, curated for a Singaporean audience, or stop to shop from the collections on sale. The art house also offers a curated "Living Room Art" service, where the staff can hand-select designs to suit your own space. ✉ 01–03 Tanglin Place, 91 Tanglin Rd., Orchard ☎ 6733–0283 ⊕ www. brunoartgroup.com Ⓜ Orchard.

Goodwood Park Hotel

HOTEL—SIGHT | Though it's 30 years younger than the more widely known Raffles, this hotel is just as much a landmark. Built in 1900, it was previously used as a German club and, during World War II, as a Japanese army headquarters. In 1989, the Tower Wing, with its pointy terracotta-colored roof, was named a national monument. Today, the interior is modeled on European designs, and, in true British fashion, you can enjoy an elegant afternoon tea near the lobby at L'Espresso—the perfect break from all that shopping. High tea is served from 2 pm to 5:30 pm and costs about S$45. ✉ 22 Scotts Rd., Orchard ☎ 6737–7411 ⊕ www.goodwoodparkhotel.com Ⓜ Orchard.

ION Art Gallery

ART GALLERIES—ARTS | ION Art showcases modern and contemporary art and design, including multimedia and digital works. Part of the ION Mall, this free gallery focuses on Asian artists—both emerging and established—with a spectrum of art-based events and exhibitions held throughout the year. ✉ #4 ION Orchard Mall, 2 Orchard Turn, Orchard ✛ ION Orchard - Level 4 next to lobby ☎ 6238–8228 ⊕ www.ionorchard.com/ion-art Ⓜ Somerset.

★ ION Sky

VIEWPOINT | ION Sky offers panoramic views of Singapore from the 56th floor of ION Mall, 718 feet above the ground. It's technically free to enter, but only after spending S$20 in ION Mall (you need to download the ION Orchard app, then scan your receipt to receive your QR ticket). Alongside the great views are a number of interactive exhibits, including films screened on the glass walls and historic portrayals of how Singapore once looked. ⊠ *Level 56, 2 Orchard Turn, Orchard* ⊕ *www.ionorchard.com/ion-sky* Ⓜ *Orchard.*

The Istana

GOVERNMENT BUILDING | Built in 1869, this elegant neo-Palladian style building set in extensive tropical gardens once served as the British colonial governor's residence. Today, it is the official residence of the president of Singapore (Istana means "palace" in Malay). The building and grounds are open to the public only on the holidays listed on its website. On the first Sunday of each month, a changing-of-the-guard ceremony at the main gates on Orchard Road is held at 5:45 pm. ⊠ *35 Orchard Rd., Orchard* ⊕ *www.istana.gov.sg* ⊠ *Self-guided tour S$4, guided tour S$10* Ⓜ *Dhoby Ghaut.*

Library@Orchard

LIBRARY | If you like books and appreciate beautiful design, you will enjoy an hour spent within the walls of Library@Orchard. There are more than 100,000 books housed in the swirling, spiraling bookcases, making it popular among social media users who like to snap and share the intricate designs. It's also a lovely spot to escape Singapore's scorching heat. ⊠ *277 Orchard Rd., Orchard* ☎ *6332–3255* ⊕ *www.nlb.gov.sg* Ⓜ *Somerset.*

★ Newton Food Centre

MARKET | Also known as Newton Circus, this is one of the best-known hawker centers in town. (The "circus" refers to a round-about, as in Piccadilly Circus.) It's a great place to visit at night, when the atmosphere is buzzing, and it's usually very busy no matter which evening you go. Food vendors here often get pushy with their menus, so walk with confidence if you don't want to be accosted. Note that you can sit anywhere: it can feel strange buying food at one stall, then sitting down in front of another, but that's the practice. In fact, it can sometimes be hard to find a table, so grab whatever you can get. The barbecue seafood stalls are famous here, though things like tiger prawns and chili crab are priced by weight, so have the bill tallied up ahead of time to avoid expensive surprises. ⊠ *500 Clemenceau Ave. North, Orchard* Ⓜ *Newton.*

KEY

- ● Exploring Sights
- ● Restaurants
- ● Hotels

0 — 1,000 ft
0 — 200 m

Orchard [M]

Sights	Restaurants	
Art Forum, **7**	Akashi, **3**	Nassim Hill Bakery Bistro Bar, **1**
Bruno Gallery, **2**	Aoki, **11**	Patara, **2**
Goodwood Park Hotel, **6**	Din Tai Fung, **20**	Pete's Place, **17**
ION Art Gallery, **3**	Food Opera @ ION Orchard, **9**	PS. Cafe, **5**
ION Sky, **4**	Food Republic @ Shaw House, **14**	The Rice Table, **10**
The Istana, **13**	Hai Di Lao, **22**	Soup Restaurant, **21**
Library@Orchard, **9**	Hainanese Delicacy, **18**	Sun with Moon, **7**
Newton Food Centre, **8**	Iggy's, **6**	Thai Tantric, **4**
Opera Gallery, **5**	Jinjo, **12**	Tsuta, **15**
Orchard Central Rooftop Garden, **12**	Jollibee, **19**	
Peranakan Place, **11**	Les Amis, **13**	
Pop and Contemporary Fine Art, **10**	mezza9, **16**	
Singapore Botanic Gardens, **1**	Nam Nam Noodle Bar, **8**	

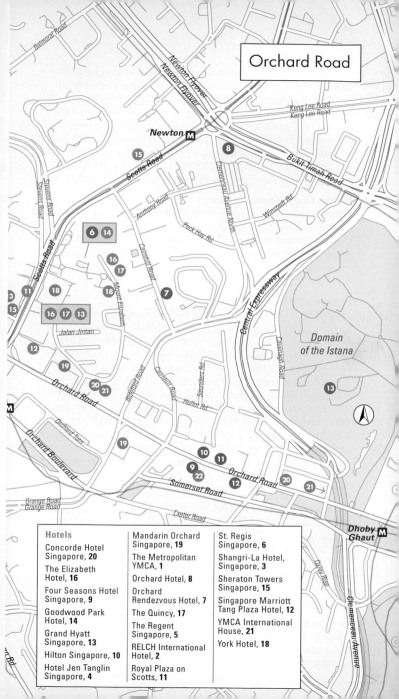

Orchard Road

Hotels

Concorde Hotel Singapore, **20**

The Elizabeth Hotel, **16**

Four Seasons Hotel Singapore, **9**

Goodwood Park Hotel, **14**

Grand Hyatt Singapore, **13**

Hilton Singapore, **10**

Hotel Jen Tanglin Singapore, **4**

Mandarin Orchard Singapore, **19**

The Metropolitan YMCA, **1**

Orchard Hotel, **8**

Orchard Rendezvous Hotel, **7**

The Quincy, **17**

The Regent Singapore, **5**

RELCH International Hotel, **2**

Royal Plaza on Scotts, **11**

St. Regis Singapore, **6**

Shangri-La Hotel, Singapore, **3**

Sheraton Towers Singapore, **15**

Singapore Marriott Tang Plaza Hotel, **12**

YMCA International House, **21**

York Hotel, **18**

Opera Gallery

ART GALLERIES—ARTS | This cool, contemporary space is one of Singapore's most well-known galleries, with works of art from some of the greatest painters in the world, including Salvador Dali and Andy Warhol. The gallery, which also has outlets from Paris to New York, hosts a number of specialist exhibitions throughout the year in the Singapore branch. Many of the paintings and sculptures are also available to buy, though expect a hefty price tag. ⊠ *#02–16 ION Orchard, 2 Orchard Turn, Orchard* ☎ *6735–2618* ⊕ *www.operagallery.com/exhibitions/singapore* Ⓜ *Somerset.*

Orchard Central Rooftop Garden

GARDEN | This unassuming rooftop garden provides a welcome respite from the busy streets below. Located on Level 12 of the Orchard Central building, it's a small but peaceful spot to sit, think, and watch the world go by, with the sounds of the garden's tiny waterfalls tinkling in the background. ⊠ *#11–12 Orchard Central, 181 Orchard Rd., Orchard* Ⓜ *Somerset.*

Peranakan Place

PLAZA | The building on the corner of Orchard and Emerald Hill roads is a masterpiece—albeit a somewhat diluted one—of Peranakan architecture. This style, a blend of Chinese and Malay aesthetics, emerged in the 19th century, when Chinese people born in what was then called the Straits Settlements (including Singapore) adopted, and often adapted, Malay fashion, cuisine, and design. The surrounding area is now a mix of upscale residences, with renovated shophouses doubling as bars and restaurants. Parts of Emerald Hill, from Orchard Road through the Ice Cold Beer pub, are for pedestrians only; there are several outdoor cafés and restaurants along the stretch. Stroll the arcaded street, and check out fretted woodwork, pastel washes, ornate wall tiles, and other typical Peranakan touches. ⊠ *180 Orchard Rd., Orchard* ☎ *6732–6966* ⊕ *www.peranakanplace.com* Ⓜ *Somerset.*

Pop and Contemporary Fine Art

ART GALLERIES—ARTS | This vibrant, spacious gallery specializes in original paintings, limited-edition lithographs, screen prints, etchings, and sculptures in the bright and bold pop-art style. It exhibits works by the likes of Andy Warhol, Damien Hirst, Roy Lichtenstein, and Burton Morris. ⊠ *Tong Building #07–03, 302 Orchard Rd., Orchard* ☎ *6735–0959* ⊕ *www.popandcontemporaryart.com* ☞ *Closed Mon.* Ⓜ *Somerset.*

★ Singapore Botanic Gardens

GARDEN | **FAMILY** | The first site in Singapore to gain UNESCO Heritage status is also the first and only tropical botanic gardens in the world to make the list. Once you start to explore the winding trails

A "Curtain of Roots" at the Singapore Botanic Gardens leads to many stunning green spaces.

of the enormous park, which sprawls across more than 128 acres of lush greenery, you'll understand why. It is neatly segmented into different gardens featuring all the hallmarks of Victorian design—gazebos, pavilions, and ornate bandstands included. Highlights are the National Orchid Garden, showcasing over 1,000 species of brightly colored blooms, and the Ginger Garden, where several hundred varieties of ginger grow. Try to time your visit to coincide with the free guided tours that almost always take place at 9 am on Saturday. ⊠ *1 Cluny Rd., Botanic Gardens* ☎ *6471–7361* ⊕ *www.nparks.gov.sg/sbg* ✉ *Free* Ⓜ *Botanic Gardens.*

🍴 Restaurants

You could spend a lifetime trying to visit every restaurant on Orchard Road, and you still wouldn't come close. Eateries are packed into every floor of every mall in almost every building along the street. Even structures that look tired and forgotten from the outside tend to have hidden hot spots where crowds of insiders line up to get their fill during the weekday lunchtime rush.

★ Akashi

$$ | **JAPANESE** | This intimate restaurant almost succeeds in transporting you to Japan, with its traditional tea-house decor, its kimono-clad servers, and its chefs who belt out *irrashimase* (welcome). Alongside a generous sushi menu, Akashi serves delicious, beautifully presented set meals featuring green tea noodles and crispy tempura or thick udon and fried tofu. **Known for:** beautiful sashimi plates; staff in pretty kimonos; authentic Japanese atmosphere.

⑤ *Average main: S$18* ✉ *Orchard Rendezvous Hotel , 1 Tanglin Rd., Orchard* ☎ *6732–4438* ⊕ *akashi.com.sg* Ⓜ *Orchard.*

Aoki

$$$ | **JAPANESE** | Look for the fabric-covered doorway opposite the HSBC building on Claymore Hill to find this sleek Japanese restaurant. Inside, there are counters made of *hinoki* wood, a Zen minimalist design, and elegant, kimono-clad servers. **Known for:** intimate dining experience; impeccably presented dishes; fresh Japanese seafood. ⑤ *Average main: S$35* ✉ *#02–17 Shaw Centre, 1 Scotts Rd., Orchard* ☎ *6333–8015* ⊕ *www.aoki-restaurant.com. sg* ⊗ *Closed Sun.* Ⓜ *Orchard.*

★ Din Tai Fung

$ | **CHINESE** | This Taiwanese chain is respected the world over for its juicy, impossibly delicate *xiao long bao* (dumpling-like steamed buns) stuffed with fillings that include pork, chili crab, minced vegetables, and seafood. Singapore branches have been opening like crazy in recent years: there are 25 at last count, and more are undoubtedly on the way. **Known for:** xiao long baos; award-winning reputation; dumplings, dumplings, and more dumplings. ⑤ *Average main: S$10* ✉ *#B1–03, Paragon, 290 Orchard Rd., Orchard* ☎ *6836–8336* ⊕ *www.dintaifung.com.sg.*

Food Opera @ ION Orchard

$ | **CHINESE** | Celebrating Singaporean heritage dishes across 27 different vendors, this basement food court's stalls sell everything from crispy fried carrot cake to spicy prawn noodles and tangy chicken satay. The food court takes its design inspiration from the British colonial decor of the early 1990s, with a light blue, ivory, and copper-gold palette, and lush green plants. **Known for:** old-school design; Singaporean heritage dishes; friendly vendors. ⑤ *Average main: S$4* ✉ *#B4-03/04 ION Orchard, 2 Orchard Turn, Orchard* ☎ *6509–9198* ⊕ *foodrepublic.com.sg/food-republic-out-lets/food-opera-ion* Ⓜ *Orchard.*

Food Republic @ Shaw House

$ | **ASIAN FUSION** | In the basement of Shaw House, this vibrant food court has more than 20 colorful stalls selling everything from Thai curries to duck wonton. It's always busy at lunch and dinner, so do as the locals do, and *chope* (reserve) a space by leaving a packet of tissues or a personal item at the table before you order. **Known for:** lots of local dishes; contemporary design; great juices. ⑤ *Average main: S$4* ✉ *350 Orchard Rd., Orchard* ☎ *6887–5881* ⊕ *shawcentre.sg* Ⓜ *Somerset.*

Breakfast of Champions: Kaya Toast 🍴

Singaporeans love kaya toast, a traditional breakfast dish consisting of two slices of charcoal-toasted bread, slabs of chilled butter, and a generous spreading of kaya jam, which is made from coconut milk, eggs, and sugar. This is usually served alongside two soft-boiled eggs—mixed with dark soy sauce—and a strong cup of local *kopi* (coffee) sweetened with condensed milk.

The dish is said to have originated when Hainanese Chinese ship workers started adapting the food served in British shops to the local *kopi tiam* (coffee stall) culture of Singapore. Western jam was replaced with local coconut jams, and tea was replaced with local kopi.

One of the most popular outlets serving this sickly-sweet breakfast treat is **Ya Kun Kaya Toast**, a coffee shop established in 1944 that's now synonymous with the dish. There are eight outlets along Orchard Road in the space of less than 2 km (1.25 miles) and 30 across the island, as well as branches in China, Japan, Taiwan, Vietnam, and Thailand, among other countries. Another popular chain is **Killiney Kopitiam**, the oldest Hainanese coffee shop in Singapore, dating from 1919.

No trip to Singapore would be complete without trying kaya toast. Ya Kun Kaya Toast has several varieties on its menu, including cheese toast with kaya and butter sugar toast. If you haven't tired of it before, play it safe with the classic "kaya toast with butter set"—but be prepared for the inevitable sugar rush.

Hai Di Lao

$$ | CHINESE | There is always a very long line at this do-it-yourself Chinese hotpot restaurant, but in Hai Di Lao's case, that's not such a bad thing—while you wait, you can enjoy quirky (and free) services, treats, and swag like gel manicures, popcorn, ice cream, and iPhone screen-protector replacements. It can sometimes take several hours to reach the front of the line, but when you do, you'll realize what the wait was for: the dining experience is highly theatrical. **Known for:** DIY hotpot (cooking meats and veg in broth); waiters who perform "noodle dances"; free dishes in exchange for completing challenges. Ⓢ *Average main: S$20* ✉ *#04–23/24, 313 Orchard Rd., Orchard* ☎ *6835–7227* ⊕ *www.haidilao.com/sg* Ⓜ *Somerset.*

★ Hainanese Delicacy

$ | **CHINESE** | Despite being hidden away on Level 5 of the Far East Plaza mall, Hainanese Delicacy always has a long line outside at lunchtime. It's renowned among locals as serving one of the best Hainanese chicken rice dishes on Orchard Road. **Known for:** the best chicken rice around; braised eggs as a side dish; local flavors at low prices. ⑤ *Average main: S$5* ⊠ *14 Scotts Rd., #05–116 Far East Plaza,, Orchard* ⊕ *Up the escalators to level five* ☎ *6734–0639* ⊗ *Closed Mon.* Ⓜ *Somerset.*

★ Iggy's

$$$$ | **EUROPEAN** | If you're going to splurge on just one meal in Singapore, Iggy's is a good bet. Hailed as one of the top restaurants in Asia, this intimate Euro-Japanese fusion spot has mouthwatering dishes like Miyazaki Wagyu beef and Hokkaido scallop with caviar, as well as one of the best wine lists on the island. **Known for:** the gastronomic menu; 25,000 bottles of wine; Wagyu beef and black truffles. ⑤ *Average main: S$250* ⊠ *Level 3, Hilton Singapore Hotel, 581 Orchard Rd., Orchard* ☎ *6732–2234* ⊕ *www.iggys.com.sg* ⊗ *Closed Sun.–Mon.* Ⓜ *Somerset.*

★ Jinjo

$$$ | **JAPANESE** | The decor at this chic sumiyaki restaurant celebrating Japanese charcoal-grilling is as authentic as the food. It's styled after traditional Japanese izakayas, with bar seating where you can watch the chefs delicately fan the meat and vegetables cooked over open coals. **Known for:** Izakaya decor; Jinjo-branded sake; small plates. ⑤ *Average main: S$30* ⊠ *#02–19/20 Shaw Centre, 1 Scotts Rd., Orchard* ☎ *6732–2165* ⊕ *www.jinjo.com.sg* Ⓜ *Somerset.*

Jollibee

$ | **PHILIPPINE** | This Filipino fried-chicken chain, where you can get spicy wings with a side of ketchup spaghetti, was once described by the late chef Anthony Bourdain as "the wackiest, jolliest place on Earth." Each of the several branches is loved for its cheap and delicious meal deals. There's almost always a line at peak times. **Known for:** fried chicken dipped in gravy; long lines; cheap and cheerful atmosphere. ⑤ *Average main: S$6* ⊠ *#B1–038 Lucky Plaza, 304 Orchard Rd., Orchard* ☎ *6735–5117* ⊕ *www.facebook.com/JollibeeSG* Ⓜ *Somerset.*

★ Les Amis

$$$$ | **FRENCH** | Mingle with Singaporean tycoons and celebrities at the island's finest French restaurant, where you can admire the adjoining bar's grand chandelier and curtain-draped wine cabinets before adjourning to the intimate 30-seat dining area. The seasonal menu changes regularly, but expect such exquisite

French classics as foie gras, roasted whole pigeon, and razor clams. **Known for:** unmatched service; enormous wine collection; chandelier-lit dining. $ *Average main: S$150* ⊠ *#01–16 Shaw Centre, 1 Scotts Rd., Orchard* ☎ *6733–2225* ⊕ *www.lesamis. sg* Ⓜ *Orchard.*

mezza9

$$$ | **INTERNATIONAL** | There's something for everyone at Grand Hyatt Singapore's stylish 400-seat restaurant, which offers nine different "kitchens" serving everything from Thai and Chinese steamboat cuisines to yakitori, sushi, grilled meats, and some of the best martinis on the island. Whether you opt for deep-fried soft-shell crab, 28-day dry-aged Irish beef, steamed black tiger prawns, or whole Maine lobster, save room for the signature dessert: five sinful sweets and three scoops of ice cream presented on a silver platter. **Known for:** signature "five-treat" dessert; 28-day dry-aged Irish beef; delicious cocktails. $ *Average main: S$45* ⊠ *Mezzanine Level, Grand Hyatt Singapore, 10 Scotts Rd., Orchard* ☎ *6738–1234* ⊕ *www.singapore.grand.hyattrestaurants. com/mezza9* Ⓜ *Orchard.*

Nam Nam Noodle Bar

$ | **VIETNAMESE** | The enormous bowls of *pho* at this casual quick-serve noodle bar are excellent. At lunch time, you can get a bowl of any flavor, a side of crispy spring rolls, and a tea or coffee for under S$10. **Known for:** huge bowls of pho; great side dishes; beautiful tablewear. $ *Average main: S$10* ⊠ *#B2–02 Wheelock Place, 501 Orchard Rd., Orchard* ☎ *6735–1488* ⊕ *namnam.net* Ⓜ *Somerset.*

★ Nassim Hill Bakery Bistro Bar

$$ | **EUROPEAN** | This lovely bistro transforms from bakery and brunch hotspot by day to chic restaurant and bar by night. It specializes in European-style baked bread, which forms the basis of many of the brunch dishes (served until 4 pm) and then again as a delicious accompaniment to a selection of zesty dips and tapas in the evening. **Known for:** trio dip sampler; crispy, freshly baked bread; two for one beers from 9 am to 9 pm. $ *Average main: S$20* ⊠ *56 Tanglin Rd., #01–03, Tanglin Post Office Building, Orchard* ☎ *6835–1128* ⊕ *www.nassimhill.com.sg* ⊙ *Closed Mon.* Ⓜ *Orchard.*

Patara

$$ | **THAI** | This popular Thai restaurant, which also has branches in Austria, China, Switzerland, Thailand, and the United Kingdom, serves an extensive menu of classics in a serene, cozy setting. You can order everything from Thai-style soups and salads to curries and noodles. **Known for:** nua pad prik Thai (beef spare ribs sautéed in garlic and black pepper sauce); pla yang penang (sea bass grilled in penang sauce); ambience. $ *Average main: S$27* ✉ *Tanglin Mall, 163 Tanglin Rd., #03–14, Orchard* ☎ *6737–0818* ⊕ *www.patara.com.sg* Ⓜ *Orchard.*

Pete's Place

$$$ | ITALIAN | FAMILY | The dark, cozy aura at Pete's Place plays second fiddle to the hearty Italian food. Famed for its antipasto, pizza, and pasta, this family-friendly restaurant, located in the basement of Grand Hyatt Singapore, also has an enormous soup-and-salad buffet complete with warm breads and homemade butter. $ *Average main: S$35* ✉ *Grand Hyatt Singapore, 10 Scotts Rd., Orchard* ☎ *6738–1234* ⊕ *www.singapore.grand.hyattrestaurants.com/ petes-place.html* Ⓜ *Orchard.*

PS. Cafe

$$ | CONTEMPORARY | Leafy green plants fill this bright and airy café, which is on the second floor of Palais Renaissance and is a popular spot for leisurely brunches and lunches. The all-day menu is a continental mix of salads, pastas, and posh sandwiches, with heartier options like charred orange-and-thyme pork chops, or mushroom Wellington. **Known for:** large yet refined portions; beautiful decor; large glass windows letting the sun spill in. $ *Average main: S$25* ✉ *Level 2 Palais Renaissance, 390 Orchard Rd., Orchard* ☎ *6708–9288* ⊕ *www.pscafe.com/pscafe-at-palais-renaissance* Ⓜ *Orchard.*

★ The Rice Table

$$ | INDONESIAN | You get excellent value for your money at this traditional Indonesian restaurant, where you can eat as much as you like from the menu for just $19.80 at lunch or $30.80 at dinner. It's not your regular buffet-style set up, though—each dish is cooked to order and then laid out on a food warmer in the center of your table. **Known for:** slow-cooked beef rendang; unlimited small plates; traditional Indonesian aesthetic. $ *Average main: S$20* ✉ *#02–09 International Building, 360 Orchard Rd., Orchard* ☎ *6835–3782* ⊕ *ricetable.com.sg* ☾ *No dinner Sun.* Ⓜ *Orchard.*

Soup Restaurant

$$ | CHINESE | Don't be fooled: soup is hardly the only thing on the menu at this popular Cantonese chain. It's an excellent spot to taste a variety of Chinese-style food, from double-boiled pork ribs and dried scallops to tofu prawns and chicken rice, perhaps the most popular dish in Singapore. **Known for:** Chinatown cuisine; Samsui ginger chicken; excellent homemade tofu. $ *Average main: S$15* ✉ *#B1–07, Paragon Mall, 290 Orchard Rd., Orchard* ☎ *6333–6228* ⊕ *www.souprestaurant.com.sg* Ⓜ *Orchard.*

★ Sun with Moon

$$ | JAPANESE | This spacious restaurant looks a little inauthentic from the outside, but inside, the intricate meals served on beautiful Japanese tableware will quickly convince you otherwise. The set menu of main courses come with all the trimmings: miso soup, rice, and a range of side dishes to choose from, including salmon salads and deep-fried tofu. **Known for:** beautiful set-menu lunches; excellent service; delicious side dishes. $ *Average main: S$20* ⊠ *#03–15 Wheelock Place, 501 Orchard Rd., Orchard* ☎ *6733–6636* ⊕ *www.sunwithmoon.com.sg* Ⓜ *Orchard.*

★ Thai Tantric

$ | THAI | This windowless, no-frills, Thai restaurant might be tucked away on the third floor of the slightly sleazy Orchard Towers, but the locals still pile in for the delicious, authentic, and very affordable food. The menu packs all the classics, from massaman curry to traditional fishcakes, each served in generous portions. **Known for:** quick and cheap; authentic flavors and huge portions; great green curry. $ *Average main: S$10* ⊠ *#03–44 Orchard Tower, 400 Orchard Rd., Orchard* ⊕ *Head into the Orchard Towers entrance by the 7/11 and take the elevator to Level 3.* ☎ *9625–7523* ⊕ *www.facebook.com/ThaiTantricSingapore* ☽ *Closed Sun.* Ⓜ *Orchard.*

★ Tsuta

$$ | JAPANESE | Sample Michelin-starred ramen at this authentic noodle shop, which, despite the accolades, remains very affordable. The Tsuta chain was first founded in 2012 by Japan by chef Yuki Onishi, who wanted to redefine the ramen experience; it was awarded its first Michelin star in 2016. **Known for:** award-winning ramen at low prices; chef-facing dining; rich ramen broth. $ *Average main: S$15* ⊠ *#01–01 Pacific Plaza, 9 Scotts Rd., Orchard* ☎ *6734–4886* ⊕ *tsuta.com* Ⓜ *Somerset.*

🛏 Hotels

Bridging the gap between the east, west, and south of the island, Orchard Road is one of the most convenient places to stay in Singapore. There are plenty of hotels to choose from, whether you're looking for the cheap and cheerful or the best of the best. Keep in mind that Orchard Road is a busy one, so while the location might be appealing, it's not for those seeking peace and quiet.

Concorde Hotel Singapore

$$ | HOTEL | Once appropriately called the Glass Hotel, the Concorde has a glass canopy that curves down from the ninth story over the entrance, facing southeast for good fortune. **Pros:** nice swimming pool; great sushi restaurant; boutique style. **Cons:** no hotel smoking area; could do with a refresh; breakfast is average. [$] *Rooms from: S$200* ✉ *100 Orchard Rd., Orchard* ☎ *6733–8855* ⊕ *singapore.concordehotelsresorts.com* ⤳ *407 rooms* |○| *No meals* [M] *Dhoby Ghaut.*

The Elizabeth Hotel

$$ | HOTEL | This hotel is in a residential area surrounded by greenery behind Orchard Road's main shopping district and has superior and deluxe rooms done in an English country style, complete with Tudor furnishings. **Pros:** in a quieter area; free parking; has a pool and gym. **Cons:** many rooms don't have a view; staff could be friendlier; the walls are a little thin. [$] *Rooms from: S$220* ✉ *24 Mt. Elizabeth, Orchard* ☎ *6738–1188* ⊕ *www.stayfareast.com* ⤳ *256 rooms* |○| *No meals* [M] *Orchard.*

Four Seasons Hotel Singapore

$$$$ | HOTEL | FAMILY | Rooms are spacious at this refined hotel with a design inspired by the nearby Singapore Botanic Gardens, including a natural color palette with Peranakan tiles and Asian art. **Pros:** family-friendly; outside pool on the 20th floor; 24-hour gym and four tennis courts. **Cons:** on a busy road; surrounded by malls; interiors are a little dated. [$] *Rooms from: S$405* ✉ *190 Orchard Blvd., Orchard* ☎ *6734–1110* ⊕ *www.fourseasons.com/singapore* ⤳ *295 rooms* |○| *No meals* [M] *Orchard.*

Goodwood Park Hotel

$$ | HOTEL | What began in 1900 as a club for German expatriates is now a landmark hotel that's hosted the likes of the Duke of Windsor, Noël Coward, and the great ballerina Anna Pavlova, who performed here. **Pros:** beautiful Balinese-style pool; historical building; great service. **Cons:** small gym; on a busy road; a little dated. [$] *Rooms from: S$220* ✉ *22 Scotts Rd., Orchard* ☎ *6737– 7411* ⊕ *www.goodwoodparkhotel.com* ⤳ *235 rooms* |○| *Free Breakfast* [M] *Orchard.*

Grand Hyatt Singapore

$$$$ | HOTEL | The hotel's Grand Wing consists of one-, two-, and three-room apartments with extra bathrooms, study areas, and private mailboxes; the Grand Club executive floor, on Level 21, has breathtaking skyline views. **Pros:** lovely spa; wide selection of restaurants; central location. **Cons:** surrounded by malls; rooms lack personality; small standard rooms. [$] *Rooms from: S$600* ✉ *10–12 Scotts Rd., Orchard* ☎ *6738–1234* ⊕ *www.hyatt.com* ⤳ *677 rooms* |○| *No meals* [M] *Orchard.*

Hilton Singapore

$$ | **HOTEL** | At this Hilton, you can expect all the modern in-room amenities characteristic of more luxurious properties, as well as some of the country's most upscale boutiques in the on-site shopping arcade. **Pros:** Sky Bar on the 24th floor; award-winning restaurant Iggy's; near Orchard MRT. **Cons:** busy on weekends; surrounded by malls; rooms can be a little small. $ *Rooms from: S$220* ✉ *581 Orchard Rd., Orchard* ☎ *6737–2233* ⊕ *www3.hilton. com* 🛏 *423 rooms* ¶⚪ *No meals* Ⓜ *Orchard*.

Hotel Jen Tanglin Singapore

$$ | **HOTEL** | Connected to the Tanglin Mall, this hotel has all the essentials—including a lovely outdoor pool surrounded by leafy greenery. **Pros:** 24-hour room service; shuttle to MRT; chili crab at Ah Hoi's Kitchen. **Cons:** small rooms; breakfast is a little too busy; smokers have to leave the hotel for a smoking area around the corner. $ *Rooms from: S$220* ✉ *1A Cuscaden Rd., Orchard* ☎ *6738–2222, 0800/028–3337 for reservations in the U.K., 800/942–5050 for reservations in the U.S.* ⊕ *www.hoteljen.com* 🛏 *546 rooms* ¶⚪ *Free Breakfast* Ⓜ *Orchard*.

Mandarin Orchard Singapore

$$$ | **HOTEL** | The grand main lobby in this large hotel is adorned with black-and-white Italian marble and a huge mural—87 Taoist Immortals, which is based on an 8th-century Chinese scroll—and guest rooms have Asian themes with modern amenities. **Pros:** local cuisine; beautifully designed rooms; 24-hour concierge. **Cons:** tour groups can make for a crowded lobby; busy road outside; gym could be better. $ *Rooms from: S$350* ✉ *333 Orchard Rd., Orchard* ☎ *6737–4411* ⊕ *www.meritushotels.com* 🛏 *1,065 rooms* ¶⚪ *Free Breakfast* Ⓜ *Somerset*.

The Metropolitan YMCA

$$ | **HOTEL** | A 10-minute walk from Orchard Road, this YMCA has colorfully decorated rooms with all the essentials: air-conditioning, private bathrooms, in-room hot drinks stations, and free Wi-Fi. **Pros:** 25-meter pool; eclectic on-site budget restaurant; orthopedic mattresses. **Cons:** service is lacking; busy neighborhood; food is average. $ *Rooms from: S$145* ✉ *60 Stevens Rd., Orchard* ☎ *6839–8333* ⊕ *www.mymca.org.sg/stay* 🛏 *98 rooms* ¶⚪ *Free Breakfast* Ⓜ *Orchard*.

Orchard Hotel

$$ | **HOTEL** | **FAMILY** | Being close to Orchard Road, several embassies, and the Botanic Gardens has no doubt contributed to this hotel's popularity. **Pros:** recently renovated; family-friendly; business services. **Cons:** lines for reception at busy times; busy street;

restaurant staff could be better. **⑤** *Rooms from: S$210* ✉ *442 Orchard Rd., Orchard* ☎ *6734–7766* ⊕ *www.millenniumhotels.com* ⤳ *656 rooms* ⑩ *Free Breakfast* Ⓜ *Orchard.*

Orchard Rendezvous Hotel

$$$ | HOTEL | FAMILY | In this warm and colorful Mediterranean hotel, the botanical-inspired rooms are spacious, and family rooms have extra single beds and a dining area. **Pros:** family-friendly; stylish Club Lounge bar; outdoor swimming pool. **Cons:** surrounded by shopping malls; busy on the weekends; bathrooms are a little dated. **⑤** *Rooms from: S$310* ✉ *1 Tanglin Rd., Orchard* ☎ *6737–1133* ⊕ *www.rendezvoushotels.com* ⤳ *387 rooms* ⑩ *Free Breakfast* Ⓜ *Orchard.*

★ The Quincy

$$$ | HOTEL | This hotel bills itself at Singapore's first all-inclusive boutique hotel, where rates include three meals a day and complimentary cocktails during happy hour—perhaps not ideal for those excited to try the local food, but useful if you're feeding a family. **Pros:** infinity pool overlooking the city; quiet location; complimentary mini-bar. **Cons:** food is not as great as outside the hotel; limited pool seating; busy breakfast. **⑤** *Rooms from: S$280* ✉ *22 Mt. Elizabeth, Orchard* ☎ *6738–5888* ⊕ *www.quincy.com.sg* ⤳ *108 rooms* ⑩ *All-inclusive* Ⓜ *Orchard.*

The Regent Singapore

$$$ | HOTEL | A good 10-minute walk from Orchard and Scotts roads, the Regent appeals to those who want a quiet space to unwind after a busy day of shopping. **Pros:** away from the busy street; Asian artwork on display; some rooms have great views. **Cons:** 10-minute walk from MRT; difficult to catch taxis; tired in places. **⑤** *Rooms from: S$300* ✉ *1 Cuscaden Rd., Orchard* ☎ *6733–8888* ⊕ *www.regenthotels.com/regent-singapore* ⤳ *440 rooms* ⑩ *No meals* Ⓜ *Orchard.*

RELCH International Hotel

$$ | HOTEL | Doubling as an international conference center, this hotel has bargain, upper-floor guest rooms, which, though basic, are large, comfortable, and light filled. **Pros:** free Wi-Fi; balconies; quiet location. **Cons:** 15-minute walk to Orchard; difficult to hail a taxi; lacking personality. **⑤** *Rooms from: S$150* ✉ *30 Orange Grove Rd., Orchard* ☎ *6885–7888* ⊕ *www.relcih.com.sg* ⤳ *142 rooms* ⑩ *Free Breakfast* Ⓜ *Orchard.*

Royal Plaza on Scotts

$$ | HOTEL | The lobby here makes a bold statement, with Italian marble floors, two grand staircases, Burmese teak paneling, stained-glass skylights, and tapestries. **Pros:** some rooms have recently been refreshed; free minibar; pretty pool. **Cons:** some rooms are still a little dated; some rooms have street noise; room service is not 24 hours. ⑤ *Rooms from: S$210* ⊠ *25 Scotts Rd., Orchard* ☎ *6737–7966* ⊕ *www.royalplaza.com.sg* ⊃ *511 rooms* ⦿ *No meals* Ⓜ *Orchard.*

★ Shangri-La Hotel, Singapore

$$$ | **HOTEL** | For more than three decades, Shangri-La has been one of Singapore's top hotels, with some of best service in the city. **Pros:** 15 acres of flowers and plants; beautiful spa and pool; fun children's area. **Cons:** a short hike to Orchard Road; dated exterior; breakfast area can be a little too busy. ⑤ *Rooms from: S$320* ⊠ *22 Orange Grove Rd., Orchard* ☎ *6737–3644, 800/942–5050 for reservations in Canada and the U.S.* ⊕ *www.shangri-la.com/singapore/shangrila* ⊃ *747 rooms* ⦿ *Free Breakfast* Ⓜ *Orchard.*

Sheraton Towers Singapore

$$$ | **HOTEL** | Just a quick walk from Orchard Road, this relaxed hotel is also within walking distance of the hawker stalls at Newton Circus. **Pros:** good breakfast buffet; comfortable rooms; near Newton Circus. **Cons:** aging property; street noise on lower floors; Wi-Fi can be a little temperamental. ⑤ *Rooms from: S$250* ⊠ *39 Scotts Rd., Orchard* ☎ *6737–6888* ⊕ *www.marriott.com* ⊃ *420 rooms* ⦿ *No meals* Ⓜ *Newton.*

Singapore Marriott Tang Plaza Hotel

$$$ | **HOTEL** | This striking, 30-story, pagoda-inspired property anchors Singapore's "million-dollar corner"—the intersection of Orchard and Scotts roads. **Pros:** excellent location; unique architecture and design; good sports facilities nearby. **Cons:** busy street outside; street-facing rooms are noisy; slow elevators. ⑤ *Rooms from: S$290* ⊠ *320 Orchard Rd., Orchard* ☎ *6735–5800* ⊕ *www.marriott.com* ⊃ *393 rooms* ⦿ *No meals* Ⓜ *Orchard.*

St. Regis Singapore

$$$ | **HOTEL** | The high rates at this luxury hotel come with high-quality service and an array of extravagant extras. **Pros:** decadent Sunday Champagne brunch; first-rate spa; personal butler service. **Cons:** lines at breakfast; expensive; pool area is not quite as elegant as everywhere else. ⑤ *Rooms from: S$300* ⊠ *29 Tanglin Rd., Orchard* ☎ *6506–6888* ⊕ *www.marriott.com* ⊃ *299 rooms* ⦿ *No meals* Ⓜ *Orchard.*

YMCA International House

$$ | **HOTEL** | This well-run YMCA at the bottom of Orchard Road has double and dorm-style rooms, plus an impressive gym and a rooftop pool. **Pros:** low rates; central location; rooftop pool. **Cons:** only one key per room; crowded on weekdays; poor breakfast

selection. $ *Rooms from: S$120* ⊠ *1 Orchard Rd., Orchard*
☎ *6336–6000* ⊕ *www.ymcaih.com.sg* ⇄ *111 rooms* ▮◯▮ *Free
Breakfast* Ⓜ *Dhoby Ghaut.*

York Hotel

$$ | HOTEL | Despite its closeness to busy Orchard Road, this
classic European hotel is usually quiet and placid. **Pros:** quiet yet
central; friendly staff; free on-site parking. **Cons:** could use a little
updating; lacking in local style; check-in can be slow. $ *Rooms
from: S$190* ⊠ *21 Mt. Elizabeth, Orchard* ☎ *6737–0511* ⊕ *www.
yorkhotel.com.sg* ⇄ *407 rooms* ▮◯▮ *No meals* Ⓜ *Orchard.*

ⓨ Nightlife

The nightlife on Orchard Road tends to be tucked away—but it's
there in droves. Classy bars fill malls like the Shaw Centre or 313
Somerset, while clubs and pubs are often a little back from the
main road. It's not the best place to go bar-hopping (the better
bars are generally quite far apart), so it's best to pick a place to go,
and then stay put for the night.

Acid Bar

MUSIC CLUBS | This bar beside Emerald Hill has been rocking for 15
years. It has a nice outside seating area—great for people-watch-
ing—and a cozy interior where live bands play every evening. The
artists tend to be up-and-coming, so the music can sometimes be
hit or miss, but it's a good place for a few drinks and dancing. It
tends to be quite noisy, so don't come if you're looking for a quiet
conversation. ⊠ *180 Orchard Rd., Orchard* ☎ *6738–8828* ⊕ *www.
acidbar.sg* Ⓜ *Somerset.*

Alley Bar

BARS/PUBS | Tucked between two heritage Peranakan shophouses
on Emerald Hill, this low-key cocktail bar has atmospheric lanterns
hanging from its ceiling and gold and copper decorations dotting
its bar. The excellent daily happy hour (5 pm to 10 pm) makes it a
popular after-work haunt with locals. Prices are very reasonable
given the Orchard Road locale. On Wednesday, women can enjoy
free-flowing bubbly from 7 pm to 9 pm during the Singaporean
tradition of Ladies Night. ⊠ *2 Emerald Hill Rd., Orchard* ☎ *6738–
8818* ⊕ *www.alleybar.sg* Ⓜ *Somerset.*

Brix

BARS/PUBS | Renowned for being one of the hottest nightlife desti-
nations in Singapore, this hotel bar often has a line outside. Drinks
are fairly standard—expect whiskey, wine, and beer—but the
music is great, featuring everything from disco and soul to R&B
and jazz. A live band usually begins playing around 10 pm each

night, and the dance floor can get busy. ⊠ *Grand Hyatt Singapore, 10–12 Scotts Rd., Orchard* ☎ *6732–1234* ⊕ *www.singapore.grand. hyattrestaurants.com/brix* Ⓜ *Somerset.*

The Drunken Poet

BARS/PUBS | This always-lively Irish pub is well known for its revelry, especially during the sports-games screenings that take place throughout the week. Though it serves good food, the quintessentially Irish drinking atmosphere is the real draw, especially after dark. Wednesday evening sees fun pub quizzes. ⊠ *400 Orchard Rd., Orchard* ✛ *Inside Orchard Towers by the 7/11* ☎ *6734–2924* ⊕ *www.thedrunkenpoetpub.com* Ⓜ *Orchard.*

D'Underground

DANCE CLUBS | This bar-club is a popular spot among younger Singaporeans who come to play games and dance until 6 am. The bar has a range of nostalgic table games, including Crocodile Dentist, Penguin Trap, and Pirate Roulette, as well as a large area dedicated to beer pong. The free-flowing alcohol packages make it an affordable place to dance the night away, listening to live bands. ⊠ *#B1–00 International Bldg., 360 Orchard Rd., Orchard* ☎ *6834–1221* ⊕ *www.dunderground.club* Ⓜ *Orchard.*

Foc Pim Pam

TAPAS BARS | This open-air watering hole near the top of Orchard Road is popular with locals looking for a gin and tonic or glass of wine before they head home. Although it's open from the late morning, it's generally only busy in the evenings, especially Friday night, when the happy hour runs from 3 pm to 9 pm. There's also a great range of Spanish finger food, from Padrón peppers to cheese platters. ⊠ *442 Orchard Rd., Orchard* ☎ *6100–4242* ⊕ *focpimpam.com* ☞ *Closed Mon.* Ⓜ *Orchard.*

★ Ice Cold Beer

BARS/PUBS | Set in a 1910 townhouse noted for its Straits-Chinese architecture, this bustling pub attracts expats and locals alike and serves some 60 beers on tap or in bottles (they're "ice cold" from being in vast ice tanks). At the back of the bar, you can play darts; upstairs, you can play pool and arcade games. If you get peckish, the range of international bar snacks includes hot dogs, chicken wings, and mini-burgers. ⊠ *9 Emerald Hill Rd., Orchard* ☎ *6735–9929* ⊕ *www.ice-cold-beer.com* Ⓜ *Somerset.*

★ Kaku-Uchi Sake Bar

BARS/PUBS | This tiny six-seater bar is very easy to miss, tucked away as it is at the back of Isetan's supermarket near the alcohol section. It's almost always busy, so you usually have to wait for a seat. Once you've settled in, though, you can enjoy premium sake by the glass or bottle as the knowledgeable bartender talks you through the tasting notes. If you've been here for a while, and it's quiet, the staff will sometimes allow you to buy a bottle of sake from the supermarket to drink at the bar instead. ⊠ *B1 Isetan Scotts, 350 Orchard Rd., Orchard* ✛ *Inside Isetan supermarket* ☎ *6733–1111* Ⓜ *Orchard.*

KPO

BARS/PUBS | Once the Killiney Post Office, this Orchard Road landmark is now a spacious two-level indoor and outdoor bar with a great ambience in the evening. Balcony tables upstairs offer views of the traffic whizzing by, while inside the mix of raw concrete walls and steel architecture contrasts with the chill tunes that usually play, often mixed by a local DJ. ⊠ *1 Killiney Rd., Orchard* ☎ *6733–3648* ⊕ *www.imaginings.com.sg* ☞ *Closed Sun.* Ⓜ *Somerset.*

★ Manhattan Bar

BARS/PUBS | Recalling the golden age of New York, with a menu that takes you on a journey of cocktail history, this dark and sultry cocktail bar in the Regent Hotel offers more than 150 whiskeys. It's also the first in the world to craft Negronis with ingredients that have been solera-aged—and right in the hotel's own 100-barrel rickhouse. No wonder this has been named one of the top five bars in the world. ⊠ *Regent Hotel, 1 Cuscaden Rd., Level 2, Orchard* ☎ *6725–3377* ⊕ *www.regenthotels.com* Ⓜ *Orchard.*

Muddy Murphy's

BARS/PUBS | Inside Claymore Connect is this Irish pub famed for its wine-and-cheese promotions; Sunday Roast lunches; live Irish-Celtic bands; and beverage selection that includes whiskeys, draft Kilkenny Ale, and Guinness Stout. The bar was actually built in Dublin in 1996 before being reassembled in Singapore. It's one of the most popular spots on Orchard Road to catch live sports, with huge TVs showing rugby, football, boxing, tennis, and more. It also has live-music performances on weekends and Thursday quiz nights. ⊠ *#01–02 to 05 Claymore Connect, 442 Orchard Rd., Orchard* ☎ *6735–0400* ⊕ *muddymurphys.com* Ⓜ *Orchard.*

★ No. 5 Emerald Hill Cocktail Bar

BARS/PUBS | Pretty red lanterns hang above you at this chic cocktail bar inside a restored two-story Paranakan terraced house. It reflects a design style of the early-20th-century Straits-Chinese shophouses. There are a variety of enticing cocktails on offer plus an impressive selection of spirits, shooters, beers, and mocktails. You can listen to live blues and jazz while shooting some pool; sample the bar snacks, which include pizza and chicken wings;

or just sit back and enjoy the ambience. ✉ *5 Emerald Hill Rd., Orchard* ☎ *6732–0818* ⊕ *www.emerald-hill.com* Ⓜ *Somerset.*

The Other Room

BARS/PUBS | Recognized as one of Asia's 50 best bars, The Other Room is a moodily-lit speakeasy where mixologists sling cocktails until the early hours. The allure is its location: hidden behind a largely unmarked black door inside the Marriott Hotel. It's small and snug inside, so it's better to reserve ahead if you want to secure a table, especially if you want to try the classic Reuben sandwich, the plates of fresh oysters, or another of the dishes on offer. The cocktails are the real stars, though, with each one more enticing than the last—from the Old Fashioned to the Reversed gin and tonic. ✉ *Marriott Tang Plaza Hotel, 320 Orchard Rd. #01–05, Orchard* ☎ *6100–7778* ⊕ *www.theotherroom.com.sg* Ⓜ *Orchard.*

👜 Shopping

Shopping is a favorite Singaporean pastime, and no where in the country can you get a better shopping fix than along Orchard Road. The 2 km (1.25-mile) stretch of road is home to a seemingly countless number of malls, each one filled with store after shiny store promising a whole world of new belongings.

Antiques of the Orient

ANTIQUES/COLLECTIBLES | Head to this long-established store inside the Tanglin Shopping Centre for an interesting selection of vintage Southeast Asian artifacts and collectibles, including original books, photos, maps, and prints. ✉ *#02–40 Tanglin Shopping Centre, 19 Tanglin Rd., Orchard* ☎ *6734–9351* ⊕ *www.aoto.com.sg* Ⓜ *Orchard.*

★ Books Kinokuniya

BOOKS/STATIONERY | One of the largest bookstores in Southeast Asia—and *the* largest in Singapore—has separate fiction and nonfiction sections that will make bookworms want to empty their wallets and fill up their suitcases. It would be easy to spend an entire day browsing the maze of shelves with books on history, travel, poetry, adventure, politics, and so much more. ✉ *Takashimaya Shopping Centre Ngee Ann City, 391 Orchard Rd., Orchard* ☎ *6737–5021* ⊕ *kinokuniya.com.sg* Ⓜ *Orchard.*

Club 21

CLOTHING | The trendy fashion retailer Club 21 offers sharp men's and women's clothing lines from such well-known designers as Marc Jacobs, Stella McCartney, and Alexander McQueen. Naturally, the price tags match the big-brand names. There are several other branches around Singapore. ✉ #01–02 Four Seasons Hotel Shopping Arcade, 190 Orchard Blvd., Orchard ☎ 6304–1385 ⊕ sg. club21global.com/club21.

Coloc Tailor

CLOTHING | Need a stylish, well-fitting suit in a hurry? This long-time Singaporean clothing merchant is one of the few tailors in town who can whip up a high-quality suit in less than 24 hours after taking your measurements. Custom-made dresses are also an option. ✉ Mandarin Hotel Gallery, 333A Orchard Rd., #03–07, Orchard ☎ 6338–9767 ⊕ www.coloc.com.sg ☉ Sun. by appointment M Orchard.

★ Daiso

SPECIALTY STORES | If you're looking for a sushi-shaped keyring, socks for your chair legs, a pen shaped like a cat, a set of fairy lights, or a hat decorated with strawberries, then Daiso is the place for you. This department store hailing from Japan sells household gadgets and knickknacks of all types, with each item costing just $2. There are now 20 stores across Singapore, including one in the basement of Orchard's ION Mall, and each offers bargain after bargain. ✉ #B4–47 ION Mall, 2 Orchard Turn, Orchard ☎ 6634–7801 ⊕ www.daisosingapore.com.sg.

★ Don Don Donki

CONVENIENCE/GENERAL STORES | This Japanese shopping wonderland overwhelms the senses with its huge and eclectic inventory in a mishmash of vibrant colors and the "Don Don Donki" jingle that it plays endlessly (it's guaranteed to stick in your head for the rest of the day). Expect everything from hand fans to Japanese bin bags, ceramic bowls to rubber chickens. At the Orchard Central store, there is also an excellent food section, with freshly prepared bento lunches available to buy and eat at the nearby Don Don Donki bar and seating area. ✉ B1 & B2 Orchard Central, 181 Orchard Rd., Orchard ☎ 6834–4311 ⊕ www.dondondonki.sg M Somerset.

Escentials

PERFUME/COSMETICS | This shop sells rare and upscale fragrances and beauty products from more than 30 leading international brands, including Acqua Di Parma. Personal makeovers and beauty classes are available by appointment. There's an additional outlet in Tangs, another mall on Orchard Road. ✉ #03–02/05 Paragon, 290 Orchard Rd., Orchard ☎ 6737–2478 ⊕ www.escentials. com.sg M Orchard.

Far East Plaza

SHOPPING CENTERS/MALLS | Not to be confused with the nearby mall Far East Shopping Centre, Far East Plaza is a five-story mall with many stores peddling used books, trendy street wear, and much more. Although it's on the older side, it's still a popular Orchard-area hangout for local teens. Of course, it wouldn't be a Singapore mall if there weren't also dozens of restaurants, snack counters, and cafés. ⊠ # 05–134, 14 Scotts Rd., Orchard ☎ 6732–6266 ⊕ www.fareastplaza.com.sg Ⓜ Orchard.

Forum The Shopping Mall

SHOPPING CENTERS/MALLS | Forum is one of the more family-oriented shopping malls on Orchard, with more than ten kids' clothing outlets and a variety of children's learning and fitness centers. There's also a delicious Cantonese dumpling restaurant called Jade Palace alongside a dozen restaurants and coffee shops. ⊠ 583 Orchard Rd., Orchard ☎ 6732–2469 ⊕ www.forumtheshoppingmall.com.sg Ⓜ Orchard.

Francis Cheong

CLOTHING | Add a little glamour to your wardrobe with a gown fit for the red carpet from the award-winning Singaporean designer Francis Cheong. High-end jewelry and other accessories suited to fashionable finery are also available. ⊠ Delphi Orchard, 442 Orchard Rd., #02–09, Orchard ☎ 6734–9898 ⊕ www.francis-cheong.com Ⓜ Orchard.

The Hour Glass

JEWELRY/ACCESSORIES | One of the many upscale boutique jewelers located in Takashimaya, The Hour Glass carries designer watches from more than 50 international luxury brands, including Hublot, Omega, and Rolex. ⊠ #01–02 Ngee Ann City, 391 Orchard Rd., Orchard ☎ 6734–2420 ⊕ www.thehourglass.com Ⓜ Orchard.

★ ION Orchard

SHOPPING CENTERS/MALLS | With a bold, sci-fi-inspired facade and a 56th-floor viewing deck replete with high-powered telescopes, this is not your everyday megamall, even by Singapore's lofty standards. In addition to local boutiques and more than 300 luxury shops, you'll find a cavernous food hall and a gourmet supermarket. But that's still not all: the fourth floor has the 3,640-square-foot ION Art Gallery, which regularly exhibits works by local and international artists. ⊠ 2 Orchard Turn, Orchard ☎ 6238–8228 ⊕ www.ionorchard.com/en Ⓜ Orchard.

Justmen's

CLOTHING | You'll find a number of men's and women's tailors in the Tanglin Shopping Centre, but Justmen's has a well-earned reputation as being one of the best. ⌧ *#01–36/39, 19 Tanglin Rd., Orchard* ☎ *6737–4800* ⊕ *www.justmens.com.sg* ⊗ *Closed Sun.* Ⓜ *Orchard.*

Loang & Noi

JEWELRY/ACCESSORIES | Oversized, gem-encrusted pendants, bracelets, rings, and other glitzy wearables are on offer at this shop, one of a number of high-end jewelers in the upscale Paragon shopping center. ⌧ *#01–23 Paragon, 290 Orchard Rd., Orchard* ☎ *6732–7218* ⊕ *www.loang-noi.com.sg* Ⓜ *Orchard.*

Lucky Plaza

SHOPPING CENTERS/MALLS | An old Orchard Road mainstay that now seems somewhat out of a place among the area's more modern and fashionable megamalls, Lucky Plaza is packed with six floors and a basement full of trinkets, clothing, jewelry, luggage, fashion accessories, and electronics—some of questionable authenticity. On the weekend, it's packed with locals looking for a bargain. ⌧ *304 Orchard Rd., Orchard* ☎ *6235–3294* ⊕ *www.luckyplaza. com.sg* Ⓜ *Orchard.*

★ Muji

HOUSEHOLD ITEMS/FURNITURE | There are four branches of this minimalist Japanese lifestyle chain on Orchard Road, but the flagship is in Plaza Singapura mall. Muji has a range of high-quality Japanese products, from sleek and simple dresses to artisanal lamps, portable aroma diffusers, and folding floor chairs—each item reflecting Japan's traditional Zen philosophy of natural simplicity. The flagship branch also offers a customized embroidery service for any textiles you purchase, with letters and graphics starting from $3. ⌧ *#01–10 16 Plaza Singapura, 68 Orchard Rd., Orchard* ☎ *6264–5838* ⊕ *www.muji.com/sg* Ⓜ *Dhoby Ghaut.*

★ Ngee Ann City

SHOPPING CENTERS/MALLS | The Japanese department store Takashimaya dominates this gigantic shopping mall, but there are also more than 130 other shops and dining outlets packed into the somewhat outdated building. The basement food center is fun for snacking on everything from Hokkaido-style ice cream and Italian-style gelato to marinated meats and freshly baked breads, and there's also, of course, a large food court if you're craving something more substantial. Books Kinokuniya—a must-visit—is one of the biggest bookstores in Southeast Asia, and special sales on clothing, housewares, and other goods are regularly held in the basement-level square. ⊠ *391 Orchard Rd., Orchard* ☎ *6506–0461* ⊕ *www.ngeeanncity.com.sg* Ⓜ *Orchard.*

Opera Gallery

ART GALLERIES | Expect works from some of the world's most-renowned contemporary artists at Opera Gallery, one of a dozen global branches of this elite Parisian art dealer. ⊠ *#02–16 ION Orchard, 2 Orchard Turn, Orchard* ☎ *6735–2618* ⊕ *www.operagallery.com* Ⓜ *Orchard.*

Palais Renaissance

SHOPPING CENTERS/MALLS | Though it has lost some of its more prominent tenants in recent years, this extravagantly marbled shopping emporium still features a handful of recommended hair salons and the much-praised international restaurant PS.Café. ⊠ *390 Orchard Rd., Orchard* ☎ *6737–6992* ⊕ *www.palais.sg* Ⓜ *Orchard.*

Paragon

SHOPPING CENTERS/MALLS | The glossy Paragon is worth a stroll, whether you're just window shopping or on the hunt for high-end fashions, jewelry, and accessories at boutiques such as Gucci, Ermenegildo Zegna, Salvatore Ferragamo, or Prada. Marks & Spencer, Metro, and Muji all have outlets here, plus there are branches of popular chain restaurants like Din Tai Fung, Nando's, and Ya Kun Kaya Toast. ⊠ *290 Orchard Rd., Orchard* ☎ *6738–5535* ⊕ *www.paragon.com.sg* Ⓜ *Orchard.*

The Planet Traveller

SHOES/LUGGAGE/LEATHER GOODS | Upgrade your banged-up bags at The Planet Traveller, which carries backpacks, full-sized suitcases, and carry-on bags from Eagle Creek, Victorinox, and other high-quality labels. Additional outlets are at Marina Square and Changi International Airport Terminal 3. ⊠ *#04–15/16 Paragon, 290 Orchard Rd., Orchard* ☎ *6732–5172* ⊕ *www.theplanettraveller.com* Ⓜ *Orchard.*

Plaza Singapura

SHOPPING CENTERS/MALLS | Need an air-conditioned escape from the afternoon heat? Daiso and Marks & Spencer department stores, a Golden Village movie theater, a supermarket, and more than 50 food outlets are among the tenants of this enormous nine-level building. ⊠ *68 Orchard Rd., Orchard* ☎ *6332–9248* ⊕ *www.capitaland.com/sg* Ⓜ *Dhoby Ghaut.*

Robinsons The Heeren

SHOPPING CENTERS/MALLS | Now a household name, this enormous department store first opened in Singapore in 1858. It spans six floors and 150,000 square feet and sells some of the most sought-after brands and labels in Singapore. On Black Friday, thousands of Singaporeans camp outside the night before ito get to Robinson's bargains first, whether fashion, furniture, or kitchenware. Outside of the sales, prices can be a little steep, but the quality is always good. ⊠ *260 Orchard Rd., Orchard* ☎ *6735–8838* ⊕ *www.robinsons.com.sg* Ⓜ *Orchard.*

Scape

SHOPPING CENTERS/MALLS | This is the place to drop off teens for a few hours while you shop your way through Orchard Road's manifold megamalls. Clothes and accessories from up-and-coming designers can be found in the Scape Underground basement space, while upstairs legions of cool kids browse streetwear and guitar shops, hang out in gaming centers and karaoke rooms, or snack at fast-food chains. The main attraction, though, is the 32,000-square-foot outdoor Somerset Skate Park, where kids whiz around on skateboards and scooters. There's also a movie theater next door, at Cathay Cineleisure Orchard. ⊠ *#04–01, 2 Orchard Link, Orchard* ☎ *6521–6565* ⊕ *www.scape.sg* Ⓜ *Orchard.*

Scotts Square

SHOPPING CENTERS/MALLS | One of Singapore's best places for close-to-haute couture at affordable prices is Scotts Square. The mall has a basement food court, plus a changing roster of farmer's markets, craft fairs, and other offerings to keep shoppers entertained. Check the website for the latest events. ⊠ *6–8 Scotts Rd., Orchard* ⊕ *www.scottssquareretail.com* Ⓜ *Orchard.*

The Shopping Gallery Hilton Singapore

SHOPPING CENTERS/MALLS | High-end fashion from some of the world's most recognized designers is the focus at the Hilton's triple-level shopping center. The latest collections from Stella McCartney, Paul Smith, and Alexander Wang are all here; take the underground passage to the Four Seasons Hotel Singapore for more options. ⊠ *The Shopping Gallery Hilton, 581 Orchard Rd., Orchard* ☎ *6737–2233* ⊕ *www.hiltonshoppinggallery.com* Ⓜ *Orchard.*

Tanglin Mall

SHOPPING CENTERS/MALLS | Not to be confused with Tanglin Shopping Centre or Tangs, this aging four-level mall tends to get lost in the Orchard Road shuffle, given that it's tucked away at the far west end of Orchard Road. It nevertheless remains popular with local expats thanks to its Tasty Food Court, as well as the somewhat upscale Tanglin Market Place, which sells a fine selection of international foods. ⊠ *163 Tanglin Rd., Orchard* ☎ *6736–4922* ⊕ *www.tanglinmall.com.sg* Ⓜ *Orchard.*

Tanglin Shopping Centre

SHOPPING CENTERS/MALLS | This is a recommended first stop if you're in the market for Asian antiques or Persian carpets. Antiques of the Orient, which deals in vintage charts, maps, and other antiquities, provides a unique shopping experience, plus there are more than 10 tailors here specializing in custom-made suits and alterations. ⊠ *19 Tanglin Rd., Orchard* ☎ *6737–0849* ⊕ *www.tanglinsc.com* Ⓜ *Orchard.*

Tangs

DEPARTMENT STORES | Tangs is a much-loved department store selling all the major brands. Its basement is particularly good for household items, from Le Creuset pans to the latest coffee machines—less practical for short-term visitors to Singapore but a great place to shop if you plan to stick around a little longer. ⊠ *310 Orchard Rd., Orchard* ☎ *6737–5500* ⊕ *www.tangs.com.sg* Ⓜ *Orchard.*

★ 313@Somerset

SHOPPING CENTERS/MALLS | One of Orchard Road's best-loved megamalls contains eight levels of shopping and dining distractions. Key fashion tenants include UNIQLO, Zara, and Timberland, though there are plenty of tech, jewelery, and home-ware stores, too. Along the mall's open-air Discovery Walk is a clutch of buzzing bars and restaurants, including a branch of the ever-busy Brotzeit German Bier Bar & Restaurant and the JiBiru Japanese Craft Beer Bar, which deals in local and imported microbrews. ⊠ *313 Orchard Rd., Orchard* ☎ *6496–9313* ⊕ *www.313somerset.com.sg* Ⓜ *Somerset.*

TianPo Jewellery

JEWELRY/ACCESSORIES | The Orchard Road location of this jeweler is the most convenient of the four branches it has in Singapore. Here, you can access the new collections that are released every few months. TianPo is also the island's exclusive provider of such international labels as Yvel and Hearts on Fire. ⊠ *#01–43/46 Centrepoint, 176 Orchard Rd., Orchard* ☎ *6235–1889* ⊕ *www.tianpo. com* Ⓜ *Orchard.*

Tokyu Hands

HOUSEHOLD ITEMS/FURNITURE | This quirky Japanese lifestyle store stocks all kinds of made-in-Japan products, from cutesy stationery and notebooks to pretty bento boxes and high-quality kitchenware. This is the kind of shop you visit to browse but end up leaving with bags full things you didn't know existed and can't live without. There are two branches in Singapore: one in Orchard and one in Suntec City. ⊠ *B1–07 Somerset 313 Mall, 181 Orchard Rd., Orchard* ☎ *6834–3755* ⊕ *www.tokyu-hands.com.sg* Ⓜ *Somerset.*

Wisma Atria

SHOPPING CENTERS/MALLS | The Japanese department store Isetan anchors the five floors of dining and retail revelry at Wisma Atria. There's also a fourth-floor Food Republic, which offers more than 20 hawker-style food stalls with kitschy, retro design highlighted by mosaic tile floors and vintage bric-a-brac along the walls and the dining area. ⊠ *Wisma Atria, Level 1, 435 Orchard Rd., Orchard* ☎ *6235–2103* ⊕ *www.wismaonline.com* Ⓜ *Orchard.*

🏃 Activities

★ Cosmic Bowling at K Bowling Club

BOWLING | "A bowling experience like no other" is what this venue promises at its cosmic-themed alley. Neon lights twirl, music blares, the drinks keep flowing, and the balls keep rolling. If you're not in the mood for bowling, there are also darts machines, karaoke booths, arcade games, and more—enough to keep you entertained all evening. ⊠ *#03–27 313@Somerset, 313 Orchard Rd., Orchard* ☎ *6737–5313* ⊕ *kbowlingclub.com* Ⓜ *Somerset.*

Remède Spa

SPA—SIGHT | From its eucalyptus steam room to its customized massages, the decadent spa at the St. Regis Singapore has the revitalizing experiences every traveler needs after a long day of shopping on Orchard. ⊠ *The St. Regis Singapore, 29 Tanglin Rd., Orchard* ☎ *6506–6876* ⊕ *www.remedespasingapore.com* Ⓜ *Orchard.*

Yoga at COMO Shambhala Urban Escape

AEROBICS/YOGA | Work up a sweat at this perfumed spa and yoga studio, a holistic wellness center that caters to some of Singapore's most affluent clientele. Tucked away on Level 6 of the Delfi Orchard, it's small, but it has an extensive range of classes, from Reformer Pilates, using props and machines, to Suspend Yoga, where you perform the usual yoga moves suspended in a harness. Sipping free ginger tea in the cozy lounge area is a relaxing way to finish a tough class. The center also offers excellent massages. ⊠ *#06–01/02, 402 Orchard Rd., Orchard* ☎ *6304–3552* ⊕ *www. comoshambhala.com* Ⓜ *Orchard.*

EASTERN SINGAPORE

WITH CHANGI, GEYLANG SERAI, AND KATONG/JOO CHIAT

Updated by
Audrey Phoon

👁 Sights	🍴 Restaurants	🛏 Hotels	🛍 Shopping	🌐 Nightlife
★★★★☆	★★★★★	★★★☆☆	★★☆☆☆	★★☆☆☆

NEIGHBORHOOD SNAPSHOT

TOP EXPERIENCES

■ **Jewel Changi Airport:** The world's largest indoor waterfall, an indoor forest, and more than 280 shops and eateries are here, under a gigantic glass dome.

■ **East Coast Road:** A stroll down this street in Katong, with its brightly colored shophouses, is an immersive introduction to Singapore's Peranakan culture.

■ **Private dining:** Some of the best food in Singapore is served in private homes, where you can immerse yourself in the local culture and flavors.

■ **Seafood at sunset:** Dinner at East Coast Seafood Centre is a memorable affair, as is fishing for your dinner at Smith Marine.

■ **Beaches and parks:** Picnic in the sun at Pasir Ris Park; spot sea turtles at Changi Beach, or go biking at East Coast Park.

GETTING HERE

The airport and Joo Chiat are easily accessible via the MRT, and buses serve the rest of the area. Paya Lebar, on the Circle Line (yellow) and East West Line (green), and Eunos, on the East West Line (green), all stop along Sims Avenue in Geylang, about a mile north of Katong. Joo Chiat Road and East Coast Road, in the heart of Katong, are accessible via buses 10, 14, and 16. Come 2023, the area will be served by a new Thomson–East Coast MRT line.

PLANNING YOUR TIME

Plan a day in Eastern Singapore when you arrive or depart from nearby Changi Airport, devoting a few hours to Katong for lunch. Weekends are busiest.

QUICK BITES

■ **328 Katong Laksa.** At this cult-favorite cafeteria—Singapore's most well-known for laksa—you can tuck into rich, spicy, coconutty bowls of noodles. ⊠ *51 East Coast Rd., Katong, Singapore 428770 Buses: 10, 12, 32, 36, 40*

■ **Sinpopo Brand Restaurant.** It feels like the '60s in this retro cafe, which serves up reinvented local specialities and baked goods, like the Gula Melaka Cake made with palm sugar. ⊠ *458 Joo Chiat Rd., Joo Chiat* ⊕ *www. sinpopo.com Buses: 16, 36, 48*

■ **Alibabar The Hawker Bar.** Several noteworthy stalls can be found at this tiny food court, including Yong Huat and its delicious pork-and-prawn Hokkien noodles. ⊠ *125 East Coast Rd., Katong* ⊕ *www.alibabar. com.sg Buses: 16, 36, 48*

Eastern Singapore may be the smallest of Singapore's five regions, but it's the most densely populated. It's also home to the country's two airports, Changi International Airport (a destination in itself) and the military-use Paya Lebar Air Base, with economic activity driven by aviation and manufacturing. While the region isn't typically on first-time tourist hit lists because there aren't any big monuments or headline attractions, there is perhaps no better place to immerse yourself in true Singaporean culture and authentic local cuisine.

The pretty Katong neighborhood, the beating heart of Singapore's Peranakan and Eurasian culture, has the largest cluster of preserved Peranakan shophouses from the 1800s. Changi, at the easternmost tip of the island, is home to both the state-of-the-art Changi International Airport (with its newly opened retail, dining, and entertainment extension, Jewel) as well as the country's most rustic throwbacks: Changi Village and the island of Pulau Ubin, which you'll find in the Side Trips chapter. And a trip to Geylang Serai, the home of Singapore's Malay community, affords a living, breathing look into the rich Singaporean Malay culture. For foodies in particular, Eastern Singapore is a must-visit: many of the best hawker, Peranakan, and Malay bites are here, though most places are scattered throughout the area and may require more than one trip. Three of Singapore's most popular beaches—East Coast Park, Pasir Ris Park, and Changi Beach—are also in Eastern Singapore and provide a breezy breather from the urban landscape.

Changi

The northeastern section of Singapore is seldom visited by out-of-towners, but it has some worthwhile temples, beaches, and the showstopping Changi International Airport, which has been called one of the best airports in the world. If you have a long layover or are staying in the area to catch a flight, there are certainly a few good options to fill your time. The area is also a jumping off point for trips to the island Pulau Ubin.

Sights

★ Changi International Airport

STORE/MALL | FAMILY | Singapore's slick airport hasn't just won multiple awards for World's Best Airport—it's also been named one of the world's most outstanding retail real-estate projects. And it's no wonder: The sprawling four-terminal complex houses hundreds of stores and restaurants, many of which can't be found elsewhere. If shopping and eating—the country's most popular pastimes—aren't your thing, there are plenty of other draws, like the **Butterfly Garden**, a **Canopy Park** (where you can walk across bouncy nets suspended across the top floor), and the **Rain Vortex**, a seven-story (and the world's tallest) indoor waterfall. ⊠ *Changi International Airport, 70 Airport Blvd., Changi* ☎ *6595–6868* ⊕ *www.changiairport.com.*

Changi Sree Ramar Temple

RELIGIOUS SITE | This breezy, tranquil Hindu temple by the sea is the only one of its kind in Southeast Asia devoted to the Hindu god Rama. Interestingly, it also serves as the spiritual center for many non-Hindus living in Eastern Singapore, because it houses Buddha and Goddess of Mercy idols. ⊠ *Changi Sree Ramar Temple, 51 Changi Village Rd., Changi.*

Loyang Tua Pek Kong Temple

RELIGIOUS SITE | Tens of thousands of devotees visit this sprawling multi-religious temple every month to pay their respects to the Buddhist, Taoist, and Hindu deities and worship in the Muslim shrine here. Elaborately carved patterns on the ceilings demarcate the different areas in the temple, which is especially popular with those seeking wealth and good fortune. During the Nine Emperor Gods Festival in the ninth lunar month (from late October to early November), the temple takes on a carnival atmosphere as some 100,000 Taoist pilgrims descend on it, bringing exotic foods, flowers, joss sticks, and candles as offerings for their prayers. ⊠ *Loyang Tua Pek Kong Temple, 20 Loyang Way, Changi* ⊕ *www.lytpk.org.sg.*

Beaches

Changi Beach Park

BEACH—SIGHT | One of Singapore's oldest and quietest coastal parks, Changi Beach is a two-mile stretch of sand dotted with coconut trees and public barbecue pits. Although its tranquility belies its dark history—this was one of the main sites of the Sook Ching massacre during the Japanese Occupation—today the area is a popular spot for couples as well as fishing and photography enthusiasts. **Amenities:** food and drink; toilets. **Best for:** solitude; swimming; walking. ⊠ *Nicoll Dr., Changi* ⊕ *Near Changi Village* ☎ *6471–7300* ⊕ *www.nparks.gov.sg.*

Pasir Ris Park

BEACH—SIGHT | **FAMILY** | This green lung within the Pasir Ris residential area is a popular picnic spot with families, thanks to its kid-friendly facilities that include one of Singapore's biggest (and free) outdoor playgrounds. The park is also home to a 15-acre mangrove forest, which you can explore via several walking trails, a wheelchair-accessible boardwalk, and a three-story birdwatching tower. **Amenities:** food and drink; parking; toilets. **Best for:** solitude; swimming; walking. ⊠ *Pasir Ris Central, Changi* ☎ *6471–7300* ⊕ *www.nparks.gov.sg* Ⓜ *Pasir Ris.*

🍽 Restaurants

Beauty In The Pot

$$$ | **CHINESE** | **FAMILY** | Hotpot meals are a big part of modern local culture, as the communal dining experience is considered a convenient way to celebrate special occasions with family and friends. Homegrown chain Beauty In The Pot is one of the country's most popular, serving up tasty collagen-infused broth into which you can dip gourmet cuts of meat, handmade noodles, and other ingredients. **Known for:** collagen broth with beauty benefits; top hotpot meals; excellent service. ⓢ *Average main: S$50* ⊠ *Jewel Changi Airport, 78 Airport Blvd, #B2–224, Changi* ☎ *6242–5131* ⊕ *www.paradisegp.com/brand-beauty-in-the-pot* Ⓜ *Changi Airport.*

Little Island Brewing Co

$$ | **INTERNATIONAL** | **FAMILY** | This laid-back, open-air microbrewery is a rare gem in the quiet Changi Village area, serving up house brews with whimsical, psychedelic labels alongside hearty roasts and weekend brunches. Pour yourself a glass from the DIY draft counter and sit at a table under the fairy lights—it's the perfect place to while an evening away. **Known for:** tasty craft beers; laid-back vibe; good location. ⓢ *Average main: S$20* ⊠ *6 Changi Village Rd., #01–01/02, Changi* ☎ *6543–9100* ⊕ *libc.co.*

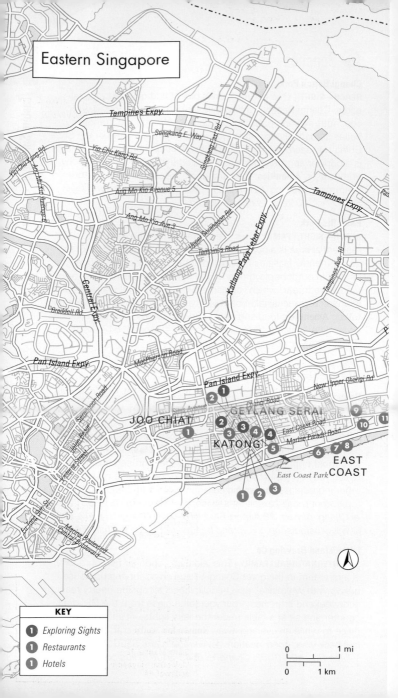

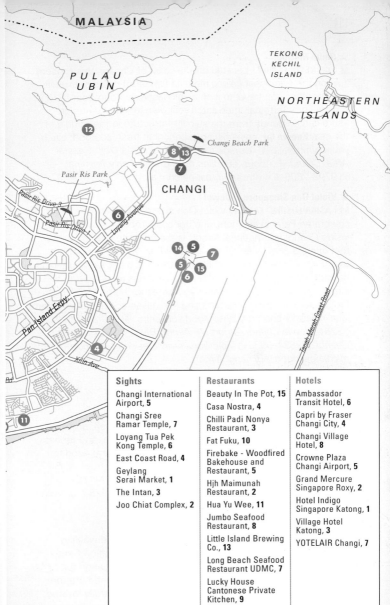

Sights

Changi International Airport, **5**

Changi Sree Ramar Temple, **7**

Loyang Tua Pek Kong Temple, **6**

East Coast Road, **4**

Geylang Serai Market, **1**

The Intan, **3**

Joo Chiat Complex, **2**

Restaurants

Beauty In The Pot, **15**

Casa Nostra, **4**

Chilli Padi Nonya Restaurant, **3**

Fat Fuku, **10**

Firebake - Woodfired Bakehouse and Restaurant, **5**

Hjh Maimunah Restaurant, **2**

Hua Yu Wee, **11**

Jumbo Seafood Restaurant, **8**

Little Island Brewing Co., **13**

Long Beach Seafood Restaurant UDMC, **7**

Lucky House Cantonese Private Kitchen, **9**

PS. Cafe East Coast Park, **6**

Sin Huat Eating House, **1**

Smith Marine, **12**

Violet Oon Singapore at Jewel, **14**

Hotels

Ambassador Transit Hotel, **6**

Capri by Fraser Changi City, **4**

Changi Village Hotel, **8**

Crowne Plaza Changi Airport, **5**

Grand Mercure Singapore Roxy, **2**

Hotel Indigo Singapore Katong, **1**

Village Hotel Katong, **3**

YOTELAIR Changi, **7**

★ Smith Marine

$$ | **CHINESE** | **FAMILY** | Located off the coast of Changi, this modern spin on the traditional *kelong* (floating fish farm) doles out meals to remember. You travel to it on an old-fashioned bumboat from Changi Ferry Terminal, then catch your own lunch or dinner in "sure-catch" ponds from the ship-like structure in the middle of the sea. **Known for:** novel dining experience; fresh seafood; catch-your-own meals. $ *Average main: S$30* ⊠ *Pulau Ubin Coastal Area, Changi* ✛ *About 3.6 miles from Changi Ferry Terminal* ☎ *9792–7609* ⊕ *www.smithmarine.com.sg.*

★ Violet Oon Singapore at Jewel

$$ | **ASIAN FUSION** | **FAMILY** | Violet Oon is one of Singapore's most celebrated Peranakan chefs, and her eponymous restaurant inside Changi International Airport is the only one with a terrace that offers a direct view of the airport's Rain Vortex, the world's tallest indoor waterfall. In addition to treats like her signature (and delightfully tangy) dry laksa, the restaurant has an open grill, a long bar, and a retail area where you can stock up on Oon's beautifully packaged pineapple tarts and Peranakan cookies. **Known for:** local celebrity chef; dry laksa; food souvenirs. $ *Average main: S$25* ⊠ *Jewel Changi Airport, 78 Airport Blvd., #01–205/206, Changi* ☎ *9834–9935* ⊕ *violetoon.com/violet-oon-singapore-at-jewel-changi-airport* Ⓜ *Changi Airport.*

🛏 Hotels

Ambassador Transit Hotel

$$ | **HOTEL** | Rooms at this airport hotel are clean, fresh, and basic, and include use of the swimming pool, sauna, and fitness center. **Pros:** includes use of swimming pool and gym; good for early flights and layovers; bargain prices. **Cons:** basic rooms; far from the city; little atmosphere. $ *Rooms from: S$141* ⊠ *Changi International Airport, Airport Blvd., Changi* ☎ *6507–9788,* ⊕ *www.harilelahospitality.com* ↴ *171 rooms* ⦿ *No meals.*

Capri By Fraser Changi City

$$ | **HOTEL** | Located within Changi Business Park and walking distance to the Singapore Expo Convention & Exhibition Centre is this modern apartment-hotel. **Pros:** convenient location for business travelers working in the East; free high-speed Internet; rooms have kitchenettes for cooking. **Cons:** not centrally located; area has little personality; limited dining options nearby that aren't in a mall. $ *Rooms from: S$154* ⊠ *Changi City Point, 3 Changi Business Park Central 1, Changi* ☎ *6933–9833* ⊕ *singapore.capribyfraser.com* ↴ *313 rooms* ⦿ *No meals* Ⓜ *Expo.*

Changi Village Hotel

$$ | **HOTEL** | It's only 10 minutes from the airport and near many attractions, including a beach, boat rides to other islands, cafés, pubs, shops, golf facilities, and a museum; free shuttle buses are available to the airport and downtown. **Pros:** near the airport; infinity pool; a quiet hideaway. **Cons:** far from the city; limited dining and retail options nearby; inaccessible via public transport. $ *Rooms from: S$128* ⊠ *1 Netheravon Rd., Changi* ☎ *6379–7111* ⊕ *www.villagehotels.asia/en* ↘ *380 rooms* ◎ *No meals.*

Crowne Plaza Changi Airport

$$$ | **HOTEL** | **FAMILY** | What may be the world's best airport hotel has many (soundproof) rooms that face the runway, as well as more tranquil terrace rooms that lead directly to the lushly landscaped pool. **Pros:** connected to the airport and MRT station; comfortable rooms; unique views of the runway. **Cons:** not centrally located; area isn't interesting; no free in-room WiFi. $ *Rooms from: S$300* ⊠ *Changi International Airport, 75 Airport Blvd., #01–01, Changi* ☎ *6823–5300* ⊕ *changiairport.crowneplaza.com* ↘ *320 rooms* ◎ *No meals* Ⓜ *Changi Airport.*

YOTELAIR Changi

$$ | **HOTEL** | Opened in 2019, this airport hotel offers modern, windowless cabins by the hour as well as day and overnight rates. **Pros:** close to the airport and shops in Jewel Changi Airport; brand new; free Wi-Fi and use of gym. **Cons:** windowless cabins; small rooms; a tad pricey. $ *Rooms from: S$175* ⊠ *Jewel Changi Airport, 78 Airport Blvd., #04–280, Changi* ☎ *6407–7888* ⊕ *www. yotel.com* ↘ *130 rooms* ◎ *No meals* Ⓜ *Changi Airport.*

● Shopping

Changi City Point

OUTLET/DISCOUNT STORES | **FAMILY** | One of the rare outlet malls in Singapore, Changi City Point houses more than 140 shops, including the factory stores of big-name sports and fashion brands like Nike, Adidas, Clarks, and Esprit. The landscaped rooftop garden of the three-story mall is a great place to take a breather in between shopping, and the top floor also houses a free playground and tree-house trail for kids. ⊠ *5 Changi Business Park Central 1, Changi* ✥ *Inside Changi Business Park* ☎ *6511–1088* ⊕ *www. changicitypoint.com.sg* Ⓜ *Expo.*

★ Jewel Changi Airport

SHOPPING CENTERS/MALLS | **FAMILY** | This sprawling 280-store complex is a one-stop shop for top Singapore labels, local gourmet snacks, and more than a handful of first-in-Southeast Asia brands.

Highlights include In Good Company for sleek, minimalist womenswear; Pazzion for chic, cheerful shoes (this flagship boutique also houses the first-of-its-kind Pazzion Cafe); and the wildly popular Irvins Salted Egg snacks. If you're on your way in or out of Singapore, leave ample time for browsing. ⊠ *Changi International Airport, 78 Airport Blvd., Changi* ⊹ *Connected to Terminal 1* ☎ *6956–9898* ⊕ *www.jewelchangiairport.com* Ⓜ *Changi Airport.*

m)phosis

CLOTHING | There are a few outlets of this trendy women's clothing boutique across Singapore. With all the chic handbags, footwear, and stylish tops and skirts available, you'll have no trouble pulling together a fashionable, reasonably priced outfit. ⊠ *#01–05 Century Square, 2 Tampines Central 5, Changi* ☎ *6781–0037* ⊕ *www. mphosis.sg* Ⓜ *Tampines.*

Activities

In addition to shopping, having a picnic on Changi's beach, or fishing for your dinner, you can take a half day or full day trip to Pulau Ubin (see Side Trips chapter), an island just off the coast.

Free Singapore Tour

WALKING TOURS | If your layover at Changi International Airport is more than 5½ hours but less than 24 hours, check your bags at left luggage, and head to Terminal 2 or 3's Level 2 to sign up for a free English-language walking tour of the city (you can also pre-book on the airport's website). There are three 2½-hour options: the Jewel Tour, which takes you to the airport's jaw-dropping Jewel development, housing the Rain Vortex, Forest Valley, Canopy Park, and Singapore Coffee Museum; the Heritage Tour, which takes you into the city to see top neighborhoods including the Civic District and Merlion Park, Chinatown, Little India, and Kampong Glam; or the City Sights tour, covering Marina Bay Sands and Gardens by the Bay. To register, you'll need your passport, boarding passes, and valid entry visa. The tours are first-come, first-served, and note that you can only exit and enter the airport once during your layover. ⊠ *Changi International Airport, 75 Airport Blvd., T2 or T3, Level 2 Departure Transit Hall, Changi* ⊕ *www.changiairport. com/en* Ⓜ *Changi Airport.*

Geylang Serai

Farther inland and closest to the city is Geylang Serai, which was once a red-light district but is now a thriving area with robust dining and shopping options. Whether you grab a bite at the market or stroll by the traditional shophouses, you'll surely catch a glimpse of traditional Singapore and its rich culture.

👁 Sights

Geylang Serai Market
LOCAL SPECIALTIES | FAMILY | This double-story Minangkabau-style market and hawker center is the beating heart of Singapore's Malay community. Here, you can pick up a vast range of Malay groceries, fashion accessories, and some of the best—and most reasonably priced—Muslim food in town. The ground floor of the open-air structure contains a wet market that peddles everything from halal meat to the fabled *tongkat ali* drink (meant to help with male fertility). The second floor has a dry-goods bazaar and food center. ⊠ *1 Geylang Serai, Geylang* Ⓜ *Paya Lebar.*

Joo Chiat Complex
HOUSEHOLD ITEMS/FURNITURE | Take a trip back to Singapore in the '80s at this retro two-complex shopping center filled with stores bursting at the seams with fabric, home furnishings and a hodgepodge of kitchenware. It's a chaotic riot of color and a lively change from the slick, polished malls of Orchard Road. ⊠ *Joo Chiat Complex, 1 Joo Chiat Rd., Geylang* Ⓜ *Paya Lebar.*

🍴 Restaurants

Hjh Maimunah Restaurant
$ | MALAYSIAN | FAMILY | One of the most beloved Malay restaurants in Singapore offers more than 40 tasty dishes at any one time, which you can have with steaming white rice. It's easy to tailor a plate to your palate, since the range includes everything from more adventurous recipes like *sambal goreng pengantin* (stir-fried offal with prawns and spices) to tamer but no less tasty favorites like chicken curry. **Known for:** authentic Malay cooking; impressive variety; hard-to-find dishes. Ⓢ *Average main: S$10* ⊠ *20 Joo Chiat Rd., Geylang* ☎ *6348–5457* ⊕ *hjmaimunah.com* Ⓜ *Paya Lebar.*

East Coast and Katong/Joo Chiat

The intersection of East Coast Road and Joo Chiat Road is the heart of Katong, a district steeped in the culture of the Peranakans, the descendants of 17th-century Chinese immigrants who married local Malays. This part of town is where you will find the island's largest assortment of heritage shophouses, many painted in pretty pastel colors and featuring traditional Peranakan motifs.

Colorful Peranakan houses line Joo Chiat's Koon Seng Road and East Coast Road.

This is a popular dining enclave and the birthplace of one of Singapore's most famous local dishes, Katong laksa (rice vermicelli in a spicy coconut-based broth). The Betel Box hostel and bistro is known for organizing informative food tours of the neighborhood. Nearby, running along the southeastern coast, is East Coast Park, the biggest park in the country.

◉ Sights

★ East Coast Road

HISTORIC SITE | One of the earliest delineated thoroughfares in Singapore, East Coast Road is also one of the prettiest, with more than 800 heritage buildings from the early to mid 1900s, a time when the area served as a seaside retreat for the wealthy. Today, a stroll along this spirited enclave will give you a taste of the country's diverse culture—the stretch is dotted with colorful Peranakan shophouses, museums, and quaint stores, as well as eateries that serve up everything from traditional rice dumplings to Thai *mookata* and Greek-influenced wood-fired breads. ⊠ *East Coast Rd., Katong.*

The Intan

MUSEUM | "Intan" refers to the rose-cut diamonds popularly used in Straits Chinese jewelry, and this privately owned, by-appointment-only Straits Chinese museum is a gem in its own right. Owner Alvin Yap amassed a vast collection of Peranakan paraphernalia in his quest to find out more about his culture, and then decided to open his home to the public so others could learn more about it, too. In this intimate space, you experience the Peranakan life as Yap takes you on a personally guided tour of the artifacts he's collected. ⊠ *69 Joo Chiat Terr., Joo Chiat* ☎ ⊕ *www. the-intan.com* ☞ *By appointment only* Ⓜ *Eunos.*

Beaches

East Coast Park

BEACH—SIGHT | **FAMILY** | This breezy, 460-acre seaside park isn't just one of Singapore's largest beaches, it's also the most popular, with a plethora of dining and recreational activities. There's fun for the whole family here, whether you choose to cycle along the bike-dedicated paths, go waterskiing, have a seafood dinner, or even camp overnight (just remember to apply for an electronic camping permit first). A cable-ski park, SKI360, is set up around a lagoon for wakeboarding enthusiasts. You can also go windsurfing, sailing, or simply take a dip in the sea. There are public barbecue pits, 4.7 miles (7.5 km) of sandy beaches, and a hawker center. Before the upcoming Thomson–East Coast MRT Line connects the park with other parts of Singapore in 2023, a taxi or public bus is your best bet for getting here. **Amenities:** food and drink; parking; toilets; water sports. **Best for:** swimming; walking; windsurfing. ⊠ *Along East Coast Pkwy. and East Coast Park Service Rd., Katong* ⊕ *www.nparks.gov.sg.*

Restaurants

★ Casa Nostra

$$$$ | **ITALIAN** | At this private dining experience, you get excellent pasta and pizza that's as close to perfection as they come, hand-made by a passionate Italian. Antonio Miscellaneo has pizza dough down to an art, experimenting with different types of flour, water, and ratios in his quest to achieve the ideal formula. **Known for:** private dining; artisanal pizzas and pastas; foodie insider favorite. Ⓢ *Average main: S$120* ⊠ *Tembeling Rd., Katong* ⊕ *www.casanostra.sg* ⊗ *By appointment only* ▭ *No credit cards.*

Chilli Padi Nonya Restaurant

$ | **ASIAN FUSION** | **FAMILY** | The Peranakan-style cuisine here is delicious and fiery, so be sure to specify exactly how tongue tingling you'd like your order to be. Signature dishes include *bakwan kepiting* (minced crab and pork soup), assam fish head (in spicy gravy), *ayam sio* (chicken with coriander), and *udang masak nenas* (prawns cooked with tamarind and pineapple). **Known for:** Peranakan cuisine; homey setting; catering. Ⓢ *Average main: S$13* ⊠ *#01–03, 11 Joo Chiat Pl., Katong* ☎ *6275–1002* ⊕ *www.chillipadi.com.sg* Ⓜ *Paya Lebar.*

★ Fat Fuku

$$$$ | **ASIAN FUSION** | **FAMILY** | Food writer and host Annette Tan brings Peranakan cuisine to life at this breezy, loft-like, home-dining experience through dishes made with her mother's recipes and stories of her own experiences. Expect a modern take on classics, like Tan's divine crispy *mee siam* (rice vermicelli married with piquant spices and pan-fried to a crisp), which is truly photo-worthy. **Known for:** private dining; modern Peranakan food; unique local experience. $ *Average main: S$110* ⊠ *Upper East Coast Rd., Marine Parade* ☎ *9387–6399 For reservations; text only* ⊕ *fatfuku.com* ☞ *By appointment only* ▭ *No credit cards.*

Firebake - Woodfired Bakehouse and Restaurant

$$ | **EUROPEAN** | **FAMILY** | Alongside the local chicken rice and laksa hawker stalls lining East Coast Road is this gem of a European cafe, which is as faithful to its roots as its neighbors. What you get here are hearty meals and artisanal bread baked in a full-scale, 37-ton wood-fired oven, all made with ingredients that are as natural and sustainable as possible. **Known for:** brunch; prawn capellini aglio olio; "cheesymite" sourdough roll. $ *Average main: S$25* ⊠ *237 East Coast Rd., Katong* ☎ *6440–1228* ⊕ *www.firebake.sg* ⊗ *Closed Mon.-Tues.* Ⓜ *Eunos.*

★ Hua Yu Wee

$$ | **CHINESE** | **FAMILY** | Time seems to stand still at this nostalgic, convivial Chinese restaurant that's the only survivor from an era when seafood restaurants used to line East Coast Road. Parked in a 1920s bungalow, the restaurant's menu, decor, and presentation touches—like the fresh purple orchids that top off delicious dishes—are old-school. **Known for:** unique local experience; reasonable prices; chilli crab. $ *Average main: S$15* ⊠ *462 Upper East Coast Rd., Marine Parade* ☎ *6442–9313* ⊗ *No lunch.*

★ Jumbo Seafood Restaurant

$$$ | **SEAFOOD** | **FAMILY** | This atmospheric East Coast Seafood Centre staple is the perfect place to crack into a chili or black pepper Sri Lankan crab, a glorious, delicious mess of a dish that's a true Singaporean specialty—be sure to order it with sides of fried buns to sop up the sauce. Prices are by the kilogram; some crabs are large enough to feed up to four people, but smaller ones for two are also available. **Known for:** chili crabs; live seafood cooked to order; seaside location. $ *Average main: S$34* ⊠ *#01–07/08 East Coast Seafood Centre, Block 1206, East Coast Pkwy., Katong* ☎ *6342–3435* ⊕ *www.jumboseafood.com.sg* ⊗ *No lunch Mon.–Sat.*

Long Beach Seafood Restaurant UDMC

$$$ | SEAFOOD | FAMILY | This seaside branch of one of Singapore's most long-standing seafood restaurant chains lets you pick your own fish, crab, lobsters, and more from tanks, then have it cooked the way you like. Whatever you choose, don't miss the black pepper crabs; Long Beach is the creator of the now-iconic Singaporean dish, and its version is still tops. **Known for:** live seafood; black pepper crab; seaside location. $ *Average main: S$25* ⊠ *East Coast Seafood Centre, 1202 East Coast Pkwy., #01–04, Singapore* ⊕ *longbeachseafood.com.sg.*

★ Lucky House Cantonese Private Kitchen

$$$$ | CANTONESE | Slow-food champion Sam Wong runs this private dining experience from his vintage-furnished terrace house, at the back of which sits his wildly untamed fruit and vegetable garden. You'll have to book months ahead for a table, but the wait for his painstakingly made food—like a signature roast duck that undergoes three days of preparation and features homemade spices—is worth it. **Known for:** private dining; roast duck; locavore culture. $ *Average main: S$80* ⊠ *Upper East Coast Rd., Marine Parade* ☎ *9823–7268 For reservations; text only* ⊗ *By appointment only* ▭ *No credit cards.*

PS. Cafe East Coast Park

$$ | AUSTRALIAN | FAMILY | Part of the popular PS. Cafe chain, this stylish, sun-lit cafe by the sea is one for the Instagram, and a perfect spot for weekend brunch (although you'll likely have to wait in line). **Known for:** photo-worthy setting; brunch; delicious desserts. $ *Average main: S$26* ⊠ *Cyclist Park, 1110 East Coast Pkwy., #01–05/06/07, Katong* ☎ *6708–9288* ⊕ *www.pscafe.com/ pscafe-east-coast-park.*

★ Sin Huat Eating House

$$$$ | SEAFOOD | It may be rough around the edges, it's in the red-light district of Geylang, and the cost of a full meal would make some fine-dining establishments blush, but there's good reason why the late food magnate Anthony Bourdain named Sin Huat one of the "10 places to eat before you die." Chef Danny's rich, gooey, briny, magnificent crab (or prawn) *bee hoon* (vermicelli-like rice noodles) is stunning. Pair it with on-the-shell scallops slathered in black bean sauce and a plate of *kailan* (fresh greens) with garlic for a meal to remember. **Known for:** crab noodles; on-the-shell scallops; edgy neighborhood. $ *Average main: S$100* ⊠ *659/661 Geylang Rd., Geylang* ☎ *6744–9755.*

Hotels

Grand Mercure Singapore Roxy

\$\$ | **HOTEL** | **FAMILY** | This modern if sparsely furnished hotel is a smart choice for those who want to experience Singapore's bohemian East Coast lifestyle or explore East Coast Park. **Pros:** plenty of dining and shopping options nearby; cool neighborhood; free airport shuttle. **Cons:** rooms look bare; no MRT station within walking distance (although there are bus stops); not centrally located. $ *Rooms from: S$160* ✉ *Roxy Square, 50 East Coast Rd., Katong* ☎ *6344–8000* ⊕ *www.grandmercureroxy.com.sg* ⤴ *576 rooms* ⦿ *No meals.*

Hotel Indigo Singapore Katong

\$\$ | **HOTEL** | **FAMILY** | A stay here puts you in the heart of Singapore's bohemian Katong district and in one of the hotel's 131 colorful rooms decorated in vibrant, modern Peranakan style. **Pros:** plenty of food options nearby; rooftop infinity pool; interesting neighborhood. **Cons:** a distance from the city center; no free airport shuttle, as other hotels in the neighborhood have; no on-site bar. $ *Rooms from: S$205* ✉ *86 East Coast Rd., Katong* ☎ *6723–7001* ⊕ *www.hotelindigo.com* ⤴ *131 rooms* ⦿ *No meals.*

Village Hotel Katong

\$\$ | **HOTEL** | Located in a building that was formerly the Paramount Hotel, one of Katong's most iconic landmarks, this hotel sits at the top of East Coast Road. **Pros:** all rooms have balconies; walking distance to food, museums, and East Coast Park; free airport shuttle. **Cons:** no MRT station nearby (although there are bus stops); somewhat simple rooms; not centrally located. $ *Rooms from:* ✉ *25 Marine Parade Rd., Katong* ☎ *6344–2200* ⊕ *www.stayfareast.com* ⤴ *229 rooms* ⦿ *No meals.*

🍸 Nightlife

The Cider Pit

BREWPUBS/BEER GARDENS | Home to an expansive range of English ale and cider, this casual bar is run by a British owner passionate about his brew. The music tends to linger a few decades behind the times. There's also a menu of typical pub grub. ✉ *328 Joo Chiat Rd., Joo Chiat* ☎ *6344–5759* Ⓜ *Eunos.*

🛍 Shopping

City Plaza

CLOTHING | Shop the latest Korean, Chinese, and Thai fashions at this retro, under-the-radar mall, where wholesalers plug their wares to local stores. You'll have to do some digging, but the thrill of finding a chic piece at a great price will likely make up for that. ⊠ *810 Geylang Rd., Katong* ⊕ *www.cityplaza.sg* Ⓜ *Paya Lebar.*

★ Kim Choo Kueh Chang

GIFTS/SOUVENIRS | FAMILY | Although this store is best-known for its traditional Peranakan rice dumplings and cakes, you can also pick up Peranakan porcelain pieces and other Peranakan-themed knickknacks here. If you have more time, it also offers heritage tours and free sarong kebaya fitting sessions. ⊠ *111 East Coast Rd., Katong* ☎ *6741–2125* ⊕ *www.kimchoo.com.*

Parkway Parade

SHOPPING CENTERS/MALLS | FAMILY | If the myriad megamalls of central Singapore just aren't enough, head east to wander through this multilevel shopping center, with more than 250 stores and restaurants. You can shop in relative peace and quiet during the week, but it tends to get uncomfortably crowded on weekends. ⊠ *80 Marine Parade Rd., Katong* ☎ *6344–1242* ⊕ *www.parkway-parade.com.sg.*

★ Rumah Bebe

ANTIQUES/COLLECTIBLES | This lavishly decorated heritage shophouse peddles all manner of Peranakan goods, from traditional sarong kebaya clothing to snacks. It's owned by Peranakan beadwork specialist Bebe Seet, who also offers classes on beadwork and embroidery. ⊠ *113 East Coast Rd., Katong* ☎ *6247–8781* ⊕ *www. rumahbebe.com.*

🏃 Activities

★ Betel Box Food Tours

WALKING TOURS | Eastern Singapore is one of Singapore's best-known regions for food, so it's no surprise the area has numerous food tours. One of the most established and popular is the Joo Chiat/Katong Food Walk conducted by Betel Box, which takes participants on a 1.8-mile cultural and educational journey through the Joo Chiat and Katong neighborhoods and includes a sampling of more than 30 local specialities. Along the way, you'll learn about the history of the area, Singapore's housing system and architecture, the Peranakan culture, and much more. Wear comfortable walking shoes, be prepared for a brisk pace—and bring that appetite. ✉ *Betel Box Hostel, 200 Joo Chiat Rd., Katong* ☎ *6247–7340* ⊕ *www.betelboxtours.com.*

Glamping City

CAMPING—SPORTS-OUTDOORS | FAMILY | Camping never used to be common in Singapore—perhaps because it's only legal in three areas and you have to apply for a permit first. But the activity is gaining popularity thanks to new glamping (glamorous camping) operators like Glamping City that are making it simpler to sleep under the stars. From around S$170 a night, you can book a picture-perfect tent (permit included) at East Coast Park complete with fairy lights, a fan, and a queen-size bed. You can also spend a bit more for extras that range from a picnic basket to a full movie theater set-up. There are also bigger tents that sleep up to eight people. ✉ *East Coast Park Area G, 1500 East Coast Pkwy.* ☎ *9651–1114* ⊕ *www.glampingcity.com.*

Singapore Wake Park

WATER SPORTS | FAMILY | At the city's only cable-ski park, you can wakeboard and kneeboard from day to night on the calm (and filtered) waters of East Coast Lagoon. The sprawling space caters to both beginners and experts, with three state-of-the-art cable systems that stretch over a total of 1,755 ft and have variable speeds and an obstacle course. Equipment, showers, lockers, and even free Wi-Fi—so you can upload photos of yourself riding the waves onto Instagram—are all provided. The on-site Coastal Rhythm cafe is a tasty place to refuel and wakeboarder-watch when you need a break. ✉ *1206A East Coast Pkwy.* ☎ *6636–4266* ⊕ *www.singaporewakepark.com.*

Chapter 8

WESTERN SINGAPORE

WITH DEMPSEY HILL, HOLLAND VILLAGE, AND CLEMENTI

Updated by
Olivia Lee

⦿ Sights	🍴 Restaurants	🛏 Hotels	🛍 Shopping	🍸 Nightlife
★★★★★	★★★★☆	★★☆☆☆	★★☆☆☆	★★☆☆☆

NEIGHBORHOOD SNAPSHOT

TOP EXPERIENCES

■ **Wine and dine on Dempsey Hill:** Some of Singapore's chicest shops, restaurants, and bars are tucked into the lush greenery on the hill's peak.

■ **Go out in Holland Village:** Drink, eat, and be merry alongside the expats that call this international neighborhood home.

■ **Explore nature reserves:** From the rain forest of Bukit Timah to the tangle of trees at MacRitchie, there's plenty of wild green space to see.

■ **Day-trip to wildlife parks:** The Singapore Zoo, Night Safari, and Jurong Bird Park top the list of many travelers.

■ **Discover the magic of Haw Par Villa:** At this treasure trove of a park, you'll learn all about Chinese legends and mythology.

GETTING HERE

Western Singapore is made up of a number of sprawling neighborhoods. Fortunately, the entire area is well connected, with the Circle (orange) MRT Line serving Holland Village and the East-West (green) Line connecting the farther regions of Clementi and Jurong. On the East-West (green) line, Queenstown has a well-connected MRT station of the same name. Where the MRT lines don't go, there's usually a bus that does.

PLANNING YOUR TIME

Western Singapore is largely residential, so it can feel quiet during the week. This is a good time to visit the west's attractions, including the wildlife reserves or museums. Plan for a half day or full day for each major neighborhood.

QUICK BITES

■ **New Century Cafe.** This casual, open-air restaurant at the edge of Ghim Moh wet market offers cheap, local dishes served in huge portions. ⊠ *19 Ghim Moh Rd., 270019* Ⓜ *10-minute walk from Buona Vista MRT*

■ **Island Creamery.** A charming ice cream shop not far from the Botanic Gardens, Island Creamery serves up unusual local flavors, including soursop, dragon fruit, and durian. ⊠ *569A Bukit Timah Rd., 269702* ⊕ *www.islandcreamery.com* Ⓜ *10-minute walk from Botanic Gardens MRT*

■ **Tiong Hoe Specialty Coffee.** The trendy artisanal café serves beautiful bean-to-cup flat whites and lattes from more than 20 origins. ⊠ *170 Stirling Rd., Queenstown* ⊕ *www.tionghoe.com* Ⓜ *10-minute walk from Queenstown MRT*

Western Singapore is not so much a neighborhood as an entire corner of the country, sprawling from leafy Mount Faber park in the south to the industrial tip of Jurong in the far west. In between, you'll find malls, markets, museums, nature reserves, and residential pockets, where the local way of life thrives in a way you can't see in Singapore's glitzy center.

You could spend days visiting the many nature reserves, parks, museums, landmarks and wetlands of the area and still not see them all. Visiting each will take some careful planning: the west is very spread out, and will likely require rides on both the MRT and buses (30-minutes to an hour or more) to reach the more remote attractions. It's worth the effort though—western Singapore is a welcome breath of fresh air after spending time in the more touristy neighborhoods down south.

There are four major neighborhood groupings that can be easily be paired together: Holland Village and Dempsey Hill for great restaurants and bars; Bukit Merah and Queenstown for the cool Henderson Waves and Mount Faber; Bukit Timah and its neighbors to the north (Kranji and the Central Water Catchment) for parks and the zoo; and Clementi and Jurong for an up-and-coming area with the Jurong Bird Park. The best way to explore is just to pick a neighborhood and walk around, dipping into the many malls, market places, and hawker centers scattered about the region.

Dempsey Hill and Holland Village

Dempsey Hill first served as British Army barracks, then as a local military base. These days, it's a place to see and be seen—a refurbished enclave filled with tropical trees and some of the city's best restaurants, bars, and lifestyle shops, many of them in restored, black-and-white, 19th-century colonial houses.

Nearby, you'll find Holland Village, Singapore's best-known expat district, with many terraced homes remaining from the British

KEY

🔵 Exploring Sights

🔴 Restaurants

🟠 Quick Bites

🟣 Hotels

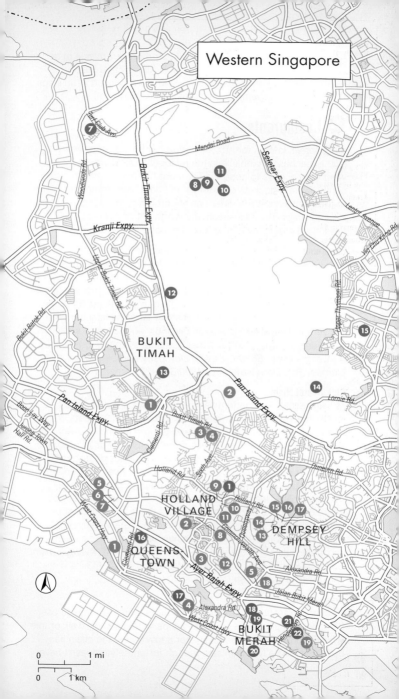

Army before World War II. This small community, a village of sorts as it encompasses just a few streets, is filled with a buzzing selection of modern restaurants and bars that make it a fun place to explore in the evenings (particularly on weekends).

🍴 Restaurants

Singapore is known for its food countrywide, but the culinary scene reaches its pinnacle in the residential west where locals want easy access to good food without having to travel into the center. Vibrant pockets of eateries and bars have sprung up in all of the west's most prominent neighborhoods, including Dempsey Hill and Holland Village—each one worthy of an evening of your time. It's a great way to see how the locals like to dine.

Candlenut

$$$ | CHINESE | Candlenut is the world's first Michelin-starred Peranakan restaurant, serving a little-known traditional cuisine that blends Chinese ingredients with Malaysian and Indonesian spices and cooking methods. The restaurant's design reflects this style, with intricate tiles on the floor and straw lanterns hanging from the ceiling. **Known for:** Peranakan cuisine; "ah-ma-kase" set lunch and dinner menus; colorful dishes like blue swimmer crab curry. ⑤ *Average main: S$30 ⊠ COMO Dempsey complex, Block 17A, Demsey Rd., Dempsey Hill* ☎ *1800/304–2288.*

Chikuwatei Nishi

$$ | JAPANESE | This modern Japanese izakaya is split across two levels: the stylish ground-floor snack bar offers street eats like *takoyaki* (battered octopus balls) and *yakitori* (grilled chicken), and the second-level sake bar serves more than 50 kinds of rice wine, craft beer, and Japanese-inspired cocktails alongside dishes like *sukiyaki* (a kind of beef hotpot) and *chirashi* (a rice bowl topped with vegetables, meat, or fish). The restaurant is tucked away from the main strip of Holland Village, which means the atmosphere can be less buzzing at times, but don't let the lack of people put you off—the food is authentic, the drinks are varied, and the staff is always very friendly. **Known for:** great sake; authentic Japanese cuisine; bright and bold interior design. ⑤ *Average main: S$15 ⊠ 48 Lor Mambong, Holland Village* ☎ *6734–4436* ⊕ *www. chikuwateinishi.com.sg.*

Crystal Jade Kitchen

$ | CHINESE | FAMILY | With nearly 50 outlets (and counting) across Singapore, chances are you'll always be within a short walk of this wildly popular Cantonese chain. For a few years, the chain has been awarded a Michelin star, though fortunately it doesn't have

Michelin-star prices to match. **Known for:** some of the best dim sum in Singapore; affordable sharing plates; ordering system of marking paper menus. ⑤ *Average main: S$12* ✉ *2 Lor Mambong, Holland Village* ☎ *6469–0300* ⊕ *www.crystaljade.com* Ⓜ *Holland Village.*

Jones the Grocer

$$ | INTERNATIONAL | Partly a casual café and partly an upscale grocery, Jones the Grocer is packed with expat families during the weekend brunch, but on the quieter weekday evenings, you'll likely share this roomy, industrial-style space with just a handful of others. Salads, sandwiches, pastas, and light seafood platters are among the foods on the seasonal menu (the concept hailing from Woollahra in Sydney, where the first branch opened over two decades ago). **Known for:** Sunday brunch crowd; elegant, high-quality produce; great vegetarian selections. ⑤ *Average main: S$25* ✉ *#03–03/04, 9D Dempsey Hill, Dempsey Hill* ☎ *6476–1518* ⊕ *www.jonesthegrocer.com.*

★ Long Beach Seafood Restaurant

$$$ | SEAFOOD | Cracking into a a black-pepper or chili crab is one of those signature Singapore dining experiences, and there are few places that do it better than Long Beach. There are five restaurant locations across Singapore, including the main branch on the East Coast, near where it first opened in 1946, but this Dempsey Hill branch stands out for its convenience and outdoor seating deck (plus you can stop for a pre-dinner pint or two of tasty micro-brews at the nearby RedDot Brewhouse). **Known for:** crab, crab, and more crab; Singapore's original seafood restaurant; open-air dining. ⑤ *Average main: S$32* ✉ *Blk. 25, Dempsey Rd., Dempsey Hill* ☎ *6323–2222* ⊕ *www.longbeachseafood.com.sg.*

★ Samy's Curry

$$ | INDIAN | Because of its airy, colonial edifice with wooden-louvered windows and overhead fans, Samy's Curry has a casual canteen feel that is distinct from the more upscale ambience typical of many Dempsey Hill eateries. Although the wait staff can be a little brisk, the restaurant remains a firm favorite among the locals thanks to the flavorful and filling north and south Indian dishes on offer at very affordable prices. **Known for:** delicious fish head curry; banana leaves in place of plates; classic Indian dishes including chicken tikka. ⑤ *Average main: S$15* ✉ *Civil Service Club, Block 25, Dempsey Rd., Dempsey Hill* ☎ *6472–2080* ⊕ *www.samyscurry.com* ⊗ *Closed Tues.*

Dempsey Hill Through the Years

On a small hill near the center of Singapore you will find one of the country's chicest lifestyle destinations, home to Michelin-star restaurants and fashion outlets—with price tags to match. But it hasn't always been this way.

EARLY YEARS

Dempsey Hill began its life as Mount Harriet, the site of an enormous nutmeg plantation that stretched from the hill to what is now the Singapore Botanic Gardens. A beetle blight devastated the plantation in the 1850s, and the land was sold to the British Forces, who cut down the trees and replaced them with the Tanglin Barracks.

WWII

The hill was named for General Sir Miles Christopher Dempsey, the commanding officer of the Second Army, the main British force involved in the 1944 D-Day landings. He served throughout World War II and the Japanese occupation. In 1945, the Japanese troops surrendered, and Singapore was returned to the British, who maintained the barracks until their withdrawal in 1971.

TODAY

The area gradually transformed into a retail enclave using the former soldier's barracks as shops and warehouses. Today, it is a place to see and be seen as you shop in the beautiful (if overpriced) produce stores, and wine and dine in the expensive but elegant restaurants, each housed in an original colonial building, with low-lying red-brick roofs and white-washed walls.

Sanpoutei

$$ | **JAPANESE** | This lively ramen restaurant at the edge of Holland Village hails from Niigata in Japan. It specializes in *shoyu* (soy sauce ramen with homemade noodles served alongside thin slices of chashu pork and nori). **Known for:** rich bowls of ramen; a history that dates from 1967; gooey soft-boiled eggs. $ *Average main: S$15* ✉ *253 Holland Ave., #01–01, Holland Village* ☎ *6463–7277* ⊕ *www.sanpoutei.sg.*

★ The White Rabbit

$$$$ | **MODERN EUROPEAN** | This former church's compelling interior—soaring ceilings, ample arched windows, stained glass, and rows of chandeliers hanging over curved banquettes—has helped draw many faithful diners to this European restaurant. The kitchen takes an artsy, nouveau approach to a menu of dishes designed to "transport you down the rabbit hole," from classic bouillabaisse to lobster and kombu linguine. **Known for:** the laid-back outdoor

garden; a striking setting in a former chapel; its reputation as one of the best dining experiences in Singapore. $ *Average main: S$50* ⊠ *39C Harding Rd., Dempsey Hill* ☎ *6473–9965* ⊕ *www. thewhiterabbit.com.sg* ☾ *Closed Mon.*

☕ Coffee and Quick Bites

Craftsmen Coffee

$ | CAFÉ | At the edge of Holland Village, this independent speciality shop is a rare treat in a country where good coffee can be hard to come by. It sources single-origin beans from around the world, focusing on the aromas and tastes of each variety, and serves its coffee alongside simple snacks and meals, from fresh salads and pastas to sandwiches and croissants. **Known for:** coffee beans from around the world; cool brunch spot; sandwiches and pastries. $ *Average main: S$5* ⊠ *275 Holland Ave., Holland Village* ☎ *9658–0769* ⊕ *www.craftsmencoffee.com.*

☾ Nightlife

The nightlife in western Singapore seems elusive, but it's there if you know where to look. One place you'll have no difficulty finding it is Holland Village, with its many bars and eateries. Dempsey Hill, too, is a nice place to stroll at night, dipping into the various watering holes. Outside of these two expat enclaves, though, the nightlife options are more spread out. You won't be able to do much bar-crawling, but if you pick a spot and hunker down for the evening, you'll get a taste of how the locals like to drink.

CM-PB

BARS/PUBS | Set amid the tropical trees that fill Dempsey Hill, this rustic bungalow bar (the acronym used for its name stands for Contemporary Melting-Pot and Bar) is a great place to spend an evening with good food, great drinks, and plenty of live music. A selection of tapas inspired by the flavors of Asia counterbalances a wide array of beer, ciders, cocktails, and alcohol-free mocktails, and a comprehensive brunch menu is offered until late afternoon on the weekends. ⊠ *#01–05, Blk 7 Dempsey Rd., Dempsey Hill* ☎ *6475–0105* ⊕ *www.cm-pb.net.*

RedDot Brewhouse

BREWPUBS/BEER GARDENS | Come for the excellent microbrews, stay for the location amid the lush greenery of Dempsey Hill. The food is satisfying—pizzas, grilled meats, and Spanish tapas—but it's the range of delicious beers that take center stage, from IPAs to Czech pilsners. The most commonly served drink is RedDot's own

Monster Green Lager, a tall glass of fluorescent beer that gets its hue from spirulina. It tastes better than it looks. ⊠ *#01–01, Blk. 25A, Dempsey Rd., Dempsey Hill* ⊕ *www.reddotbrewhouse.com.sg*.

Wala Wala

BARS/PUBS | Holland Village has seen many bars open and close, but this wildly popular watering hole has stayed the same for decades, pairing its jugs of cocktails and other drinks with Western favorites like pizza and steak. Live music often plays upstairs, and there's a bustling bar downstairs that has a welcoming outdoor sitting area, which occasionally spills out onto the street on a Saturday night. ⊠ *31 Lorong Mambong, Holland Village* ☎ *6462–4288* ⊕ *www.walawala.sg*.

👜 Shopping

Shops in the west vary wildly depending on where you visit. Around Holland Village and Dempsey Hill, they tend to be high-end boutiques, catering to the affluent residents. Outside these wealthier pockets, you will find all manner of shops, from giant malls that keep local teenagers endlessly entertained to neighborhood stores that seem to sell everything from slippers to ironing boards. If you want to try some cheap local shopping, head to one of Singapore's many wet markets, where little stalls selling knick-knacks and trinkets pop up among the fruit and vegetable stands on weekend mornings.

Affordable Style Files

HOUSEHOLD ITEMS/FURNITURE | Though perhaps geared more to the expats who flock to Dempsey Hill, this beautiful boutique has a range of home and lifestyle products that would add color and elegance to any room. Although it's not quite as affordable as its name might imply, the items for sale—intricately woven rugs, boldly patterned plant pots, and fragrantly scented candles—are the kinds of things you don't need but definitely want. Be prepared to break your wallet. ⊠ *6A Dempsey Rd., Dempsey Hill* ☎ *6909–0115* ⊕ *affordablestylefiles.com* ⊙ *Closed Sun.*

Asiatique Collections

ANTIQUES/COLLECTIBLES | Occupying a 5,000-square-foot space on Dempsey Hill, this store specializes in jewelry, art, and home furnishings from around the world and with a focus on natural and recycled materials. Even if, as a short-term visitor, you aren't in a position to purchase some of the larger items, it's still a fun shop to walk around, getting lost in the maze of old goods. There are also personalized services like custom-made furniture.

✉ *Henderson Industrial Park Wing B, Blk 203 Henderson Rd. #04–07, Dempsey Hill* ☎ *6471–3146* ⊕ *www.asiatiquecollections. com* ⊗ *By Appointment Only.*

★ Bynd Artisan

HOUSEHOLD ITEMS/FURNITURE | Having a personalized notebook made for you by hand might be one of the greatest gifts in our digital age. In around 20 minutes, the artisans at Bynd can create a bespoke leather-bound notebook, complete with foil stamping on the cover forming your desired lettering. They can also personalize other gifts, including wallets and phone cases. ✉ *44 Jln Merah Saga, Holland Village* ☎ *6475–1680* ⊕ *www.byndartisan. com* ⊗ *Closed Mon.*

★ Emgallery

TEXTILES/SEWING | This gorgeous shop works with skilled artisans throughout Southeast Asia to create unique textile products, from delicate Cambodian tie-dye dresses to intricately woven Laos rugs. The shop—nestled amid greenery in an old heritage building—is run by founder and owner Emiko, whose inspiration comes from the culture of her native Japan. She also creates and sells a range of fabric-themed accessories, including hand-made wooden necklaces and silk organza scarves. ✉ *#01–03A, Blk 26 Dempsey Rd., Dempsey Hill* ☎ *6475–6941* ⊕ *www.em.gallery.*

Lim's Arts and Living

ANTIQUES/COLLECTIBLES | Located in the Holland Road Shopping Centre, which is an expat landmark, Lim's Arts and Living carries colonial furniture, silks, paper products, Asian-style housewares, and sundry knickknacks. Even if you don't buy anything, it's a fun shop to browse. This is just one of several of Lim's outlets across the city. ✉ *#02–02 Holland Road Shopping Centre, 211 Holland Ave., Holland Village* ☎ *6467–1300* ⊕ *www.limslegacy.com.*

REDSEA Gallery

ART GALLERIES | Contemporary works from more than 50 international artists are displayed in this gallery housed in a former army barracks. All pieces are handpicked by the gallery's owner, Chris Churcher, who meets with each artist before showcasing his or her work. ✉ *Dempsey Hill, Block 9 Dempsey Rd., #01-10, Dempsey Hill* ☎ *6732–6711* ⊕ *www.redseagallery.com.*

The Star Vista

SHOPPING CENTERS/MALLS | This excellent mall, within walking distance of Holland Village, is a great place to lose a few hours shopping and eating. The stores seem especially geared towards Japanese culture, with a great Japan Home shop for lifestyle products and a number of well-reviewed Japanese restaurants. There's also a selection of lovely boutiques selling hand-made jewelery, scarves, and trinkets, plus a 5,000-seat theater on Level 4 that hosts music performances and plays. ✉ *1 Vista Exchange Green, Holland Village* ⊕ *www.capitaland.com/sg/malls/thestarvista/en.html.*

Bukit Merah and Queenstown

The southwest coast of Singapore stretches from Queenstown to Bukit Merah, encompassing the iconic Southern Ridges—a seamless span of green parks linked by a 10-km (6.2-mile) trail. Queenstown is home to the National University of Singapore, so you'll often find crowds of young people in the local bars. Bukit Merah, near Tiong Bahru and Chinatown, is a popular residential area thanks to its many green parks, including Mount Faber, and its close proximity to the city center. Holland Village is just a 10 to 15 minute walk away from Queenstown.

Sights

Berlayer Creek Boardwalk

TRAIL | The ½-mile Berlayer Creek Boardwalk near the neighborhood of Alexandra runs through one of the two remaining mangrove forests in southern Singapore. The boardwalk is raised, letting you peer over the sides at the swampy undergrowth, where 60 bird species, 19 fish species, and 14 mangrove plant species have been recorded. There are informative storyboards along the route, as well as look-out points where you can get closer to the area's unique biodiversity. ✉ *Bukit Merah* ✛ *Join the trail from Labrador Park MRYT* ⊕ *nparks.gov.sg* Ⓜ *Labrador MRT.*

Gillman Barracks

MUSEUM | This wonderful art space started out life in 1936 as a barracks for the British Army. Today, it champions Singaporean and Southeast Asian art in a number of galleries housed in the original army blocks. There are also regular events and workshops, including film weeks, rotating exhibitions, and evening talks. After you've browsed the galleries, kick back at one of the pretty on-site cafés or bars, each one surrounded by leafy foliage. ✉ *9 Lock Rd., Bukit Merah* ⊕ *www.gillmanbarracks.com* ☽ *Closed Mon.* Ⓜ *Labrador Park.*

Haw Par Villa

AMUSEMENT PARK/WATER PARK | **FAMILY** | Formerly known as Tiger Balm Gardens, Haw Par Villa is a charmingly bizarre park dedicated to Chinese legends and myths. Once part of an estate owned

Curving and twisting 118 feet above ground, Henderson Waves is Singapore's highest pedestrian bridge.

by the two eccentric brothers who created Tiger Balm ointment, the gardens were opened to the public after World War II and later transformed into this theme park. A highlight of the intriguing treasure trove of Chinese mythology, religion, and social mores is the walk-through "Ten Courts of Hell" display, which depicts a tale of life after death designed to teach traditional Chinese morality. ⊠ *262 Pasir Panjang Rd., Bukit Merah* ☎ *6773–0103* ⊕ *www.hawparvilla.sg* 🎟 *Free* Ⓜ *Buona Vista.*

★ Henderson Waves
BRIDGE/TUNNEL | Singapore's highest pedestrian bridge is a fantastical, wave-like span suspended 118 feet above lush rain forest. It was built in 2008 to connect Mount Faber Park and Telok Blangah Hill Park and quickly became a social media photo phenomenon thanks to its distinctive shapes and undulating design. It's just under 1,000 feet long, making it fairly quick to cross, but you'll want to allot extra time to capture the cool shapes on camera. Come early in the morning to avoid crowds. ⊠ *Henderson Rd., Bukit Merah* Ⓜ *Telok Blangah.*

Mount Faber
NATIONAL/STATE PARK | The tall hill of Mount Faber Park is one of the oldest green spaces in Singapore, with excellent views across the city. While you can drive or walk to the top, taking the cable car from the Harbourfront station, the same cable car that continues on to Sentosa Island, is the most scenic way to reach the peak. The park has a number of dining and entertainment complexes at the top where you can grab a meal or a drink and look out over the

park's vibrant lush rainforest, with the city in the distance beyond. ⊠ *Mount Faber Park, Telok Blangah Rd., Bukit Merah* ⊕ *www. nparks.gov.sg* Ⓜ *Telok Blangah.*

★ NUS Museum

ARTS CENTERS | Located within the main campus of the National University of Singapore, the NUS Museum is the nation's oldest university museum. At any one time, it displays some 1,000 of its roughly 8,000 artifacts and artworks, which were first introduced by museum curator Michael Sullivan as a teaching collection in 1955. The works are split across four major exhibits, including the South and Southeast Asian Collection and the Straits Chinese Collection. Temporary exhibitions also pop up from time to time, alongside educational workshops. If you can't make the trip to the museum itself, you can also view more than 2,000 of the fascinating artifacts via the museum's online database. ⊠ *National University of Singapore, 50 Kent Ridge Crescent, Queenstown* ☎ *6516–8817* ⊕ *museum.nus.edu.sg* ⊠ *Free* ↻ *Closed Sun.-Mon.*

Southern Ridges

NATIONAL/STATE PARK | The Southern Ridges is the collective name for the hilly green parks that lie in Singapore's southwestern tip: Mount Faber Park, Telok Blangah Hill Park, HortPark, Kent Ridge Park and Labrador Nature Reserve. This is a great place to go hiking, with a number of trails, including the Forest Walk and Canopy Walk, that wind alongside creeks, over bridges, and through the secondary rain forest that covers the area. ⊠ *Bukit Merah* ☎ *800/471–7300* ⊕ *nparks.gov.sg.*

🍴 Restaurants

★ ABC Brickworks Food Centre

$ | **CHINESE** | Tucked behind an imposing IKEA building, one of the island's oldest food centers is particularly popular with locals in the Alexandra area; expect lines on weekend mornings to snake across the hall. But the wait is worth it, as you'll find some of Singapore's best hawkers here. **Known for:** char siew BBQ pork buns; Michelin Bib Gourmand noodle stall; busy weekend lines. ⑤ *Average main: S$5* ⊠ *6 Jalan Bukit Merah, Bukit Merah* ☎ *6225–5632* Ⓜ *Redhill.*

Beauty in The Pot at The Star Vista

$$ | **CHINESE** | **FAMILY** | One of six outlets, Beauty in The Pot at The Star Vista mall specializes in hotpot, which employs rich, fragrant broths to cook an assortment of extras waiting on the table. This branch is an easy introduction to the world of hotpot: a spacious, art deco–themed room with space for bigger groups (and you'll

Saturdays at Ghim Moh Market

In Queenstown, not far from Holland Village, lies the bustling Ghim Moh market. It's not well publicized to tourists, but it's the place to be on a Saturday morning for locals. The wet market overflows with produce fresh from the farms in Malaysia, offering some of the cheapest vegetables around. At the food center behind, people line up for breakfast from the many delicious stalls.

need them to finish that broth!). **Known for:** hotpots; pork bone broth; excellent vegetarian selection. ⑤ *Average main: S$20* ✉ *#02–24 The Star Vista, 1 Vista Exchange Green, Bukit Merah* ☎ *6262–1692* ⊕ *www.paradisegp.com* Ⓜ *Buona Vista.*

Cable Car Sky Dining

$$$$ | ASIAN | This dining-in-the-sky experience ticks a number of boxes: it's unique, the food is good, and it features an incredible view. As you travel up and down Mount Faber in a private cable-car cabin, you'll tuck into a four-course dinner (Stardust Standard Cabin) or a more communal local offering (Singapore Flavours Cabin). **Known for:** unique dining experience; spectacular views; private setting. ⑤ *Average main: S$65* ✉ *109 Mount Faber Rd., Level 2 Faber Peak Singapore, Bukit Merah* ☎ *6771–5000* ⊕ *www. onefabergroup.com.*

Colbar

$ | ASIAN FUSION | Built in 1953 as a canteen for the British army (and seemingly unchanged since), this gem of a cafe lies in a secluded spot near Queenstown. Although the building itself is a little rustic, the garden tables outside are perfect for lazy weekend afternoons, especially those with young children. **Known for:** colonial decor; ales and fruit ciders; lovely outside seating area. ⑤ *Average main: S$8* ✉ *9A Whitchurch Rd, Queenstown* ☎ *6779–4859* ◷ *Closed Mon.* Ⓜ *One North.*

🛏 Hotels

Hotels in the west are few and far between, mainly because visitors to Singapore prefer to stay a little closer to the center. Still, if you're planning a trip to one of the sights in the far west—or if you want to get closer to the local way of life—there are a few good options.

Citadines Fusionopolis

$$ | RENTAL | The stylish serviced apartments of this sleek property have all conveniences of a home and all the facilities of a hotel. **Pros:** excellent facilities; quiet location; amazing views from the loft apartments. **Cons:** a little far from Singapore's main bustle; impersonal design; can only accommodate two people per room. $ *Rooms from: S$250* ✉ *Symbiosis Tower, 3 Fusionopolis Way, Queenstown* ☎ *6248–3333* ⊕ *www.citadines.com/en* ⤴ *50 rooms* ❖| *Free Breakfast* Ⓜ *One North.*

K2 Guesthouse

$$ | HOTEL | Offering basic but comfortable rooms with free Wi-Fi, this budget-friendly guesthouse has a nice garden and a convenient airport pick-up service. **Pros:** quiet, residential location; very affordable; nice outside terrace. **Cons:** shared bathrooms could be cleaner; can sometimes hear noise from other guests; Wi-Fi can be patchy. $ *Rooms from: S$100* ✉ *15 South Buona Vista Rd., Bukit Merah* ☎ *8686–2444* ⊕ *k2guesthouse.com* ⤴ *24 rooms* ❖| *No meals.*

Park Avenue Rochester

$$ | HOTEL | This shiny hotel is located next to a number of great shopping malls, including Rochester Mall and The Star Vista, plus it's only a two-minute walk from Buona Vista MRT, connecting you directly to Tiong Bahru and Raffles Place. **Pros:** friendly, professional staff; great breakfast; good facilities, including a pool and gym. **Cons:** a little far from the center; expensive considering location; lack of TV channels. $ *Rooms from: S$220* ✉ *31 Rochester Dr., Bukit Merah* ☎ *6830–8360* ⊕ *parkavenueintl.com/parkavenuerochester* ⤴ *351 rooms* ❖| *No meals* Ⓜ *Buona Vista.*

★ Park Hotel Alexandra

$$ | HOTEL | Set against the leafy backdrop of the Southern Ridges, this elegant hotel has far-reaching views from the floor-to-ceiling windows that line many of the rooms. **Pros:** residential neighborhood; great views from the pool; boutique-style design. **Cons:** 15-minute walk from nearest MRT; on the junction of a busy road beside IKEA; parking is not on site. $ *Rooms from: S$200* ✉ *323 Alexandra Rd., Bukit Merah* ☎ *6828–8888* ⊕ *www.parkhotelgroup.com/en/alexandra* ⤴ *440 rooms* ❖| *No meals.*

🍸 Nightlife

The Good Beer Company

BARS/PUBS | This laid-back local spot, often full of workers and students finishing long days, is a bottle shop mecca for beer aficionados. From the same team who run Smith Street Taps—the hidden gem of a beer bar in Chinatown—the brews here are eclectic, interesting, and often very reasonably priced. There's a rotating selection on draft, with a good discount during happy hour, and some delicious pizzas that make this the perfect stop before heading home. ⊠ #01–23 Ascent, 2 Science Park Dr., Queenstown ☎ 9859–7386 Ⓜ Kent Ridge.

Hooha! Café

BARS/PUBS | Music industry insiders, club owners, and musicians congregate at this club in the small but busy Pasir Panjang Village entertainment hub. The Saturday night jamming and sing-along action may go into the early hours upstairs, with people leaving the bar to go directly to Mass in the morning. There's no band, but drum sets and guitars are available upstairs. Downstairs, there's a bar and restaurant, though the drinks are better than the food. ⊠ Viva Vista Mall #B01–06/11/50, 3 South Buona Vista Rd., Bukit Merah ☎ 6250–6348 ⊕ www.hoohacafe.com Ⓜ Pasir Panjang.

Hopscotch

BARS/PUBS | Fresh from a pop up in Chinatown's much-loved Maxwell Food Centre, this laid-back bar located in the art complex of Gillman Barracks has some serious cocktail credentials. Try Singaporean twists on classics (Sidecar, S$20), something a little more adventurous (the Peranakan-inspired, tequila-soaked Little Nonya, S$21) or even one of their bespoke creations (from S$20). Food ranges from yakitori-style grilled meat sticks, pizzas, pasta and sliders, all good to soak up those boozy drinks. ⊠ Gillman Barracks, 45 Malan Rd., Bukit Merah ☎ 6339–0633 ⊕ www.hop-scotch.sg ☞ Closed Sun. Ⓜ Labrador Park.

★ Timbre+

GATHERING PLACES | This vibrant urban food park is a great place to while away an evening, with live music performances every night of the week. You can watch the bands play on the big stage as you eat your way around the hipster food vans serving everything from charcoal-grilled kebabs to lip-smacking bowls of ramen. There's also an excellent bar and bottle shop, where you can order craft beer on tap or choose from more than 120 beer and cider bottles. Timbre+ is located by One North MRT, one stop away from Holland Village on the circle (orange) line. ⊠ JTC LaunchPad @ one-north, 73A Ayer Rajah Crescent, Queenstown ☎ 6252–2545 ⊕ timbreplus.sg Ⓜ One North.

🛍 Shopping

VivoCity

SHOPPING CENTERS/MALLS | FAMILY | Step aside ION Orchard and Marina Square—this is the largest shopping mall in Singapore, at least for now. Located on the southwestern tip of the island—about 10 minutes by taxi from Orchard Road—and doubling as a de facto gateway to Sentosa, this monolithic complex has, as expected, hundreds of retailers and restaurants and a 15-screen movie theater. But it also has art installations, an outdoor playground for kids, and a rooftop amphitheater near huge pools of water in which you can splash about. Expect a full house during the weekend. ⊠ *1 Harbourfront Ave., Bukit Merah* ☎ *6377–6860* ⊕ *www.vivocity.com.sg* Ⓜ *HarbourFront*.

Bukit Timah and Around

The residential area of Bukit Timah lies close to the center of the island, sandwiched between the green lungs of the Botanic Gardens to the south and the Bukit Timah Nature Reserve to the north. The area is known for its great culinary scene, especially when it comes to brunching. In part, that's thanks to the number of locals and expats that call the sprawling neighborhood home.

To the north of Bukit Timah, heading all the way up to the border with Malaysia, you'll find the scenic sights of Kranji, a small suburb known for its countryside and artisanal farms. Between the two lies the enormous Central Water Catchment, a huge sprawl of parkland containing recreational sites like the Singapore Zoo and Night Safari.

👁 Sights

Bukit Timah Nature Reserve

NATURE PRESERVE | Step away from Singapore's manicured urban parks and into 405 acres of wild rain forest at this sprawling nature reserve. The walking paths are well marked, but exploring here still gives you a sense of what the island was like when tigers still roamed the jungle. Towering trees, tangled vines, and prickly rattan palms line the footpaths, while long-tailed macaques, squirrels, and tree shrews scamper overhead. The trails circle Singapore's highest hill (535 feet), with some of the routes leading to the peak for spectacular views of the dense greenery. Wear good walking shoes—the trails are rocky and muddy after the rain—and make sure you bring water. You can buy maps from the visitor center. ✉ *177 Hindhede Dr., Bukit Timah* ☎ *1800/471–7300* ⊕ *www.nparks.gov.sg* 🏷 *Free.*

Chestnut Nature Park

NATIONAL/STATE PARK | Hikers and bikers can enjoy about 200 acres of greenery at Singapore's largest nature park, located just outside of the Central Catchment Nature Reserve. Its two hiking trails (a 2-mile route on the north side and a 1.3-mile route on the south side) and 5 miles of mountain biking trails offer adventurous escapes from the hustle and bustle of the city for a day. ✉ *Chestnut Ave., Bukit Timah* ☎ *1800/471–7300* ⊕ *www.nparks.gov.sg.*

Kong Meng San Phor Kark See Monastery

RELIGIOUS SITE | The Bright Hill Temple, as it's commonly known due to its location on Bright Hill Drive, is Singapore's largest Mahayana monastery. Built in the 1920s, it's in a relatively modern complex made up of colorful buildings decorated with gilded carvings, as well as pretty gardens and a large number of Buddha statues. The closest MRT station, Bishan, is a couple of kilometers away, so prepare to catch a bus or take a taxi to reach the monastery without breaking too much of a sweat. ✉ *88 Bright Hill Dr., Bukit Timah* ☎ *6849–5300* ⊕ *www.kmspks.org* 🏷 *Free* Ⓜ *Bishan.*

Kranji War Memorial

MEMORIAL | More than 4,400 white gravestones line the manicured hillside in neat rows at this World War II memorial site, honoring the men and women who died in the line of duty for Singapore. You'll also find a number of larger memorial stones, one of which bears the names of more than 24,000 Allied soldiers and airmen killed in Southeast Asia who have no known grave. Visiting is a poignant experience—a reminder of the greatness of the loss in this and all wars. ✉ *9 Woodlands Rd., Bukit Timah* ☎ *6269–6158* ⊕ *www.cwgc.org* 🏷 *Free* Ⓜ *Kranji to Bus 170.*

★ MacRitchie Reservoir

TRAIL | **FAMILY** | This 30-acre park is a lush green wilderness, crisscrossed by a 10 km (6.2-mile) walking trail that loops around the reservoir. The trail is mostly flat and shaded, with only the warbling of birds and chatter of the park's many monkeys to break the peaceful reverie. Pick up the trail from MacRitchie Reservoir Park in the south, near the trail's main car park, where you can grab a drink from the cafés and kiosks before heading off. From here, you can follow signs towards the TreeTop Walk, which lies at around midway mark in the north of the park. This 820-foot-long suspension bridge soars above the trees, with spectacular views across the wild rain forest to the city skyscrapers in the distance. After completing the TreeTop Walk, continue following the trail

The Night Safari offers a unique chance to spot Singapore's wildlife after dark.

towards Jelutong Tower—another spot with scenic views that lies in the west of the park—before looping back to the MacRitchie Reservoir Park along the picturesque waterside boardwalk. ✉ *Lornie Rd., near Thomson Rd., Bukit Timah* ☎ *1800/471–7300* 🎟 *Free* Ⓜ *Marymount.*

Night Safari

ZOO | FAMILY | Right next to the Singapore Zoo, the safari is the world's first wildlife park designed exclusively and especially for night viewing. More than 80 acres of secondary jungle provide a home to more than 2,500 animals that are more active after the sun sets. Some 90% of tropical animals are, in fact, nocturnal, and to see them do something other than snooze gives their behavior a new dimension. From elephants, lions, and clouded leopards to flying foxes and rare pangolin, the Night Safari is an unusual way to spy animals after dark. Their habitats have been designed to come as close to their natural setting as possible, with just enough light for you to see what they're doing but not enough to limit the animals' normal activity. ✉ *80 Mandai Lake Rd., Bukit Timah* ☎ *6269–3411* ⊕ *www.wrs.com.sg/en/night-safari* 🎟 *S$57* Ⓜ *Ang Mo Kio to Bus 138.*

Rainforest Lumina

ZOO | FAMILY | Rainforest Lumina is a 1-km (0.62-mile), multimedia night walk through lush greenery. Using fluorescent lighting, interactive activities, and audiovisual displays, the fun 45-minute journey teaches you about creatures that come out after dark. It's particularly popular among families, with the stroller-friendly walking trails well-lit and geared towards children. The experience is technically part of Singapore Zoo, though separate tickets need to be purchased. ⊠ *80 Mandai Lake Rd., Bukit Timah* ☎ *6269– 3411* ⊕ *rainforestlumina.wrs.com.sg/index.html* ⛟ *S$18* Ⓜ *Ang Mo Kio to Bus 138.*

River Safari

ZOO | FAMILY | Asia's first and only river-themed wildlife park is inspired by eight of the world's most iconic waterways. It's home to more than 7,500 aquatic and terrestrial animals, including Kai Kai and Jia Jia—Singapore's resident pandas—plus the world's largest collection of freshwater fauna, a squirrel monkey forest, and several themed restaurants. Most of the park is designed to be explored on foot, but the fun Reservoir Cruise lets you enjoy its pretty nature from the water. ⊠ *80 Mandai Lake Rd., Bukit Timah* ☎ *65/6269–3411* ⊕ *www.wrs.com.sg/en/river-safari* ⛟ *S$36* Ⓜ *Ang Mio Kio.*

Singapore Zoo

ZOO | FAMILY | Sprawling over 69 acres of a 220-acre natural rain-forest, this zoo has stunning views of nearby reservoir lakes. Wet or dry moats are used to separate the animals from the people. A 3-foot-deep moat, for instance, will keep humans and giraffes apart, since a giraffe's gait makes even a shallow trench impossible to negotiate. A narrow water-filled moat prevents spider monkeys from leaving their home turf for a closer inspection of visitors. The zoo uses massive glass viewing windows to great effect: not only can you watch polar bears perform "ballet" underwater and pygmy hippos do less graceful things, but you can also observe such big cats as lions and jaguars close up. At the reptile house, be sure to seek out the Komodo dragons, which can grow to 10 feet in length. The primate displays are striking, too, and the orangutan enclosure shows off the world's largest captive orangutan group. In all there are about 3,000 animals from around 300 species here. ⊠ *80 Mandai Lake Rd., Bukit Timah* ☎ *6269–3411* ⊕ *www.wrs.com.sg/en/singapore-zoo* ⛟ *S$39* Ⓜ *Ang Mo Kio.*

★ Sungei Buloh

NATURE PRESERVE | The Sungei Buloh wetlands are a true breath of fresh air in Singapore. They lie at one of the most north-westerly points of the island, a sprawling 500-acre ecological site of man-groves and mudflats. Migratory birds, crabs, and mud lobsters can be found in abundance, viewable from the trails or observation posts that dot the park. The site was designated as a nature park by the government in 1989, before being designated Singapore's first ASEAN Heritage Park in 2003. Stroll the raised boardwalks, watch a prawn-harvesting demonstration, or pick up a free guided tour from the visitor center. ⊠ *301 Neo Tiew Cres, Bukit Timah* ☎ *6794–1401 Visitor center* ⊕ *www.nparks.gov.sg.*

🍴 Restaurants

Brazil Churrascaria

$$$$ | **BRAZILIAN** | Carnivores with a taste for succulent slices of marinated beef, pork, lamb, and other meats sliced off jumbo-sized skewers can take a 20-minute cab ride from downtown to this busy all-you-can-eat *churrascaria* (barbecue) restaurant in the affluent Bukit Timah neighborhood. You'll pay a set price for the meats, sides, and desserts. **Known for:** all-you-can-eat barbecued meats; lively atmosphere with classic Brazilian music; huge buffet of hot and cold dishes. ⑤ *Average main: S$52* ⊠ *14–16 Sixth Ave., Bukit Timah* ☎ *6463–1923* ⊕ *www.brazilchurrasco.com* ⏱ *No lunch* Ⓜ *Sixth Avenue.*

★ Bukit Timah Food Centre

$ | **ASIAN** | This bustling food center is a true local's haunt, with more than 80 hawker stalls selling everything from succulent Hainanese chicken rice to tangy satay. When it comes to picking where to eat, use the golden rule of every hawker center in Singapore: choose the stalls with the longest lines. **Known for:** cheap eats; huge variety of hawker stalls; delicious fish soup. ⑤ *Average main: S$4* ⊠ *Bukit Timah Market & Food Centre, 51 Upper Bukit Timah Rd., Bukit Timah* Ⓜ *Beauty World.*

★ Riders Café

$$ | **INTERNATIONAL** | The airy, old colonial-style space of this charming café is set amid the rolling hills and verdant greenery of the Bukit Timah Saddle Club—you'll need to take a taxi to get here, but it's worth the effort. Expect Western-style comfort foods like steak frites and portobello burgers for lunch and dinner; the weekend brunch menu, served from 8 am to 3 pm, includes indulgences like burnt banana brioche and homemade potato rosti with sausage or seafood risotto. **Known for:** beautiful location; open-air seating; classic comfort foods. ⑤ *Average main: S$27* ⊠ *Bukit Timah Saddle Club, 51 Fairways Dr., Bukit Timah* ☎ *6466–9819* ⊕ *www.riderscafe.sg* ⏱ *Closed Mon.* Ⓜ *Taxi or 20-min walk from Sixth Avenue.*

★ Violet Oon's Kitchen

$$ | **ASIAN FUSION** | Black-and-white tile flooring, polished marble countertops, and colorful Peranakan tiles from an old shophouse highlight the bistro aesthetic of this buzzing restaurant. It's a true family effort here: the well-known Singaporean food personality

Violet Oon handles the kitchen, her fashion-designer daughter was charged with the restaurant's design, and her son manages day-to-day operations. **Known for:** Peranakan cuisine; kesturi lemon pie with clotted cream; owner-chef and Singaporean food personality Violet Oon. $ *Average main: S$28* ✉ *881 Bukit Timah Rd., Bukit Timah* ☎ *9834–9935* ⊕ *www.violetoon.com* ☉ *Closed Mon.* Ⓜ *Sixth Avenue.*

🍸 Nightlife

OnTap Craft Bistro

BREWPUBS/BEER GARDENS | OnTap's in-house microbrewery serves 11 kinds of freshly brewed craft beer, one of which won a silver medal in the Asian Beer competition. The bar, tucked away on the second floor of a slightly dilapidated-looking building, is tricky to find but worth the perseverance for its delicious brews and friendly staff. Bar snacks and meals are also served, including fish and chips and fried chicken. ✉ *#02–01, 31 The Splendour, Bukit Batok Crescent, Bukit Timah* ☎ *9247–7385* ⊕ *ontap-craft-bistro-bar.business.site* ☞ *Closed Sun.* Ⓜ *Bukit Batok.*

👜 Shopping

Junkie's Corner

ANTIQUES/COLLECTIBLES | Everything from intricately carved wooden figurines to shiny marble tables and 1970s jukeboxes can be discovered in this dilapidated Asian antiques warehouse (or Aladdin's cave of collectibles, depending on your view). It's not easy to comb through the slightly claustrophobic shop, but it is fun, especially when you unearth a bargain. ✉ *2 Turf Club Rd., Bukit Timah* Ⓜ *Sixth Avenue.*

🏃 Activities

★ Bollywood Veggies

TOUR—SPORTS | This lush sanctuary of a farm transports you far from the noise of the city and into the wild countryside of Kranji in the north. There's always something to do here, from touring the farm and getting your hands dirty in the paddy fields, to taking part in a cooking class or listening to a talk from the resident medicine woman about which plants and herbs can be used for medicinal purposes. There's also a great on-site bistro that celebrates farm-to-table dining in its most literal sense. ✉ *100 Neo Tiew Rd., Bukit Timah* ☎ *6898–5001* ⊕ *bollywoodveggies.com* ☞ *Closed Mon.-Tues.*

Ikeda Spa

SPA—SIGHT | There's no better place to de-stress in Singapore than this spa outside the city center and in the midst of calming nature reserves. The Japanese-style spa is known for its customized treatments, VIP couples suite, Japanese Zen Garden, and outdoor onsen (hot tub). There is also a location in Clarke Quay on the Singapore River. ⊠ *787 Bukit Timah Rd., Bukit Timah* ☎ *6388–8080* ⊕ *www.ikedaspa.com* Ⓜ *Sixth Avenue.*

Kebun Baru

BIRD WATCHING | One of the last surviving bird-singing clubs in Singapore, Kebun Baru is a fascinating spot for bird-watchers. Onlookers watch as melodic song birds are hoisted 20 feet up in their cages to compete for the best tune. While songbird training takes place on site nearly every day, Sunday mornings are the best times to visit, when the cacophony of birdsong reaches its pinnacle during the competitions. The songbird owners—mainly men of the older generation—kick-back in the shade and natter, using the opportunity to gather and socialize. *There's no denying that the birds are caged (though all signs point to them being well-looked after and well-loved by their owners), so if that bothers you, you may want to reconsider a visit.* ⊠ *Ang Mo Kio Ave 5, Bukit Timah* ⊕ *Open field near Blk 159* ☎ *8182–2943* ⊕ *kebunbaru-birdsingingclub.weebly.com* Ⓜ *Ang Mo Kio.*

Prawning at Ah Hua

FISHING | FAMILY | Prawning, or prawn-fishing, is a fun Singaporean past time in which families or groups of friends gather round purpose-made ponds to fish for their lunch. Using rods or poles, you can catch prawns to grill up at the site's barbecue pit. You pay by the hour, not by the number of prawns you catch, so you might want to brush up on your fishing skills. The rate is inclusive of rods, bait, and all the prawns that you catch. ⊠ *10 Neo Tiew Ln. 2, Bukit Timah* ☎ *9125–2088* ⊕ *www.facebook.com/ahhuafishing* ☞ *S$20 per hour (inclusive of rods, bait, and all the prawns you catch).*

Clementi and Jurong

Clementi is the definition of up-and-coming. High-rise condos and malls are constantly sprouting up across the area as more people move out of Singapore's center and into the suburbs. Despite the modern transformation, Clementi still manages to maintain some of its traditional charm in its wet markets, hawker centers, and iconic landmarks that scatter the neighborhood.

Jurong Bird Park is home to more than 5,000 birds from all over the world.

To the west of Clementi lies Jurong, one of Singapore's westernmost regions. This is primarily a residential and industrial area separated into smaller neighborhoods, including Jurong East, Jurong West, and Boon Lay. It makes for a good day trip from the city center, with a number of Singapore's larger sights found here, including the expansive Jurong Bird Park.

◉ Sights

Jurong Bird Park
ZOO | FAMILY | This iconic Singaporean wildlife park is home to one of the world's most comprehensive avian collections, providing the opportunity to look at, learn about, and appreciate more than 5,000 birds, including hornbills, hummingbirds, parrots, and penguins. Highlights of the park's enormous grounds include the world's largest walk-in aviary; the "Wings of Asia" aviary, home to many threatened Asian species; and one of the world's tallest man-made waterfalls, at 100 feet. There are two colorful bird displays shown twice daily (at 10 am and 4 pm, and 11 am and 3 pm), as well as wildlife tours and "feed the bird" experiences for children. ✉ *2 Jurong Hill, Clementi* ☎ *6269–3411* ⊕ *www.wrs. com.sg/en/jurong-bird-park* 🎫 *S$32* Ⓜ *Boon Lay.*

★ Science Centre Singapore
COLLEGE | FAMILY | Aviation, nuclear science, robotics, astronomy, space technology, and Internet technology are entertainingly explored through audiovisual and interactive exhibits housed in the 14 galleries here. You can walk into a "human body" for a

closer look at vital organs, test yourself via computer quiz games, or settle into the **Omni Theatre**, where movies and planetarium shows are screened. Other fascinating exhibitions include "Butterflies Up-Close," an immersive journey through the stages of butterfly metamorphosis, and "Climate Change Climate Challenge," which shows what life will be like if global warming continues—and what we can do to prevent it. ✉ *15 Science Centre Rd., Clementi* ☎ *6425–2500* ⊕ *www.science.edu.sg* 🖘 *S$12, including Omni Theatre* Ⓜ *Jurong East.*

Singapore Discovery Centre

COLLEGE | FAMILY | This world-class children's center makes education entertaining through a large number of multimedia attractions that aim to engage the senses via demonstrations and digital animation, including 3D films and 4D simulations. In "On Location Reporter," for instance, children can practice announcing the news on "live" TV. In "Crisis Simulation," a thought-provoking video helps explore what would happen if a bomb were to explode at one of the busiest MRT stations in Singapore. ✉ *510 Upper Jurong Rd, Clementi* ☎ *6792–6188* ⊕ *www.sdc.com.sg* 🖘 *S$10 ("basic" entry)* Ⓜ *Joo Koon.*

Snow City

AMUSEMENT PARK/WATER PARK | FAMILY | Snow is a novelty when you live in a country where it's tropical all year-round. Locals endure freezing temperatures for a rare chance to touch and play in real snow at the only permanent indoor snow center in Singapore. Although it's geared more toward locals, it's a fun way to spend some time if you're not used to experiencing freezing temperatures. Admission includes the use of winter jackets and boots. ✉ *21 Jurong Town Hall Rd., Clementi* ☎ *6337–1511* ⊕ *www.snow-city.com.sg* 🖘 *Two hours of Snow Play Time: S$29* Ⓜ *Jurong.*

Tiger Brewery

WINERY/DISTILLERY | Tiger Beer is one of the most popular local beers in Singapore. You'll probably drink it (or at least see it) more than once on your trip, so why not visit where it is made? At the official Tiger Brewery, on the far west of the island, you can take a 45-minute guided tour of the facilities every afternoon from Tuesday to Sunday to see how the brewery process works. At the end of the tour, cool off during the "beer appreciation session" as you drink a one (or more) icy-cold Tiger beers. Don't forget to bring your ID or passport. ✉ *459 Jalan Ahmad Ibrahim, Clementi* ☎ *6860–3005* ⊕ *tigerbrewerytour.com.sg* 🖘 *S$18 (weekday), S$20 (weekend)* ☯ *Closed Mon.*

 Restaurants

Clementi Central Market and Hawker Centre
$ | **CHINESE** | This highly popular local hawker cen
stalls serving all kinds of delicious Singapore fav
duck noodles to succulent chicken and rice. As
hawker centers in Singapore, it's hot and a little messy, but the
food is always great—especially if you pick a stall with a long line.
Known for: huge variety of hawker stalls; local flavors at low prices;
covered, open-air setting. ⑤ *Average main: S$4* ⊠ *448 Clementi
Ave 3, Clementi* ▭ *No credit cards* Ⓜ *Clementi.*

★ Prata Alley
$ | **INDIAN** | This hipster south Indian restaurant is king of the *prata*
(an Indian flatbread made by frying stretched dough flavored with
ghee), and it is the centerpiece of their menu. The owners are
especially proud of the "Big One," a Sicilian prata stuffed with pes-
to chicken, mozzarella cheese, shitake mushrooms, pineapples,
and more. **Known for:** prata, especially the "Big One"; cozy bench
seating; dosas (savory pancakes). ⑤ *Average main: S$8* ⊠ *#01–12
, 321 Clementi Ave. 3, Clementi* ☎ *9181–4511* ⊕ *www.prataalley.
com* Ⓜ *Clementi.*

Tianfu Szechuan Cuisine
$ | **SICHUAN** | Located inside the City Vibe mall, this unpretentious
restaurant prides itself on its highly-authentic Szechuan menu
with plenty of choice. Bold, spicy dishes, including mapo tofu and
double-cooked pork, are served alongside a selection of beers,
wines, teas, and traditional Sichuan spirits. **Known for:** hearty use
of Szechuan pepper; low-key atmosphere; Kung Pao chicken.
⑤ *Average main: S$12* ⊠ *#01–17/18 City Vibe Mall, 3151 Common-
wealth Ave. West, Clementi* ⊕ *tianfu-szechuan-cuisine.business.
site* Ⓜ *Clementi.*

🛏 Hotels

Oasia Residence Singapore
$$ | **HOTEL** | Located near the ocean-facing West Coast Park in a
residential part of Singapore, the apartments of Oasia Residence
feel like little homes away from home. **Pros:** great for longer-stay
guests; great facilities, including a pool and gym; free parking.
Cons: far from the city and MRTs; no breakfast on weekends;
minimum six-night stay required. ⑤ *Rooms from: S$200* ⊠ *123
W Coast Cres., Clementi* ☎ *6428–8600 Reservations, 6254–1746
Operator* ⊕ *www.oasiahotels.com/en* ⇱ *140 rooms* ⦿❙ *No meals.*

Activities

There's a lot to do in the west if you know where to look. Most of the activities aren't geared towards international visitors, but to the people that call the surrounding neighborhoods home. This means you can expect fair prices and fewer tourists, as well as a chance to mingle with locals.

The Rink
ICE SKATING | FAMILY | If you've had enough of Singapore's heat, head to the country's Olympic-sized ice rink for a cool skating session. Housed within JCube mall, the largest rink in Singapore regularly hosts skating events such as *Saturdays on Ice*, where you can skate to themed music like '80s Rock 'n' Roll. If you dress in the appropriate themed costume, you can get in for free. If you're a little shaky on your skates, they also offer lessons and workshops. Visit the website to find out what events are taking place. ✉ *#03–11 JCube, 2 Jurong East Central 1, Clementi* ☎ *6684–2374* ⊕ *www.therink.sg* Ⓜ *Jurong East.*

Thwo Kwang Pottery Jungle
LOCAL INTEREST | FAMILY | Part workshop, part education center, this family-run operation is home to some of Singapore's most beautiful pottery, which you can admire, buy, or even try making for yourself. The regularly scheduled workshops will have you rolling up your sleeves and turning clay into mugs, vases, and bowls. The center uses one of the oldest surviving brick-built kilns in Singapore, the Dragon Kiln, to create its intricate works of art. ✉ *No. 85 Lorong Tawas, Clementi* ☎ *6265–5808* ⊕ *thowkwang.com.sg.*

Chapter 9

SIDE TRIPS

WITH SENTOSA ISLAND, PULAU UBIN, AND BINTAN ISLAND

Updated by
Charlene Fang

◉ Sights	🍴 Restaurants	🛏 Hotels	◑ Shopping	🍸 Nightlife
★★★★☆	★★★★☆	★★★★☆	★☆☆☆☆	★☆☆☆☆

NEIGHBORHOOD SNAPSHOT

TOP EXPERIENCES

■ **Sentosa Island:** This beachy wonderland just south of Singapore is the perfect escape for lying on the sand in front of a resort (or going on a beach-bar crawl).

■ **Theme parks:** Get your scream on at Universal Studios Singapore, an outpost of the famous thrill-seeker's theme park.

■ **Fine dining:** Make a reservation at one of Sentosa Island's high-end eateries.

■ **Pulau Ubin:** Hop on a bumboat to this island and spend a day experiencing old-school Singapore.

■ **Indonesia's Bintan:** Catch a ferry to this island for an action-packed or utterly indulgent weekend.

GETTING HERE

Sentosa Island is connected to mainland Singapore by a causeway bridge that takes less than 3 minutes to cross. To get here for free, you can walk or bike across the 765-yard-long Sentosa Boardwalk, or drive an electric car. Otherwise, you can take a cable car or taxi, or use the Sentosa Express, a form of public transportation from VivoCity (MRT: Harbourfront). A selection of small "bumboats" and ferries will take you to Singapore's other islands.

PLANNING YOUR TIME

Set aside at least one day for Sentosa Island or two if you're combining it with an excursion to Universal Studios Singapore, S.E.A. Aquarium, or Adventure Cove. A visit to one of Singapore's smaller islands will likely take a full day given travel time.

QUICK BITES

■ **Old Chang Kee.** Known for its legendary curry chicken puff, this is the spot for mouthwatering Halal-friendly street snacks. ✉ 50 *Beach View, Sentosa Island* ⊕ *www. oldchangkee.com* Ⓜ *Beach Station*

■ **Co+Nut+ink.** As you might guess from the name, this casual stall sells coconut ice cream desserts and fresh coconut water. ✉ 5 *Siloso Beach Walk, Sentosa Island* ⊕ *www.conutink. com* Ⓜ *Siloso Point Station*

■ **Baristart Coffee.** This Japan-based cafe outpost uses imported Hokkaido dairy to make the filling for its signature oversized cream puffs. ✉ 40 *Siloso Beach Walk, Sentosa Island* ⊕ *www. baristartcoffee.com* Ⓜ *Beach Station*

Though it's small, Singapore is actually made up of 63 different islands. Although the bulk of sights and attractions are on the mainland, other islands like Sentosa (incidentally the largest island of the 62 other islands) and smaller ones like Pulau Ubin and Kusu Island are well worth a visit. If time permits, consider venturing a bit farther to Bintan Island, which is just a 75-minute ferry ride away.

Proving a respite from Singapore's hustle and bustle, the nearby islands like Pulau Ubin and Kusu Island are examples of Singapore's rich biodiversity and also serve as a gentle reminder that this city-state wasn't always a bustling metropolis.

If there is one spot in Singapore that has undergone a major transformation, it is Sentosa Island. What was once a British military base and a Japanese prisoner-of-war camp during World War II has evolved into an island focused on fun. Located just off Singapore's southern coast, Sentosa draws visitors eager to soak up the sun on one of its many beaches. Along with a string of high-end hotels, a world-class golf course and marina, numerous restaurants, and more than a few lively beach bars, sights, and attractions, it's an ideal outing for all ages, whether you stay for a half day or an extended weekend.

Sentosa Island

Sentosa, which means "peace and tranquility" in Malay, is far from tranquil these days. Located to the south of the main island, and connected to it via a causeway, this former fishing village was converted into a vacation resort back in 1968. Today, it's filled with pristine artificial beaches, golf courses, the hotel-and-casino hub Resorts World, and various other hotels, bars, and restaurants.

Sentosa can take up anywhere from the time it takes for a few afternoon cocktails on the beach to a long weekend devoted to Universal Studios, the S.E.A. Aquarium, and one of its five-star hotels. HarbourFront MRT station is on the North East (purple)

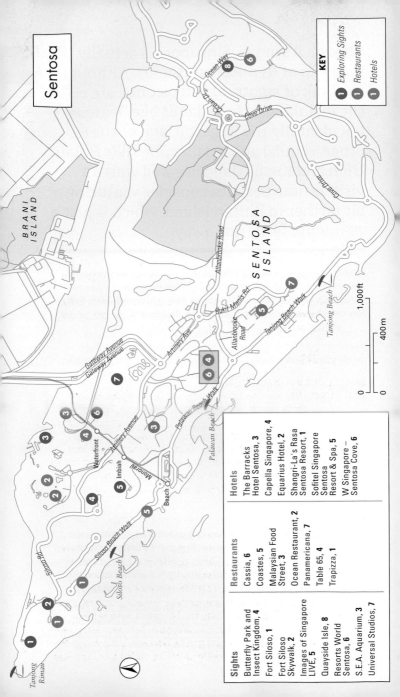

Sentosa

KEY
- ● *Exploring Sights* **1**
- ● *Restaurants* **1**
- ● *Hotels* **1**

BRANI ISLAND

SENTOSA ISLAND

Tanjong Rimau

Siloso Beach

Tanjong Beach

Palawan Beach

Siloso Rd.
Siloso Beach Walk
Artillery Avenue
Gateway Avenue
Waterfront
Imbiah
Monorail
Beach
Palawan Beach Walk
Allanbrooke Road
Bukit Manis Rd.
Tanjong Beach Walk
Attamdraoke Road
Cove Drive
Ocean Way
Ocean Drive

0   400m
0   1,000ft

Sights
Butterfly Park and
Insect Kingdom, **4**
Fort Siloso, **1**
Fort Siloso
Skywalk, **2**
Images of Singapore
LIVE, **5**
Quayside Isle, **8**
Resorts World
Sentosa, **6**
S.E.A. Aquarium, **3**
Universal Studios, **7**

Restaurants
Cassia, **6**
Coastes, **5**
Malaysian Food
Street, **3**
Ocean Restaurant, **2**
Panamericana, **7**
Table 65, **4**
Trapizza, **1**

Hotels
The Barracks
Hotel Sentosa, **3**
Capella Singapore, **4**
Equarius Hotel, **2**
Shangri-La's Rasa
Sentosa Resort, **1**
Sofitel Singapore
Sentosa
Resort & Spa, **5**
W Singapore –
Sentosa Cove, **6**

Cable cars connect mainland Singapore to Sentosa, a resort-filled island just offshore.

and Circle (yellow) lines. From here Sentosa is accessible via the Sentosa Express Monorail, cable cars, buses, and on foot by way of the outdoor Sentosa Boardwalk.

👁 Sights

Butterfly Park and Insect Kingdom

ZOO | FAMILY | Set within a rain forest—and featuring an Asian landscape complete with a moon gate, streams, and bridges—this park has a collection of 1,500 live butterflies from 50 species, as well as 3,000 insects that creep, crawl, or fly. Look for tree-horn rhino beetles, scorpions, and tarantulas. A number of free educational and feeding experiences with iguanas, tortoises, and other creatures are scheduled daily. ✉ *51 Imbiah Rd., Sentosa Island* 🕾 *6275–0013* ⊕ *www.jungle.com.sg* 💲 *S$20* ⊗ *Closed Mon.-Tues.*

Fort Siloso

MILITARY SITE | FAMILY | This well-preserved fort covers 10 acres of gun emplacements and tunnels created by the British to fend off the Japanese. Unfortunately, the Japanese arrived by land (through Malaysia) instead of by sea, so the huge guns were pointed in the wrong direction. Fort Siloso is now home to a treasure trove of World War II memorabilia, including coastal guns and the remains of fortified structures. The displays have been successfully revamped with lots of interactive high-tech audiovisual and animatronic effects. Photographs document the war in the Pacific, and dioramas depict the life of POWs during the Japanese occupation. Free guided tours are available every second and third Saturday of the month from 3 pm to 4:30 pm. Register with history@sentosa.com.sg as limited slots are available. ⊠ *Siloso Point, 33 Allanbrooke Rd., Sentosa Island* ☎ *6736–8672* ⊕ *www. sentosa.com.sg/explore/attractions/fort-siloso* ▣ *Free.*

Fort Siloso Skywalk

VIEWPOINT | Singapore loves treating visitors to sky-high views. This one on Sentosa Island might not be the tallest at just 11 stories, but it is free to enter, and there's a short, scenic, treetop walkway leading to Fort Siloso. To gain access, climb the staircase, or ride the elevator. Either way, the view of Keppel Harbour and the Southern Islands in the distance is pretty rewarding. ⊠ *Siloso Rd., Sentosa Island* ☎ *6736–8672* ⊕ *www.sentosa.com.sg/en.*

Images of Singapore LIVE

TOUR—SIGHT | **FAMILY** | A 45-minute show using live actors, special effects, and 11 immersive, themed areas teaches visitors about Singapore's history, from its beginnings as a Malay Fishing Village to its current status as a metropolis. The tour ends with the Spirit of Singapore Boat Ride, in which iconic landmarks and Sir Stamford Raffles (the founder of modern Singapore) make an appearance. The entry fee includes admission to Madame Tussauds Singapore, Marvel 4D Cinema, and Ultimate Film Star Experience. ⊠ *Imbiah Lookout, 40 Imbiah Rd., Sentosa Island* ☎ *6715–4000* ⊕ *www.imagesofsingaporelive.com* ▣ *S$42.*

Quayside Isle

NEIGHBORHOOD | The Quayside Isle complex is a cluster of international restaurants near Sentosa Cove's flashy yachts and sailboats moored in the marina. Less family-focused than the rest of Sentosa Island, it's kind of a Southeast Asian Capri—the perfect place for sunset cocktails and an evening meal. ⊠ *Sentosa Cove, 31 Ocean Way, Sentosa Island* ☎ *6887–3502* ⊕ *www.quayside.sg.*

Resorts World Sentosa

AMUSEMENT PARK/WATER PARK | **FAMILY** | This giant hotel-and-entertainment hub has an oceanarium; the Adventure Cove Waterpark; the Universal Studios' theme park; Resorts World Casino, an assortment of restaurants with famous chefs at their helm; and eight hotels. It's a good place for keeping kids entertained, but laid-back adults with little interest in gambling might want to steer clear. There are also multimedia shows like *Lake of Dreams* staged nightly (11 pm at Festive Walk). ⊠ *8 Sentosa Gateway, Sentosa Island* ☎ *6577–8888* ⊕ *www.rwsentosa.com.*

★ S.E.A. Aquarium

ZOO | **FAMILY** | One of the world's largest aquariums, this underwater wonderland provides views of more than 1,000 species from around the world. Gaze into a shipwreck habitat; walk through a tunnel surrounded by various shark species; and gape at goliath groupers, Napoleon wrasses, and a squadron of magnificent manta rays. There are educational shows on dive feeding and understanding dolphin behavior scheduled throughout the day. VIP tours can be organized. ✉ *Resorts World, 8 Sentosa Gateway, Sentosa Island* ☎ *6577–8888* ⊕ *www.rwsentosa.com/en/attractions/sea-aquarium* ✆ *S$41.*

★ Universal Studios

AMUSEMENT PARK/WATER PARK | **FAMILY** | Packed with cutting-edge rides, shows, and movie-themed attractions, this world-famous theme park located inside Resorts World Sentosa is a family favorite. Eighteen of the 24 movie-themed rides were designed or adapted for the Singapore park, including the world's first *Puss in Boots' Giant Journey* and the dueling *Battlestar Galactica: Human vs Cyclone* roller-coaster. Spread across seven themed sections, the park has a number of kid-friendly rides and shows, including Waterworld, Dino-Soarin', and Donkey-Live. The five-hour guided VIP tour includes priority access to popular rides like *TRANSFORMERS* The Ride: The Ultimate 3D Battle and photo ops with characters. Popular dining spots like Mel's Drive-In and Fairy Godmother's Juice Bar provide fuel for what will be a busy day. ✉ *8 Sentosa Gateway, Sentosa Island* ⊕ *www.rwsentosa.com* ✆ *S$81* Ⓜ *Harbourfront.*

🏖 Beaches

Sentosa may be a small island but it has a 2-mile stretch of white sand separated into a few small beaches. Each has its own distinct character and attractions.

Palawan Beach

BEACHES | **FAMILY** | The most family-friendly beach in Sentosa, Palawan has fine sand and waves so gentle the little ones can frolic freely. There's also a small island reachable via a short swim or a walk across a photo-worthy suspension rope bridge. The reward at the end of it? Reaching what's allegedly the southernmost point of continental Asia. **Amenities:** food and drink; showers; toilets. **Best for:** sunset; swimming. ✉ *Sentosa Island.*

Siloso Beach

BEACHES | This wide, sandy beach is a hive of activity thanks to the concentration of beach clubs, water-sports centers, and nearby attractions such as the Mega Adventure Park. It's also home to big events like the annual New Year's Eve countdown party. There are a number of casual eateries along the stretch of sand, and in-line skaters zoom up and down the promenade. For swimmers, there are red and yellow flag markers (swim here), as well as beach patrol officers if help is required. **Amenities:** food and drink; showers; toilets; water sports. **Best for:** partiers; sunset; swimming. ⊠ *Sentosa Island* ⊕ *www.sentosa.com.sg.*

Tanjong Beach

BEACHES | Shaped like a numeral three from above, this stretch of beach is busy on weekends thanks to the beachfront Tanjong Beach Club. It's also popular with dog owners and their water-trained pooches. Come on a weekday if you fancy having the beach all to yourself. **Amenities:** food and drink; showers; toilets. **Best for:** sunset; swimming solitude. ⊠ *Tanjong Beach, Sentosa Island* ⊕ *www.sentosa.com.sg.*

Tanjong Rimau

BEACHES | Sentosa Island isn't all fancy hotels and beach bars—there's also the natural, biodiverse area of Tanjong Rimau. Located at the far end of Siloso Beach, it is home to many creatures like red egg crabs, hairy crabs, sea snails, and occasionally, octopuses that can be spotted at low tide. The closest amenities are at Fort Siloso Skywalk or Silver Shell Cafe. **Amenities:** none. **Best for:** solitude; walking. ⊠ *Tanjong Rimau, Sentosa Island.*

🍽 Restaurants

Cassia

$$ | **CHINESE** | Traditional Cantonese dishes are presented with modern flair in an understated setting at this award-winning Chinese restaurant. Plush banquettes and elegant wallpaper by designer Andre Fu grace the dining room, and an outdoor seating area overlooks lush grounds. **Known for:** Peking duck; dim sum afternoon tea on weekends; elegant setting. ⑤ *Average main: S$24* ⊠ *Capella Hotel, 1 The Knolls, Sentosa Island* ☎ *6591–5045* ⊕ *www.capellahotels.com/en* ☉ *Mon.-Thurs.*

Coastes

$$ | **INTERNATIONAL** | **FAMILY** | At this kid-friendly hangout, adults can unwind over pizza and watch the little ones take a dip in the shallow water or play with the restaurant's sand toys. Expect a laid-back vibe and a self-ordering food and drink system; there are also sunbeds and deck chairs for customers. **Known for:** laid-back beachfront setting; family-friendly atmosphere; curry laska and chicken wings. $ *Average main: S$16* ✉ *50 Siloso Beach Walk, #01–05, Sentosa Island* ☎ *6631–8938* ⊕ *www.coastes.com.*

★ Malaysian Food Street

$ | **MALAYSIAN** | Who wins the great debate over which country has the best hawker food, Singapore or Malaysia? Judge for yourself without crossing the causeway at this cluster of hawker stalls (thankfully air-conditioned), which has all the signature Malaysian hawker noshes in one spot. The variety (and aromas) can prove overwhelming, so your best (and safest) bet is opting for the places with the longest lines. **Known for:** authentic Malaysian hawker food such as clay pot chicken rice; affordable prices; wide variety. $ *Average main: S$8* ✉ *8 Sentosa Gateway, Waterfront Level 1, Sentosa Island* ⊕ *www.rwsentosa.com/en/restaurants/malaysian-food-street/overview* ▭ *No credit cards.*

Ocean Restaurant

$$$ | **MEDITERRANEAN** | The sight of sharks and manta rays swimming past your dinner table at this elegant restaurant in the S.E.A. Aquarium makes for quite the memory. **Known for:** romantic atmosphere; fresh Mediterranean-California creations; unusual destination dining experience. $ *Average main: S$40* ✉ *Resorts World Sentosa, 22 Sentosa Gateway, #B1–455 & 456 S.E.A. Aquarium, Sentosa Island* ⊹ *West zone carpark B1M* ☎ *6577–6688* ⊕ *www.rwsentosa.com.*

Panamericana

$$$ | **SOUTH AMERICAN** | Come for the view, stay for the food and laid-back vibes. The menu of farm-to-fire dishes spans the Americas with standouts like the slow-cooked lamb charred on the asador, Argentinian empanadas, and market-fresh ceviche swimming in coconut milk. **Known for:** lamb cooked over an asador; large platters and cocktails; view of the South China Sea. $ *Average main: S$32* ✉ *Sentosa Golf Club, 27 Bukit Manis Rd., Sentosa Island* ☎ *6253–8182* ⊕ *www.panamericana.sg* ⊗ *Closed Tues.*

★ Table 65

$$$$ | **MODERN EUROPEAN** | For a really special treat, this Singapore eatery by chef Richard van Oostenbrugge of Amsterdam's one-Michelin-starred Restaurant 212 will do the trick. The tasting menus (the five-course Discovery or eight-course Experimental) are pricey, but they're served in a convivial, communal setting where you might sit next to strangers. **Known for:** precise, elegant cuisine; communal fine-dining experience; theatrical presentations. $ *Average main: S$148* ✉ *26 Sentosa Gateway, #01–104 &*

10 Hotel Michael, Sentosa Island ☎ *6577–7939* ⊕ *www.rwsentosa.com/en* ⊙ *Closed Sun. and Mon.*

Trapizza

$$ | ITALIAN | FAMILY | Channeling a Palm Springs vibe with cacti and palm-tree landscaping, this family-friendly Italian eatery on Siloso Beach has a dedicated children's water play area and coloring corner. Order the thin-crust, wood-fired pizzas—including a shareable 16-inch pie—or a hearty burger. **Known for:** family-sized 16-inch pizza; chill beachfront setting; kid-friendly facilities. ⑤ *Average main: S$28* ⊠ *Shangri-La Rasa Sentosa , 10 Siloso Beach Walk, Sentosa Island* ☎ *6376–2662* ⊕ *www.shangri-la.com.*

🛏 Hotels

The Barracks Hotel Sentosa

$$$$ | HOTEL | For those who appreciate luxe heritage spaces, the Barracks Hotel provides an intimate setting on the premises of an old British artillery outpost. **Pros:** extras like the heritage tour; ground-floor rooms have direct pool access; nightly happy hour. **Cons:** pricier than other nearby hotels; shared gym facilities; expensive in-room dining. ⑤ *Rooms from: S$450* ⊠ *2 Gunner Ln., Sentosa Island* ☎ *6722–0802* ⊕ *www.thebarrackshotel.com.sg* ⇨ *40 rooms* ⍥ *Free Breakfast.*

★ Capella Singapore

$$$$ | HOTEL | Situated on a lush 30-acre property, this word-class hotel is made up of a pair of restored colonial bungalows from the 1880s and a modern wing designed by Foster + Partners. **Pros:** direct access to Palawan Beach; triple-tier infinity pool; several award-winning eateries. **Cons:** small spa (advanced booking recommended); pricey; breakfast not included. ⑤ *Rooms from: S$780* ⊠ *1 The Knolls, Sentosa Island* ☎ *6377–8888* ⊕ *www.capellahotels.com* ⇨ *112 rooms* ⍥ *No meals.*

Equarius Hotel

$$$$ | RESORT | FAMILY | This hotel feels less like a family theme park than the five other hotels that make up **Resorts World Sentosa**. **Pros:** some rooms have direct pool access; a tranquil escape; access to amenities at other Resorts World hotels. **Cons:** not centrally located; could use more character; very expensive. ⑤ *Rooms from: S$800* ⊠ *Resorts World, 8 Sentosa Gateway, Sentosa Island* ☎ *6577–8899* ⊕ *www.rwsentosa.com* ⇨ *172 rooms* ⍥ *No meals.*

Shangri-La's Rasa Sentosa Resort

$$$$ | RESORT | FAMILY | The rooms in this vast, arc-shape building all have balconies; ask for a room facing the sea, or else your view will be of a grassy knoll. **Pros:** family-friendly; beachfront location;

complimentary shuttle bus service to and from VivoCity. **Cons:** isolated; lots of kids; conference-center feel. $\boxed{\$}$ *Rooms from: S$500* ✉ *101 Siloso Rd., Sentosa Island* ☎ *6275–0100, 020/8747–8485 for reservations in the U.K., 800/942–5050 for reservations in Canada and the U.S.* ⊕ *www.shangri-la.com/en/singapore/rasasentosaresort* ⤴ *454 rooms* ⦿I *No meals.*

Sofitel Singapore Sentosa Resort & Spa

$$$ | **RESORT** | The remote location of this resort makes it good for business seminars and those looking for a real escape. **Pros:** free Wi-Fi; large pool; resort-style setting. **Cons:** away from city center; unimpressive lobby; lots of steps to the beach. $\boxed{\$}$ *Rooms from: S$325* ✉ *2 Bukit Manis Rd., Sentosa Island* ☎ *6708–8310, 800/637–7200 for reservations in the U.S.* ⊕ *www.sofitel-singapore-sentosa.com* ⤴ *213 rooms* ⦿I *No meals.*

★ W Singapore – Sentosa Cove

$$$$ | **RESORT** | At this, another of the Starwood chain's trendy W brand hotels, works by Andy Warhol and Damien Hirst are mixed in with unique art installations, and the glam-rock atmosphere starts in the lobby with an illuminated wall and fountain at WOO-BAR, where a DJ often spins. **Pros:** seaside city escape; huge pool with underwater speakers; stylish rooms. **Cons:** no beach; not centrally located; doesn't feel local, despite the lush surroundings. $\boxed{\$}$ *Rooms from: S$560* ✉ *Sentosa Cove, 21 Ocean Way, Sentosa Island* ☎ *6808–7288* ⊕ *www.marriott.com* ⤴ *240 rooms* ⦿I *No meals.*

▽ Nightlife

There isn't much real "nightlife" per se on Sentosa, but you can still find rather lively hangouts after sunset. Bob's is the most tranquil; Tanjong Beach and Rumours are good afternoon-sunset spots.

Bob's Bar

BARS/PUBS | Sentosa's resident blue-and-green peafowls are regularly sighted at this unforgettable spot—the perfect place for sunset drinks. The cocktail menu is extensive, but to try something local, order a drink containing Navegante, a rum made exclusively for the bar. Time your session to coincide with the daily "Bosum's Call" at 6:30 pm (5 pm on Sunday) when the staff hands out tasting portions of rum and canapés. ✉ *Capella Singapore , 1 The Knolls, Sentosa Island* ☎ *6591–5047* ⊕ *www.capellahotels.com.*

Rumours Beach Club

BARS/PUBS | Bringing a bit of Bali's beach swagger to Singapore, this beach club has a trio of swimming pools, a beach-facing infinity pool, and chilled beanbag seating. There's a VIP area with a private pool and family cabanas for more privacy. You won't regret ordering from the live Jimbaran seafood grill station. Otherwise, there's a selection of Indonesian dishes and an extensive menu of bar-friendly food and drinks. ⌧ *40 Siloso Beach Walk, Sentosa Island* ☎ *6970–0625* ⊕ *www.rumours.com.sg.*

★ Tanjong Beach Club

BARS/PUBS | Lounge in the sun among the palms or play outdoor games at this trendy beach-side hangout. The restaurant-bar has daybeds (prior reservations can be made) and lounge chairs, a swimming pool, and often DJs on deck. The weekend crowd is typically young professionals looking to let loose over a game of beach volleyball or beer pong. This stretch of sand, shaped like a numeral three from above, is also popular with dog owners and their water-trained pooches. To avoid the crowds; come on a weekday, and linger after sunset, which is especially pretty here. ⌧ *120 Tanjong Beach Walk, Sentosa Island* ☎ *6270–1355* ⊕ *www. tanjongbeachclub.com.*

🎭 Performing Arts

Magical Shores at Siloso

SOUND/LIGHT SHOW | **FAMILY** | This immersive light-and-sound show, staged along a stretch of Siloso Beach, has four acts: Nocturnal Awakening, Islet Whispers, Force of Nature, and New Peak. It includes two areas where you can interact with the light art on the sand. It runs from 7:30 pm to 10:30 pm every night, in 15-minute cycles. ⌧ *Siloso Beach Walk, Sentosa Island* ⊕ *www.sentosa.com. sg* Ⓜ *Harbourfront.*

Wings of Time

SOUND/LIGHT SHOW | **FAMILY** | A crowd-pleasing multisensory night show about two cranes that journey together through time, this story is told via a larger-than-life water screen programmed with 3-D effects, lasers, robotic water fountains, and spectacular pyrotechnics. For a good view of the stage, dole out extra for the premium seats. Shows take place at 7:40 pm and 8:40 pm nightly. ⌧ *Beach View, Sentosa Island* ☎ *6736–8672* ⊕ *www.wingsoftime. com.sg* 🎟 *S$18 (standard), S$24 (premium)* Ⓜ *Beach Station.*

Shopping

Unlike other parts of Singapore, Sentosa is not known for its retail stores. However, there are a decent number of luxury brands available at Resorts World Sentosa, as well as gift shops and souvenir kiosks scattered across the island.

Shopping Experiences at Resorts World Sentosa

SHOPPING CENTERS/MALLS | The bulk of the 45 retail outlets at Resorts World Sentosa are high-end luxury brands like Versace, Tiffany & Co., Rolex, and Bvlgari. For the little ones, there are shops like Candylicious, Hershey's Chocolate World, and a LEGO Certified Store. ⊠ *8 Sentosa Gateway, Sentosa Island* ☎ *6577–8888* ⊕ *www.rwsentosa.com/en/retail.*

Activities

Sentosa Island packs a punch with high-octane sports like bungee jumping and zip-lining, but it also offers the chance to be pampered in spa heaven.

AJ Hackett Sentosa

FLYING/SKYDIVING/SOARING | The bungee jump at AJ Hackett Sentosa offers a rather compelling 155-foot plunge above the palm tree–lined Siloso Beach. If that's too much of a daredevil activity for you, alternatives include the 130-foot-long Skybridge, the 138-foot Vertical Skywalk, and a group-friendly Giant Swing ride. ⊠ *30 Siloso Beach Walk, Sentosa Island* ☎ *6911–3070* ⊕ *www.ajhackett.com/sentosa* ☞ *S$159 (Bungee Jump), S$69 (Giant Swing), S$10 (Skybridge).*

Auriga Spa

SPA/BEAUTY | In this tranquil cocoon, treatments take place in spacious spa suites, each with its own private garden. There are just nine suites, so pre-booking is recommended. The Waning Moon (60 or 90 minutes) employs a detoxing lymphatic massage technique that corresponds to the different phases of the moon. Block time to have a 90-minute massage, which includes facial cleansing and a nourishing scalp massage. Pre- or post-treatment, linger in the vitality pool, steam room, or ice fountain. ⊠ *Capella Singapore, 1 The Knolls, Sentosa Island* ☎ *6591–5023* ⊕ *www.capellahotels.com.*

ESPA

SPA—SIGHT | If you're in the mood to relax, head to this enormous spa in Resorts World Sentosa to enjoy an authentic Turkish hammam as well as onsen-style pools, a crystal steam room, and private beach villa suites. ⊠ *Resorts World Sentosa, 8 Sentosa Gateway, Sentosa Island* ☎ *6577–8880* ⊕ *www.rwsentosa.com/ en/espa/overview.*

Gogreen Segway Eco Adventure

GUIDED TOURS | This outfit's fun, 60-minute, Eco Adventure+ Segway ride scoots past Palawan and Siloso beaches, while its shorter 30-minute Eco Adventure rides travel to one beach or the other. Instructions are provided beforehand, and helmets are mandatory. The last 60-minute ride departs at 6:45 pm; the last 30-minute option at 7:15 pm. ⊠ *51 Siloso Beach Walk, #01–01 Sentosa, Sentosa Island* ☎ *9825–4066* ⊕ *www.segwaytours.com. sg* ⌖ *Segways 30-min (S$39.90), 60-min (S$79.90).*

Mega Adventure Park

ZIP LINING | **FAMILY** | The 1,475-foot-long MegaZip Sentosa, the steepest zip-line in Southeast Asia, is just one of the attractions at this adventure park. There's also the ParaJump, a mini bungee jump, the kid-friendly 36-obstacle treetop MegaClimb; the Megabounce, a bungee-assisted trampoline; and the 50-foot-high MegaWall for rock climbers. Combination packages are sold online. Activities are weather dependent, so check the forecast before booking. ⊠ *10A Siloso Beach Walk, Sentosa Island* ☎ *6722–3785* ⊕ *www.sg.megaadventure.com* ⌖ *MegaZip from S$55.*

Ola Beach Club

WATER SPORTS | There's no shortage of beach clubs on Sentosa Island, but Ola Beach Club stands out for its Hawaiian-themed food (order the Lomi Lomi Salmon), tiki cocktails, private pool, and water-sports center tailored to active sun seekers. Come here to try your hand at hydro-flight with a water jet pack, a donut ride, or stand-up paddleboarding. There are also beach-facing cabanas in which to lounge. If you're here on a Saturday, expect a crowd to gather for the weekly barbecue party. ⊠ *46 Siloso Beach Walk, Sentosa Island* ☎ *6250–6978* ⊕ *www.olabeachclub.com.*

Sentosa Golf Club

GOLF | Members and guests can play two 18-hole courses at this award-winning golf club with rolling greens, mangrove swamps, and stunning city and ocean views. ⊠ *27 Bukit Manis Rd., Sentosa Island* ☎ *6275–0022* ⊕ *www.sentosagolf.com* ⌖ *Serapong course: 18 holes, 6,675 m, par 72; New Tanjong course: 18 holes, 6,210 m, par 72* ⌖ *Visitor fee on weekdays S$350; weekends S$480.*

Skyline Luge

PARK—SPORTS-OUTDOORS | FAMILY | Embrace the irony of luging—a winter sport that involves sledding down an ice track feet first—in perennially hot and humid Singapore. Here, however, you twist and turn down one of four paved tracks while seated on a luge with handlebars. If day luging is too tame, night rides are also available at no additional cost. The four-seater Skyride chairlift offers a more leisurely way to take in the view. ⊠ *45 Siloso Beach Walk, Sentosa Island* ☎ *6274–0472* ⊕ *www.skylineluge.com* ☞ *From S$24 (Luge, 2 rides), S$11 (Skyride).*

Bintan Island

Just a short ferry ride from Singapore is the Indonesian island of Bintan. A peaceful retreat from the bustling city, this leisure-focused island offers pristine beaches, luxurious day spas, championship golf courses, and a number of high-end resorts. It's an easy add-on to any stay in Singapore—one that does not require flying.

GETTING HERE AND AROUND

The best way to get to Bintan is via a fast ferry operated by Bintan Resort Ferries ⊕ *www.brf.com.sg*. It departs daily from Singapore's Tanah Merah Ferry Terminal to Bintan's Bandar Bentan Telani Ferry Terminal. Once on the island, make use of complimentary shuttle bus services ⊕ *www.bintan-resorts.com* that run between the resorts, Bandar Bentan Telani (BBT) Ferry Terminal, Plaza Lagoi and Safari Lagoi. Taxi and car rental services are also available and can be booked at the Ferry Terminal. Look for Wira Taxi Service ☎ *+62 813/7820–2111* and Global Bintan Transportaton ☎ *+62 770/691–818.*

TIMING

Depending on how long you plan to stay in Singapore, Bintan Island can be done as a day trip or as an overnight or extended weekend excursion. As the island is a popular weekend spot for both Singaporeans and Indonesians, avoid the crowds and snag better accommodation and activity deals by visiting on a weekday.

Visa: Although Bintan is just a ferry ride from Singapore, it is part of Indonesia. U.S. citizens don't need a visa for visits under 30 days but otherwise can purchase one on arrival. Currency: Some hotels charge in Singapore or U.S. dollars, but it's advisable to have some Indonesia Rupiah on you. Most resorts accept Amex, Visa, and Mastercard. Like Singapore, Bintan is humid, with a monsoon season that runs from early November to around late March. Singapore is also one hour ahead of Bintan.

Sights

Penyengat Island

ARCHAEOLOGICAL SITE | Located 15 minutes by water taxi from Bintan's Tanjung Pinang district lies Penyengat Island, once the epicenter of the Malay Riau-Lingga empire. It offers a peek into Malay cultural heritage and has been nominated as a UNESCO World Heritage Site. The main landmark is the Sultan's Palace, rumored to be built from a mixture of egg white and lime. Inside the grounds, there's a restored fort, tombs, and a handwritten and illustrated Qur'an that's more than 150 years old. To get here, hire a speed boat at Tanjung Pinang jetty (US$7). ⊠ *South China Sea, Tanjungpinang Kota* ⊕ *www.indonesia.travel/gb/en.*

Senggarang Village

TOWN | The first settlement for ethnic Chinese immigrants who arrived in Bintan sometime in the 1700s, this rustic village is home to some of Bintan's oldest temples: the complex of Lau Ya Keng and the unusual Banyan Tree Temple, a 200-year-old structure that's become intertwined with the trunk of an ancient banyan tree. The village is best reached via a 15-minute water taxi ride from Tanjung Pinang and can be combined with a visit to Penyengat Island.

 Beaches

Lagoi Beach

BEACHES | A public beach situated near the Plaza Lagoi shopping area, this pristine coastal stretch has crystal clear water and a wide variety of water sports such as kayaking, jet-skiing, and snorkeling, plus the odd game of beach volleyball. **Amenities:** food and drink; toilets; water sports. **Best for:** sunset; swimming; windsurfing. ⊠ *Lagoi Beach, Bintan Island.*

Trikora Beach

BEACH—SIGHT | Although Bintan has many swanky beach resorts, the coastline toward the east is worth a trek if you prefer to enjoy white-sand beaches without paying five-star resort prices. Located an hour's car ride from Bintan Resorts—where the ferries arrive and depart—Trikora Coast has a number of modest accommodations and eateries and is a popular spot for weekend kite surfers. There are four beaches in total and basic sheltered beach huts for rent. To get around, bring or hire a bicycle, or employ the services of a driver. **Amenities:** showers; toilets; water sports. **Best For:** sunset; swimming; snorkeling.

🍴 Restaurants

The Kelong Seafood Restaurant

$$ | SEAFOOD | Traditional *kelongs* (floating platforms built on stilts used for fishing) were once off limits to women but those that remain have mostly discarded the superstition. This one at Nirwana Gardens was transformed into a seafood restaurant and now serves fresh catches in a rustic setting overlooking the ocean. **Known for:** black-pepper crab, sea snails, and catch of the day; laid-back atompshere; scenic setting overlooking the ocean. $ *Average main: S$16* ⊠ *Jalan Panglima Pantar, Lagoi* ☎ *6323–6636* ⊕ *www.nirwanagardens.com* ☽ *Closed occasionally during lunch; it's best to call ahead.*

Nelayan

$$ | INDONESIAN | This ocean-facing alfresco restaurant at Bintan Lagoon Resort is romantic with its beach-side seating. The menu includes standard Indonesian fare like an upscale *nasi goreng* with king prawns and predictable western dishes like buttermilk chicken. **Known for:** lovely beachside setting; variety of food; family-style rijsttafel (rice table). $ *Average main: S$20* ⊠ *Bintan Lagoon Resort , Jln. Indera Segara Site A12* ☎ *770/ 691–388* ⊕ *www.bintanlagoon.com.*

🛏 Hotels

Bintan Lagoon Resort

$ | RESORT | While there are newer (and more luxurious) spots to stay, Bintan Lagoon Resort is more convenient, with a direct ferry service from Singapore. **Pros:** good location; ideal for groups; wide range of leisure activities. **Cons:** not the newest property; hard to explore outside of the resort; paid activities can be pricey. $ *Rooms from: S$90* ⊠ *Jalan Indera Segara Site A12, Bintan Utara Lagoi* ☎ *770/691–388* ⊕ *www.bintanlagoon.com* ⤴ *470 rooms* ⦿ *Free Breakfast.*

The Sanchaya

$$$$ | RESORT | It's safe to say that your privacy is assured at The Sanchaya, which is set on a 25-acre beach estate and has just 30 rooms, each with deluxe chaise longues on private verandas that offer lagoon, pool, or ocean views. **Pros:** unbeatable beach-front location; charming colonial architecture; spacious, luxurious rooms. **Cons:** small spa; expensive activities; pricey food and drink. $ *Rooms from: S$691* ⊠ *Lagoi Bay, Bintan* ☎ *770/692–200* ⊕ *www.thesanchaya.com* ⤴ *30 rooms* ⦿ *Free Breakfast.*

⚡ Activities

Mangrove Discovery Tour

BOAT TOURS | FAMILY | This 60-minute tour of the mangrove forests in Bintan's Sebung River—there are four kinds of forest to explore here—can be done either during the day or night. By day, expect to see some of the river's wildlife: snakes, lizards, monkeys, and even the occasional crocodile. By night, the fireflies come out in full force, magically lighting the route down the river. The tour departs at 9 am, 10:30 am, 1 pm, and 3 pm during the day and 7:30 at night. ⊠ *48WJ+PH Teluk Sebong, Bintan Regency, Riau Islands, Indonesia* ☎ *813/6453–7222* ⊕ *www.bintan-tour.com* ⊠ *IDR 380,000; min 2 people.*

Ria Bintan

GOLF | On weekends, many Singapore-based golfers play this championship course, one of Asia's best. Its 18-hole Ocean Course and 9-hole Forest Course cut through the island's natural junglescape and feature challenging ocean-facing holes, including a par 3 on the 9th hole (Ocean Course) that plays across the South China Sea. There's a hotel attached for overnight or longer stays, and day trips can be organized with a transfer from the ferry terminal. ⊠ *Jl Perigi Raja. Lagoi, Bintan Resorts* ☎ *770/692–837* ⊕ *www.riabintan.com* 🏌 *Weekdays: S$210. Weekends and holidays: S$310* ⛳ *Ocean Course: 18 holes, 7,075 yards, par 72; Forest Course: 9 holes, 3,266 yards, par 36.*

Pulau Ubin and Other Islands

Singapore is made up of 63 islands, so it would be a shame to explore only the mainland when several other spots are also worth a visit. A trip to Pulau Ubin offers a glimpse of what Singapore was like before modernization; ferries can also get you to to Kusu and St. John's, two of the Southern Islands, both of which have some especially good sights on offer.

⊙ Sights

Kusu Island

ISLAND | One of the Southern Islands and situated less than 4 miles southwest of Singapore, Kusu, whose name means "turtle" in Chinese, is known for its beaches and temples. One of these is Kramat Kusu, dedicated to a Malay saint named Haji Syed Abdul Rahman, who, with his mother and sister, is said to have disappeared supernaturally from the island in the 19th century.

To reach the shrine, you climb more than 100 steps that go up through a forest. Plastic bags containing stones have been hung on the trees by devotees who have come to the shrine—particularly during the ninth lunar month—to pray for forgiveness of sins and the correction of wayward children. If their wishes are granted, believers return the following year to remove their bags and give thanks. Staying overnight or camping is not permitted, and it's best to pack food and drink. ⊠ *Sentosa Island* ⊕ *www.sla. gov.sg/islands.*

★ Pulau Ubin

FOREST | FAMILY | Take a 10-minute ride on a bumboat (a small launch, prices from S$3 per person) from Changi Point Ferry Terminal to be transported back in time on this boomerang-shaped island. It's best explored by bicycle, which can be rented on the island for around S$10. There are three trails that lead past old plantations, mangrove swamps, forests, the occasional wild boar, and abandoned granite quarries that look surprisingly picturesque. You should also consider a visit to the Chek Jawa Wetlands, one of Singapore's richest ecosystems, to wander the 1-km (0.62-mile) boardwalk (Mangrove and Coastal Loops) and take in views from the 66-foot Jejawi Tower. Before heading back, cool off with a fresh coconut drink or order a kampong-style meal from one of the small seafood restaurants near the jetty. ⊕ *www.nparks.gov. sg.*

St. John's Island

ISLAND | St. John's was first a leper colony, then a prison camp, and then a place to intern political enemies of the republic. Today it's a great place for picnics and camping. You can rent colonial bungalows and there are camping facilities as well. The island is also home to a Marine Aquaculture Centre and Tropical Marine Science Institute. Visit the 2.8-km (1.7-mi.) St John's Island Trail marked by 15 stations and signboards detailing the island's history and diversity of flora and fauna. You can get to St. John's via the ferries at Marina South Pier. ⊠ *St. John's Island, Sentosa Island* ☎ *65/6534–9339* ⊕ *www.islandcruise.com.sg* ⊠ *S$15.*

🍴 Restaurants

Pulau Ubin's food options are casual and affordable, and, as there are no restrictions on what you can bring on the island, you can pack your own food and drink. If you don't have access to a kitchen, swing by the Changi Village Hawker Center near the jetty and pick up some takeout. Otherwise, make sure you have some cash on hand, as at some of the island's simple eateries, cash is the payment of choice.

Cheong Lian Yuen

$ | **ASIAN** | Simple and unassuming, this spot close to the jetty and near the bicycle rental shops is a good place to have a cold drink after exploring the island. You can't go wrong with any of the wok-friend dishes or the chili crab. **Known for:** affordable food; casual atmosphere; chili crab. $ *Average main: S$5* ⊠ *20 Pulau Ubin* ☎ *6542–1147* ▭ *No credit cards.*

Season Live Seafood

$ | **ASIAN** | One of the few restaurants on Pulau Ubin, Season Live is located close to the jetty and has a laid-back island vibe. It's a good place to grab a fresh, cold coconut drink, but if you're hungry, the dishes to try include the not-too-spicy *sambal kangkong* (stir-fried water spinach with chili) and the black-pepper crab. **Known for:** black-pepper crab; laid-back vibe; simple home-cooked food. $ *Average main: S$10* ⊠ *59E Pulau Ubin* ☎ *6542–7627* ▭ *No credit cards.*

🏃 Activities

Exploring Pulau Ubin is easily done. Whether you join a guided expedition or plan your own itinerary, resources like ⊕ *www. wildsingapore.com* (a blog dedicated to Singapore's outdoors) can come in handy.

Adventures by Asian Detours

ADVENTURE TOURS | Join this group's six-hour Ubin Bisect Kayaking tour ($95) to kayak through the mangroves of Pulau Ubin. Four hours will be spent on the water. The eight-hour Paddle to Pedal ($198) includes kayaking the backwaters of the Sungei Jelutong and cycling along Ubin's trails. ⊠ *34 Pulau Ubin* ☎ *6733–2282* ⊕ *www.adventures.network.*

National Parks Board

GUIDED TOURS | For a guided tour (90 to 120 minutes) of the intertidal flats of Chek Jawa and its rich marine life, check in with the National Parks Board, which runs regular tours ($60 per group) of the area. Booking ahead is recommended as spots fill up fast. The parks board has also mapped out two self-guided walking tours of the island for those who prefer to explore independently. ⊕ *www. nparks.gov.sg.*

Index

Photo Credits

Notes

Notes

Fodor's InFocus SINGAPORE

Publisher: Stephen Horowitz, *General Manager*

Editorial: Douglas Stallings, *Editorial Director*; Jill Fergus, Jacinta O'Halloran, Amanda Sadlowski, *Senior Editors*; Kayla Becker, Alexis Kelly, Rachael Roth, *Editors*

Design: Tina Malaney, *Design and Production Director*; Jessica Gonzalez, *Graphic Designer*; Mariana Tabares, *Design and Production Intern*

Production: Jennifer DePrima, *Editorial Production Manager*; Elyse Rozelle, *Senior Production Editor;* Monica White, *Production Editor*

Maps: Rebecca Baer, *Senior Map Editor*; Mark Stroud (Moon Street Cartography) *Cartographer*

Photography: Viviane Teles, *Senior Photo Editor;* Namrata Aggarwal, Ashok Kumar, Carl Yu, *Photo Editors;* Rebecca Rimmer, *Photo Intern*

Business and Operations: Chuck Hoover, *Chief Marketing Officer;* Robert Ames, *Group General Manager;* Devin Duckworth, *Director of Print Publishing;* Victor Bernal, *Business Analyst*

Public Relations and Marketing: Joe Ewaskiw, *Senior Director Communications a Public Relations*

Fodors.com: Jeremy Tarr, *Editorial Director*; Rachael Levitt, *Managing Editor*

Technology: Jon Atkinson, *Director of Technology*; Rudresh Teotia, *Lead Developer*; Jacob Ashpis, *Content Operations Manager*

Writers: Charlene Fang, Marco Ferrarese, Olivia Lee, Audrey Phoon, Annette Tan

Editor: Kayla Becker

Production Editor: Monica White

1st Edition

ISBN 978-1-64097-284-1

ISSN 2690-4365

All details in this book are based on information supplied to us at press time. Always confirm information when it matters, especially if you're making a detour to visit a specific place. Fodor's expressly disclaims any liability, loss, or risk, personal or otherwise, that is incurred as a consequence of the use of any of the contents of this book.

SPECIAL SALES

This book is available at special discounts for bulk purchases for sales promotions or premiums. For more information, e-mail SpecialMarkets@fodors.com.

PRINTED IN CHINA

10 9 8 7 6 5 4 3 2 1

About Our Writers

Charlene Fang, a Singapore native, is a freelance writer who splits her time between Singapore and California. She writes for a number of lifestyle and travel publications, including *Condé Nast Traveler*, *AFAR*, *Time Out*, and *SilverKris*. Charlene wrote the Little India and Kampong Glam and Side Trips chapters for this edition.

Marco Ferrarese, a freelance travel and culture writer based in Penang, is an expert on Malaysia and Borneo and has written for *Travel + Leisure Southeast Asia*, *CNN Travel*, *BBC Travel*, *The Guardian*, and *National Geographic Traveller* (UK), among others. Marco wrote the Travel Smart and Experience chapters.

Olivia Lee is a freelance writer and recent transplant to Singapore, where she writes about travel and hospitality. In the past she has contributed to *The Guardian*, *The Wall Street Journal Magazine*, *Wanderlust*, and *Adventure Travel*, as well as Fodor's *Portugal*. For this guide, Olivia wrote the Orchard Road; Western Singapore; and Chinatown and Tiong Bahru chapters.

Audrey Phoon is a Singapore-based journalist and social media strategist who has contributed to *The Wall Street Journal*, *Condé Nast Traveler*, *ELLE*, and *South China Morning Post*. Audrey has also written and edited several books on Singapore's food and culture. She wrote both the Eastern Singapore chapter and the Civic District and Marina Bay chapter.

Annette Tan is a Singapore-based writer who covers food and lifestyle. She has contributed to numerous titles, both in Singapore and internationally, such as *Condé Nast Traveler* and *Wallpaper*. She is the author of *Savour Chinatown: Stories, Memories and Recipes*, and is the founder of FatFuku, a private dining experience showcasing modern Singaporean cuisine from her home. Annette wrote parts of the Experience chapter.